Reform Without Justice

Reform Without Justice

Latino Migrant Politics and the Homeland Security State

ALFONSO GONZALES

OXFORD
UNIVERSITY PRESS

OXFORD
UNIVERSITY PRESS

Oxford University Press is a department of the University of Oxford.
It furthers the University's objective of excellence in research, scholarship,
and education by publishing worldwide.

Oxford   New York
Auckland   Cape Town   Dar es Salaam   Hong Kong   Karachi
Kuala Lumpur   Madrid   Melbourne   Mexico City   Nairobi
New Delhi   Shanghai   Taipei   Toronto

With offices in
Argentina   Austria   Brazil   Chile   Czech Republic   France   Greece
Guatemala   Hungary   Italy   Japan   Poland   Portugal   Singapore
South Korea   Switzerland   Thailand   Turkey   Ukraine   Vietnam

Oxford is a registered trademark of Oxford University Press
in the UK and certain other countries.

Published in the United States of America by
Oxford University Press
198 Madison Avenue, New York, NY 10016

© Oxford University Press 2014

Library of Congress Cataloging-in-Publication Data
Gonzales, Alfonso, 1977–
Reform without justice : Latino migrant politics and the homeland security state / Alfonso Gonzales.
pages cm
Includes bibliographical references and index.
ISBN 978–0–19–997339–2 (hardback)—ISBN 978–0–19–934293–8 (paperback)
1. Hispanic Americans—Politics and government—21st century.   2. Migrant labor—Government
policy—United States.   3. Migrant agricultural laborers—Government policy—United States.
4. Illegal aliens—Legal status, laws, etc.—United States.   5. Immigration enforcement—United
States.   6. United States—Emigration and immigration—Government policy.   I. Title.
E184.S75G644 2013
305.868'073—dc23
2013015066

3 5 7 9 8 6 4
Printed in the United States of America
on acid-free paper

Para mis abuelos, mis padres y mis hijos

CONTENTS

PREFACE

This project was born out of a frustration that I share with a generation of Chicano and Latino intellectuals and activists, most of whom either migrated to the United States as children or are the children of migrants, who came of age in the context of what historian Rodolfo Acuña calls the anti-immigrant hysteria of the last thirty years. Collectively, we have witnessed the intensification of state violence against our communities in the form of deaths at the border; mass detentions; families devastated for generations by deportation; racial profiling on streets and public places; young men gunned down by state authorities; people denied their valid asylum claims; the dehumanizing experience of being asked for "papers"; and many more quotidian injustices too detailed to list. But we have also witnessed the intensification of Latino migrant activism in many forms over the last several decades, from marches and voter registration drives to civil disobedience actions and the formation of coalitions with progressive allies in what has become a multiethnic and multisector migrant rights movement.

This book is on the relationship between Latino migrant activism and on state migration control policies and practices between 2001 and 2012, but its genesis is in California during the fight against Proposition 187 in 1994, a law that would have banned undocumented people from most public services, among other provisions. At this time, as a teenager and noncitizen, I first began to grapple with understanding how and why injustices toward migrants and Latinos come about and what it would take to stop them. Although these questions have been burning inside me for almost twenty years, this book is written from the privileged position of a political scientist and participant-observer who has lived and studied in Southern California and New York City with the goal of thinking about how to stop the injustices that have marked my generation. I do not claim that this book will provide the definitive answer to this problematic or that it will satisfy everyone who reads it. Rather, it explains the challenges facing those Latinos and their allies alike who, regardless of race or nationality, seek emancipation from human suffering in the face of a powerful and entrenched police state, even amid all the celebration around "immigration reform" and Latino political power on the horizon.

I am bound to make some mistakes and omissions in my effort to think through the relationship between Latino migrant activism and the post-9/11 security state that has emerged. Such shortcomings are entirely my own. However, the insights, knowledge, and conceptual clarity that may be gained from this book are the product of many people who have been helpful in this project in a deeply dialogical way. First and foremost among those on this long list are the more than sixty people I interviewed for this book. Indeed, these migrant activists, deportees, and policy makers shared their thoughts and time with me, often allowing me into their homes, meetings, organizations, and lives. Although it will be theoretical and challenging at times, this book is for you, for us, and for the movement of our time.

This book is also for my mentors, colleagues, and students. I want to thank Ray Rocco, Mark Sawyer, and Bill Robinson, all of whom have challenged me to think and rethink my approach to this project from its earliest stages, during my days at UCLA in the Department of Political Science. Ray has been an outstanding adviser, mentor, and friend to me, and I proudly consider myself his student. Mark has challenged me in many ways that ultimately made me a better scholar. Bill provided enthusiastic and receptive feedback while always reminding me to stay committed to my ideas.

My senior colleagues and mentors from the post doc that I completed in the Latino Studies program in the Department of Social and Cultural Analysis at New York University had a tremendous imprint on this project. While at NYU, I had the great honor of having Renato Rosaldo, René Francisco Poitevin, and Joseph Nevins provide feedback on the entire manuscript. Each provided a very specific type of feedback. Renato helped me to develop my voice and the ethnographic aspects of this project. René Francisco drew on his expertise in critical theory and encouraged me to do my "Gramsci pushups." And Joseph Nevins, an expert in the field of migration control, provided precise advice and encouragement. I also want to thank Arlene Dávila, Juan Flores, Neil Brenner, and Josie Saldaña for sharing their time and resources with me. Arlene provided help with my book proposal and early chapters, and Juan provided important feedback on different drafts of the project. Lastly from NYU, I would like to thank Cristina Beltrán for her example and for paving the way forward for my generation of theorists.

I am immensely indebted to my friends and colleagues Adrián Félix, Mark Jimenez, Aidé Acosta, Andres Garcia, Chris Zepeda, and Raul Moreno for their critical and heavy conceptual feedback on many drafts of my work at different stages in its development. I will be forever be grateful to Adrián and Andres for reading several drafts of this book cover to cover. I also want to thank Miguel Chavez, Steven Osuna, Yousef Baker, Victor Rios, Elana Zilberg, Juan de Lara, Susan Coutin, Mario Barrera, Silvia Zamora, Albert Ponce, Arely Zimmerman, Ulla Berg, Opal Tometi, Monica Novoa, and Zachariah Mampilly for reading parts of the manuscript or book proposal. Not to be forgotten, I want to thank the undergraduate researchers who provided assistance along the development of this project, including Janet Perez, Mathew Pinero, Jee Eun Mae, Diana Hernandez, Johana Rodriguez, and Fernando Venancio of Lehman College; Jazmin Molina of NYU; and Maribel Meza, Araceli Gonzalez-Flores, and Eduardo Maximo of UCLA. I also want to thank Pablo Morales, Allison Brown, Mario Rocha, and Sandy Andes.

Several individuals at various institutions helped me develop this project. Foremost among these institutions, I would like to thank Shawn Plant at the office of the Dean of the School of Natural and Social Sciences, Victoria Sanford at the Center for Human Rights and Peace Studies, and my colleagues in the Department of Political Science, especially Jeannette Graulau for her intellectual solidarity, Tom Hattori for giving me a semester off, and Chiseche Mibenge for reading the entire manuscript and providing generous feedback. I also want to thank Arlene Torres of the CUNY Latino Initiative and all of my colleagues from the Latino Caucus of the American Political Science Association.

I am also grateful to have been invited to share aspects of this project at numerous institutions. For this I am grateful to Linda Green at the Center for Latin American Studies at the University of Arizona, Ediberto Roman at the College of Law at Florida International University, Mark Noferi and his colleagues at Brooklyn Law School, and to the Department of Latin American Studies at the University of Florida. To be sure, I am immensely grateful to Oxford University Press and my editor, Angela Chnapko, for their enthusiastic support of this project. I am also indebted to the three anonymous reviewers who provided insightful and energetic suggestions on my manuscript.

There are several community members and mentors whom I would like to thank for supporting me along this journey. First and foremost, I would like to thank Jorge Hernandez, who led me to the path of higher education through a community-based Raza Studies program. Over the years many have provided me a sense of community and a sense of family from the West Coast to the East Coast, including Rosa Martha Zarate, Ward Schinke, Dariush Haghighatand, Manuela Sosa, Elizabeth Iglesias, Rossana Reguillo, Miriam Jimenez, Hector Perla Jr. Nimmi Gowrinathan, Jason Javier, Gladys Ivonne Garcia y su familia, Fabricio Herrera, Maria Huerta y su familia, and Citlali Negrete y su familia.

Last but not least, I want to thank my family. Words cannot express the deep-felt love that I have for my siblings, nephews, and my parents, John J. Gonzales and Maria Guadalupe Toribio-Gonzales. Completing this book would have been impossible without all of their love, support, and guidance. My brothers, Chris and Martin, taught me many valuable life lessons, and my sister, Jazmin, led the way forward as the first to graduate high school and attend college in our family. She is my original intellectual mentor. This book is also dedicated to my *sobrinos* Johnny, Felix, and Vicente, and my *sobrinas* Alyssa, Vanessa, and Naillila; even as children you have taught me the power of laughter and love. My father, or *jefito*, as I affectionately called him, left me many wise teachings and passed on to me his work ethic, love for *norteñas*, and sense of humor. He and my brother Chris will be missed forever. I am especially beholden to my mother, for she has taught me the value of family, perseverance, and human solidarity since I was a child in Tijuana. Indeed, it is these values that are at the heart of this book and my everyday pedagogy.

Finally, this project could not have come to fruition without the support of my brilliant and beautiful wife, Esther Maria Portillo-Gonzales, and her family. They raised her to be a humble and well-respected defender of human rights, from Southern California to New York City, from El Salvador to Mexico, and beyond. Esther's actions and intellectual interventions are written throughout this book and on my heart. Last but not least, this work is dedicated to my cherished daughter, Alitzel Guadalupe Gonzales. Your mother and I dedicate ourselves to what we do so that you may inherit a world that is more just than the one we have lived in.

Reform Without Justice

Introduction

I met Bernardo, a deportee and veteran of the 1991 US war in Iraq (Operation Desert Storm), in November 2010 at a protest in front of the US Embassy in Mexico City to denounce US immigration policies. Bernardo told his story of removal:

> I was born in Cancún and I was taken to the States when I was one year old, me and my twin sister. I lived an American life since I was one year old. I'm thirty-eight. I went to the Persian Gulf in 1991 and in 1993. I made a mistake in '93—*tres cervezas*, eighteen years ago.... Seven months ago ICE [Immigration and Customs Enforcement] agents went to pick me up from LA to San Diego, from San Diego to Eloy, Arizona, because I got this misdemeanor DUI under California law.[1]

Bernardo concisely explained how under the 1996 immigration laws passed by then president Bill Clinton, Legal Permanent Residents became retroactively deportable for prior convictions for any of the newly designated federal immigration "felonies." He then described how he was racially profiled and caught by an ICE raid in a furniture store and was detained for six months until tried before a judge:

> They lied to us! When ICE came inside this mattress company, it was like, "Anybody Latino? Get over here!" You know, separating people. "You never had a problem with the law?" "Yeah, in '93, I am not going to lie to you guys," I said. "That is probable cause for the judge to see you. Come, you are going to court tomorrow!" They lied to us! From LA they took us to San Diego. They kept telling us that we were going to court. They flew us to Eloy, Arizona. Six months fighting my papers, the judge kept telling me, "Sign the volunteer [departure]." "Your Honor, I am not going to give up my papers. I got kids to feed."[2]

Bernardo's is a tragic and complex tale that involves many points of contact between Latinos and state agencies, including being policed, detained, and deported. He went from being profiled based on his phenotypic features and cultural characteristics—in other words, because he "looked Latino"—to being detained and processed in an immigration detention center, where he was held for months, only to be deported.

What makes Bernardo's story even more tragic is that he is just one of millions of Latinos and other people of color who are subjected to a racial gaze from government officials and private individuals who view them as perpetual suspect foreigners under what anthropologist Nicholas De Genova and others have called the homeland security state.[3] De Genova uses this term to refer to a national security state similar to the one built around the specter of Communism at the beginning of the Cold War but this time with a new focus on *migration control* and anti-terrorism.[4]

The homeland security state was symbolically consolidated in the aftermath of 9/11 with the Patriot Act and the formation of the Department of Homeland Security (DHS) in 2003. However, its formation resists any facile date of birth, for it was built upon many previous efforts to increase the migration and social control capabilities of the US government, including the 1986 Immigration Reform and Control Act and the Illegal Immigration Reform and Immigrant Responsibility Act of 1996, among other congressional and executive acts.[5] Yet, for reasons that I will expand upon later, any serious analysis of the homeland security state cannot reduce it to its institutional features, nor can it avoid the war on drugs of the 1980s and 1990s. Rather, it is a deeply social and economic set of relationships.

Since 1990, the United States has deported roughly four million people, with the vast majority being deported after 9/11.[6] Under the homeland security state, the number of deportations from the year 2000 to the year 2012 has more than doubled. For instance, Figure 1 shows the rise in deportation from roughly 188,000 removals per year in fiscal year 2000 to 410,000 people in 2012. If trends continue, two million people will have been deported under the Obama administration alone. To put this in historical perspective, the United States has removed more people in the last ten years than in the last 110 years combined.[7] Moreover, the United States currently spends more on immigration enforcement than it does on all other federal law enforcement combined.[8] Today, the US government spends fifteen times more on migration control than it did in 1986, when the Immigration Reform and Control Act was passed in Congress.[9] As a result of such legislation, executive policies, and resources dedicated to enforcement, Latinos now make up one-half of those sentenced to federal prison.[10]

Yet as suggested by Bernardo's presence in 2010 at an international protest in front of the US Embassy in Mexico City organized by the International Migrant's Alliance, a global grassroots migrant organization comprised of 100 organizations and based in over 25 countries from the major migrant-sending regions of the world, Latino *migrant* activists and the broader global migrant movement have not been passive subjects.[11] The migrant rights movement is a multiethnic and multisector constellation of actors that overlap and intersect with the even broader

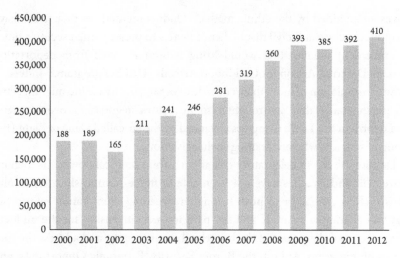

Figure 1 Removals, Fiscal Years 2000–2012.

Source: Data for this figure is drawn from two sources. The United States Department of Homeland Security, Removals Statistics, 2011 Year Book of Immigration Statistics, Table 39. ALIENS REMOVED OR RETURNED: FISCAL YEARS 1892 TO 2011 http://www.dhs.gov/sites/default/files/publications/immigration-statistics/yearbook/2011/ois_yb_2011.pdf. And from Department of Homeland Security, Immigration and Customs Enforcement, Press Release, FY 2012: ICE announces year-end removal numbers, highlights focus on key priorities and issues new national detainer guidance to further focus resources December 21, 2012. http://www.ice.gov/news/releases/1212/12 1221washingtondc2.htm

US and global Left, which includes party organizations, labor unions, faith-based organizations, nongovernmental organizations, hometown associations, affinity groups, and what scholars call the new social movements of youth, students, and racial, ethnic, and sexual minorities. Indeed, Latinos and their allies in the movement have fought back—albeit with limited success—against the encroaching homeland security state at almost every step of its development, from its embryonic stages in the 1980s and most definitely in the aftermath of 9/11.

Perhaps the most spectacular example of this resistance was during the mega-marches of 2006. In this series of massive and peaceful pro-migrant marches that took place across the country, protesters demanded legalization and voiced their opposition to the Border Protection, Antiterrorism, and Illegal Immigration Control Act of 2005 (HR 4437), which was passed in the House of Representatives of the 109th Congress. During these mass mobilizations, between 3.7 and 5 million protesters, most of whom were Latino, shocked the world by taking to the streets of over 160 cities across the United States to demand justice for migrants.[12] The movement has been able to organize mass mobilizations and actions every year after the 2006 marches. Latino migrant activists and their allies have developed a variety of tactics beyond mass mobilizations, including unprecedented naturalization, voter-registration, and get-out-the-vote drives, often aided by the ethnic media.[13] Undocumented youth activists have used direct action and civil disobedience tactics to pressure the executive office to implement policies that would bring temporary relief from deportation through Deferred Action for Childhood Arrivals (DACA) program.[14] Indeed, it is the accumulation of more than a decade of organizing by Latino migrant activists and their allies that has brought us to the historic negotiations over immigration reform in the 113th Congress advanced by the so-called Gang of Eight (the group of senators who are drafting such legislation).

Despite the recent celebratory talk about Latino political power, the migrant movement and its allies have not been able to move beyond short-term solutions such as DACA or to push through a sweeping immigration reform bill that will guarantee a simple and fair path toward citizenship for the undocumented, curtail the power of the homeland security state, and address the root causes of migration. At best, the Border Security, Economic Opportunity, and Immigration Modernization Act (S. 744) and other bills like it will bring much-needed temporary relief from deportation and the right to have a work permit for those that qualify. But it will reduce most of the eleven million undocumented people living in the United States to temporary workers and place them on a ten-year path toward a green card that is filled with legal trip wires and hurdles and that is contingent upon border security. In fact, Bernardo, and perhaps millions of others, would not benefit from this bill because of minor convictions from their past and other requirements. Most critically, most comprehensive immigration reform (CIR) proposals that have emerged in recent years are bound to preserve the very homeland security state and global economic system that has brought about mass migration over the decades.

Reform Without Justice seeks to explain what led us to this moment through an analysis of the conjuncture between 2001 and 2012 leading up to the immigration reform debate. During this period under study, through a series of contestations, Latino migrant activists and their allies have attempted to secure social justice victories for migrants in the face of mounting state violence against migrants under the auspices of the homeland security state. An analysis of any conjuncture attempts to understand the confluence of forces that define the terrain of the struggle between dominant groups and subordinate groups in any given historical moment and location.

In this regard, the book seeks to explain the complex constellation of forces and structures driving migration control policies and the challenges that they present for Latino migrant activists and their allies between 2001 and 2012. Beyond immediate short-term victories such as the DACA or any CIR bill, I seek to unearth why Latino migrant activists and their allies have not been able to win sustainable and transformative social justice victories that actually change the structures that cause migration and state violence toward migrants. My reference to justice is in the sense put forth by political theorist Iris Marion

Young—the elimination of domination and human suffering.[15] Moreover, later in the book, I discuss how Latino migrant activists and their allies could potentially turn the tide against authoritarian solutions to the so-called immigration crisis and democratize the United States.

Readers who are interested in gaining greater understanding of my theoretical framework and methods are encouraged to read the appendix. For now it should suffice to indicate that to answer my research questions, I draw upon the ideas of twentieth-century political theorist Antonio Gramsci and neo-Gramscian thinkers to develop my theoretical framework. In addition, my methodological approach is built upon critical discourse analysis and critical ethnography, a method of study that combines ten years of participant observation; over sixty interviews with migrant activist and policy makers in Los Angeles, Washington, D.C., and New York City; and interviews with deportees and policy makers in Mexico and El Salvador.

Based on this theoretical framework and methods, I argue that between 2001 and 2012, Latino migrant activists and their allies could not move beyond isolated and short-term victories because they were up against a form of political power that I call anti-migrant hegemony. This is a type of ideological leadership that naturalizes the idea that we should adopt novel authoritarian solutions to the "immigration crisis," not just within the state but in civil society—the media, religious and intellectual institutions, and other private associations located outside of the official jurisdiction of the state. While authoritarian solutions have become naturalized, there is nothing natural or inevitable about them. This form of consensual domination is the work of concrete political actors whom I conceptualize as an anti-migrant bloc, a contradictory and fluid constellation of forces composed of elected officials, state bureaucrats, think tanks, intellectuals, and charismatic media personalities who, under the influence of strategic fractions of global capital, have set the boundaries of the immigration debate around narrow questions of criminality and anti-terrorism. This narrow debate conceals the racial politics of migration control, guarantees the reproduction and expansion of the homeland security state, and obfuscates the structural causes that have displaced millions of people in the Americas and other parts of the world into the migrant stream over the last thirty years.

Anti-migrant hegemony is not a stagnant form of political power that is merely predicated on a majority in Congress, brute force, or pure domination. Rather, as Antonio Gramsci writes, hegemony is a dynamic form of power that rests upon the "combination of force and consent" in which "the fact of hegemony presupposes that account be taken of the interests and the tendencies of the groups over which hegemony is to be exercised."[16] Thus even some liberals and Latino migrant activists have come to support what the Migration Policy Institute accurately called "a strong bipartisan pro-enforcement consensus" that has resulted "in the creation of a well-resourced, operationally robust, modernized enforcement system."[17] More so than any one policy or act of Congress or the executive, this form of consensual domination is the linchpin of this modern system of migration control, and it is what leaves many elected officials, state personnel, intellectuals, and activists who are sympathetic to migrants silenced or struggling to propose a kinder, gentler version of the homeland security state rather than seeking to dismantle it. Indeed, it is this type of fluid and disparate ideological power that normalizes state violence, or what scholars Cecilia Menjivar and Leisy Abrego call "legal violence" against migrants and their families, many of whom were born in the United States.[18]

The anti-migrant bloc acts against migrants and their families in many ways; however, in this study of specific sites and localities of the homeland security state, it does so through the criminalization of migrants. I use this term in two ways throughout the book. Criminalization in the discursive sense serves as the ideological glue of the homeland security state; it is a process in which a set of discourses attribute criminal characteristics to a targeted group, in this case Latinos, to win consent for legal violence.[19] In the legal sense, criminalization also expands the grounds for removal in order to facilitate detention and deportation. Rather than being one single stagnant discourse, the exact language used to criminalize Latinos shifts in different contexts, such as in the halls of the US House of Representatives, municipal governmental bodies, in the State Department, the executive office, or in the media and in popular culture.

Despite these shifts, the criminalization of Latinos functions to legitimize state violence against women and entire Latino families and maps out polemical but simple "common sense" and "race neutral" "solutions" to a complex problem rooted in the evolution of US-led global capitalism and the displacement of millions of people from Latin America and the Caribbean from their traditional means of survival. Regardless of the context, the criminalization of migrants is what makes it easy, almost dutiful (i.e., "common sense"), for a judge to deport someone like Bernardo, without thinking about the impact of the deportation on his wife, children, mother, community, or even his very life. It also leaves some liberals asking what *else* did someone like Bernardo do to be deported instead of questioning the system of mass deportation that cast him and millions of other migrants away from their families and communities in the name of the "law." This process allows for the advocates of the homeland security state and novel police practices to make post-racial claims that enforcement is colorblind and that it is just about "enforcing the law," even when, as indicated by figure 2, Mexicans and Latin Americans comprised 97% of all removals in 2010.

Yet the most insidious consequence of the criminalization of migrants is that it allows the anti-migrant bloc to set the boundaries of the immigration debate within a binary opposition, in which they advance a one-dimensional image of "the bad immigrant" who, based solely on a few "exaggerated, simplified, and naturalized characteristics," deserves to be detained and deported and in which the traditional opposition attempts to counter with more simplified images of the

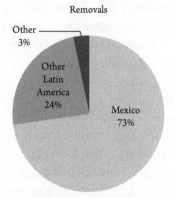

Figure 2 Pew Hispanic Center, Removals by Country of Origin 2010.

Source: http://www.pewhispanic.org/2011/12/28/ii-recent-trends-in-u-s-immigration-enforcement/

immigrant who deserves to stay.[20] This simplistic characterization forces Latino migrant activists and their allies into a false binary opposition in which the rights of the "good immigrant"—the poster child image of the palatable assimilated American kid who came to the United States—as a child may potentially stay at the expense of the "bad immigrant." The latter of whom, like Bernardo, may have made a few mistakes in their lives must be policed, detained, and deported.

Once Latino migrant activists and their allies accept this binary, they subtly consent to the production of legal violence against migrants. Moreover, advocating for the rights of the good immigrant within the binary serves to silence potentially counterhegemonic discourses that challenge the structural causes of migration and that take an unequivocally anti-racist stance to defend the human rights of Latinos (and other people of color), who, regardless of legal status or history with the law, are perpetually suspected to be deportable by virtue of their phenotypic and cultural characteristics. Thus, the ideological leadership of the anti-migrant bloc sets the boundaries of the debate and divides and disorganizes Latino migrant activists and the broader migrant rights movement between immigration reformers and oppositional forces.

Before elaborating on how the Latino migrant movement and its allies are divided and disorganized by anti-migrant hegemony, I must elaborate on the cleavages of the anti-migrant bloc. I developed this term from Gramsci's notion of the historic bloc. The anti-migrant bloc is a contradictory and discordant ensemble of forces operating at the level of the state, civil society, and the global economy that seek to expand and reproduce the homeland security state. The exact cleavages—*factions* and *fractions*—of the anti-migrant bloc are too vast and dynamic to lay out in any one study.[21]

In the period under study, some of the main sectors of the bloc include academics, charismatic television and radio personalities, elected officials, and state personnel within the bureaucracy such as DHS that have the support of strategic fractions of capital. Many of these actors take on the role of organic intellectuals whose vocation it is to educate society into supporting the expansion of the homeland security state. According to Gramsci, such a corps of intellectuals gives their particular social group awareness and greater homogeneity.[22] From this perspective, nativist academics such as the late Samuel P. Huntington—who wrote the infamous article "The Hispanic Challenge" and the book *Who Are We? The Challenge to America's National Identity,* among others—take on a critical role within the anti-migrant bloc as organic intellectuals of the homeland security state.[23] Huntington's writings in the early 1970s were a thinly veiled defense of Jim Crow racism and authoritarian state practices.[24] His more recent writings on "Hispanics" in his tradition reified the fantasy of a static and homogenous Anglo-American national identity based on Protestant values that he saw as being undermined by Latino and Mexican migration in particular at the dawn of the homeland security state. Organic intellectuals of the homeland security state are not just academics. It also includes a broad range of intellectuals including journalists and television and talk radio personalities Lou Dobbs, Glenn Beck, Michael Savage, and Rush Limbaugh.

Beyond academics and media personalities, there are set of civil society based institutions that are at the core of the anti-migrant bloc's intellectual power. Indeed, organizations such as the Federation for American Immigration Reform, the Center for Immigration Studies, the Heritage Foundation, and the Manhattan Institute, among others, are dedicated to shaping immigration policy by educating people on the virtues of the homeland security state (see chapter 1). These think tanks are funded by a select fraction of capital, such as the Scaife foundations funded by the billionaire Richard Mellon Scaife, heir to the Mellon family fortune. The Scaife foundations have given these and other ultra-Right organizations millions of dollars over the years.[25]

Operating at the level of the state, elected officials and state bureaucrats also function as organic intellectuals in a sense. Indeed, this stratum of intellectuals is strategic because they have direct decision-making power over the bureaucracy and the distinct sites of local, state, national, and transnational levels of governance. Outside of planning and codifying migration control policies, elected officials and state personnel shape and educate society about immigration issues through their connections to the media and in the halls of power. Regardless of the sector, intellectuals and intellectual power are essential to the anti-migrant bloc as it functions to shape and exploit ordinary people's common-sense thinking about immigration politics and Latinos. By "common sense," I am referring to what Gramsci described as the contradictory forms of consciousness held by ordinary people that are shaped by the dominant class's ideology and that make things appear normal and unchangeable.

The anti-migrant bloc operating at the level of the state and civil society divides and disorganizes Latino migrant activists and the broader migrant rights movement. Indeed, the movement is also not a homogenous force but rather a constellation of actors who are divided over how to respond to the good immigrant–bad immigrant binary, and they differ in their vision of what constitutes immigration reform. At the risk of oversimplification, the migrant rights movement should be conceived of as having two major factions: immigration reformers and oppositional forces. Immigration reformers, a label developed by political theorists Luis Fernandez and the late Joel Olson, seek to defend the rights of migrants by reforming the current immigration system within the dominant policy framework, whereas the oppositional sector seeks transformative change that breaks with the good immigrant–bad immigrant binary and addresses the structural causes of migration.[26]

Immigration reformers are often led by a class of professional middle-class to affluent Latino brokers who mediate between the state and the broader base of working-class Latinos in society. Many Latino immigration reformers come from the ranks of the Congressional Hispanic Caucus or other elected government bodies; the dominant Latino policy organizations in Washington, D.C., such as the National Council of La Raza, the Center for American Progress, the Center for Community Change, America's Voice, and the National Immigration Forum; the heights of the labor establishment; the Catholic Church; and select circles of academics and policy experts, among other groups.

Some Latino immigration reformers come from the ranks of the migrant working class and progressive movements and may even share much in common with their oppositional counterparts. But they are willing to accept the established terms of the debate on immigration reform within the good immigrant–bad immigrant binary. Thus immigration reformers reject using arguments around racial justice or human rights and favor a moderate discourse designed to "win over the middle," not to "offend" people who are potentially on "our side." This strategy often leads them to embrace the good immigrant–bad immigrant binary and thus focus on attempting to counter the anti-migrant bloc with the static image of the good immigrant—the straight-A undocumented student with a perfect record "who can't wait to join the Air Force," for instance—or with "data" showing that Latinos are indeed assimilating or that Latinos are more patriotic than whites.

Immigration reformers often fight for important changes that would have a real and positive impact on the lives of migrants, but they are structurally locked into a game of perpetual compromise with the dominant bloc, which often forces them to accept the established terms of the debate on migration control. This position requires immigration reformers to accept and lobby for state practices and policy proposals that include the further militarization of the US–Mexico border and interior enforcement as a "fair compromise" for immigration reform, without challenging the homeland security state, racism, and the forces of global capitalism that have displaced millions of people in the Americas. Many immigration reformers point out that the only way to win any type of legalization for some—at the moment—is to concede to the enforcement provisions proposed by mainstream political parties. Yet as we will see in the chapters that follow, CIR as it has been proposed will establish a pathway to temporary legal status and toward citizenship for only a portion of the eleven million undocumented people in the United States while entrenching the homeland security state and will lead to the mass deportation of millions through novel modes of social control at the local, national, and transnational levels of governance.

The anti-migrant bloc establishes the terms of the debate on migration control from which immigration reformers respond accordingly. Yet the immigration reformers rarely challenge the underlying forces driving migration on a global scale, nor do they effectively question the racial politics of the homeland security state. Rather they keep their critique limited to questions of tactics; the nativists propose an iron fence at the border and mandatory detention for those caught there, and they propose a smart wall and ankle bracelets for those "released"; DHS proposes a new program to deport people from communities, and the loyal opposition proposes human rights training for the police. In the most recent example of this dynamic, some immigration reformers scoffed at the idea that S. 744 would allow drones to be used by the Border Patrol up to ninety miles from the border. Instead they demanded that Border Patrol drones be limited to thirty miles from the US–Mexico border. Rarely do immigration reformers effectively question the logic of the homeland security state, global capitalism, and white supremacy.

Any effort to understand the positions taken by immigration reformers and the cleavages in the migrant rights movement cannot be reduced solely to the difference in the discourse between the two groups. Although language or discourse was important to Gramsci, he held that hegemony "must also be economic" and "must necessarily be based on the decisive function exercised by the leading group in the decisive nucleus of economic activity."[27] Capital undeniably sets the boundaries of the immigration debate among the Right and some sectors of the Left. Just as major foundations such as Scaife support sectors of the anti-migrant bloc, many of the leading immigration-reform organizations in the United States are directly funded by the leading corporate foundations or sponsored by major corporations. For example, the National Council of La Raza (NCLR) has a corporate board of sponsors, which is headed by Johnson & Johnson and includes powerful transnational corporations such as Coca Cola, AT&T, Bank of America, and Coors, among many more.[28] This sponsorship is not limited to NCLR; it is the norm for most of the influential migrant organizations across the United States. While there are many differences between immigration reformers and the anti-migrant bloc, they have reached a consensus on the boundaries of migration control that preserves the social reproduction of the global capitalist system and the institutionality of the homeland security state as a necessary and nonnegotiable part of any US migration control strategy.

While certain migrant rights organizations and corporations may seem like strange bedfellows, one must be clear on the nature of their alliances.[29] Outside the nativists and those fractions of capital that directly profit from the business of homeland security, there is a large sector of capital that seeks contained solutions to the "immigration problem" and that wants to preserve their highly flexible labor force and consumer bases. Thus the associations of growers in Alabama, select corporations in Arizona, the meatpacking industry in the Midwest, and the American Apparel company in California have come out against the most draconian immigration legislation, not because they are "pro-immigrant" or for social justice reasons—as any analysis of their labor practices would reveal—but because they seek to preserve their labor force and consumer base. The unstable and delicate coalition of convenience between these forces, and others like them, prevents immigration reformers from openly taking a position that calls into question the driving force behind migration over the last thirty years—US-led global capitalism—and divides them from the oppositional sectors of the movement.

Outside of immigration reformers, there is an oppositional faction composed of Latino migrant activists and their allies. The oppositional forces, as sporadic and disorganized as they may be, reject the good immigrant–bad immigrant binary and argue that such a binary requires that activists adopt a vision of immigration reform in which thousands of people like Bernardo would not benefit because of minor past convictions or other requirements. Moreover, the oppositional sector of the movement seeks to create an autonomous pole of political power that does not have to compromise with the authoritarian practices of the homeland security state and that could secure social justice for all migrants and their families.

The oppositional faction involves multiple sectors; it is often composed of grassroots organizations, small nonprofit organizations (many of which struggle to even pay staff members), rank-and-file union members, rebellious labor leaders, independent migrant workers, leftist intellectuals, independent labor centers, anti-globalization and anti-war activists, and a sector of the youth and student groups. The oppositional faction generally does not have the institutional resources, corporate sponsors, budgets, and salaries that immigration reformers have. Despite such disadvantages, this sector is closely linked to, or often led by, the base of migrant workers and their children who are directly affected by the homeland security state. This sector of the migrant movement is

often fiercely independent of the labor hierarchy and partisan politics. Most critically, this sector of the migrant rights movement often advances a self-conscious
critique of global capitalism and US foreign policy and argues that unless these
structural conditions are changed, no immigration reform legislation will ever
get to the root of the problem.

Both ideological poles or factions among Latino migrant activists and the
migrant rights movement have their organic intellectuals too, but they are not
as powerful or influential as the intellectuals of the anti-migrant bloc (in most
cases). Moreover, they do not have the same degree of organization and ideological unity as their counterparts in the anti-migrant bloc. There are certainly a
host of groups that are in the middle of these two factions, and there are certainly
groups that fluctuate between these two fluid ideological currents in the migrant
rights movement. Nonetheless, these are the forces that have defined Latino
migrant activism and the migrant rights movement that has emerged during the
conjuncture under study, 2001 to 2012.

The Homeland Security State and Latinos

This study requires a careful conceptual analysis of the state. Indeed, it is part of
the terrain where both the anti-migrant bloc and Latino migrant activists organize to either constrain or expand migration control policies and practices. In
the particular case of the United States, analysis requires that we have conceptual clarity on what "the state" refers to and on its relationship to the politics of
race in general and to Latinos in particular. There are competing theories on the
nature of the state and political power that I will not fully engage here. For now
it will suffice to say that postmodern theories emphasize the role of discourse
and knowledge, while Weberian accounts accentuate the bureaucratic aspects
of the state. Although language is central to any analysis of migration control
(including this one), we must remember that it is not the discourse alone that
kicks down the door to deport brown bodies in the middle of the night: it is the
state. Thus my analysis of migration control and migrant social movements rests
on a particular neo-Gramscian understanding of the state and its relationship
with Latinos.

Antonio Gramsci conceived of the state as something deeper and more complex than simply its legislative, juridical, and bureaucratic forms, such as DHS
and other police agencies. Rather, Gramsci conceptualized what he calls the
"integral state," which "contains both the apparatuses of government and the
judiciary and the various voluntary and private associations and para-political
institutions which make up civil society."[30] Gramsci uses this concept to refer
to a contradictory constellation of institutions that were rooted in a nexus

between the state, civil society, and the fundamental social group, the capitalist class. Like Nicholas De Genova and others, I view the homeland security state as the most recent configuration of a national security state that seeks to control migrant labor in the United States that includes the traditional institutions of governance, such as the Supreme Court, Congress, and the presidency, together with the bureaucracy, including DHS among other military and police institutions.[31] But departing from these scholars, I view the homeland security state as an integral state, which exists in a state–civil society nexus with other strategic sites of ideological production in civil society (such as the media, think tanks, academic experts, art, religion, and entertainment) and with fractions of capital that depend on undocumented migrant labor and the policing of migrants and people of color.

Yet as Gramsci and neo-Gramscian scholars have warned, there can never be a general theory of the state, for each state is a condensation of the specific social relations of a historically specific society.[32] When writing about the development of the state in the particular case of the United States, we must recognize its unique history based on a system of racialized class relations, that is, a class system with undeniable racial dimensions. Sociologist Aníbal Quijano writes that "in Anglo-America," there was "a racist distribution of labor and the forms of exploitation of colonial capitalism. This was, above all, through a quasi-exclusive association of whiteness with wages and, of course, with the high-order positions in the colonial administration."[33] Even though colonialism formally ended in 1776, the racial axis in the United States (and Latin America) has "proven to be more durable and stable than the colonialism."[34]

Indeed, the US state is the institutional and ideological condensation of social relations built upon a system of capitalism and white supremacy that emerged in the seventeenth century and evolved into the modern homeland security state. From this perspective, the latter is a racial state that cannot be separated from the unique history of the United States, a history in which various racial ideologies have been used to justify the dynamic system of white supremacy and the subordination of nonwhite groups throughout specific moments in history until the present.[35] By white supremacy, I am referring to what sociologist Eduardo Bonilla Silva calls "racially based political regimes that emerged post-fifteenth century" in which people "participate in race relations as either beneficiaries (members of the dominant race) or subordinates (members of the dominated race or races)."[36] The homeland security state is an integral racial state that emerged from a contentious history over the politics of race in general and with Latinos in particular.

As political theorist Cristina Beltrán emphasizes, there is nothing existentially natural about the formation of this group of peoples that we have come to call Latinos in the United States.[37] "Latinos" are a multilingual and multiracial constellation of nationalities, ethnicities, and cultures that come from all over the Americas, including the US Southwest and the Caribbean. However, departing from Beltrán, I maintain that Latinos have distinct class interests, ranging from a small—but significant—group of corporate and political elites and a growing middle class of professionals and business owners. The largest sector of Latinos, however, is the working class, which is made up of people who often live in mixed-status families and at the margins of society. In fact, the splits in the Latino migrant movement and its allies are a manifestation of two class projects: one that reflects the Latino migrant working class's popular demands and strategy for mobility, or what Fernandez and Olson call the freedom to "live, work, and love wherever you please," and one that reflects middle and affluent classes' demands and strategy of fighting for inclusion and social mobility through conventional politics and a corporate-backed immigration reform.[38]

In addition to these class cleavages, many Latinos share a history of racialization and conflict with the United States, starting with Mexicans in the 1830s and Puerto Ricans in the 1890s, and including the often dark-skinned and heavily working-class Latinos from Central America and the Dominican Republic who mostly came after 1965. While not all Latinos experience racialization in the same way, the ironic outcome of anti-migrant hegemony is that it racializes most Latinos as "foreigners" and "immigrants," including even those born in the United States, because of their phenotypic and cultural characteristics. This racialization, in turn, contributes to the further crystallization of a racialized working-class Latino identity. It is precisely because of the last few decades' anti-migrant policies and climate that we are beginning to see a strengthening of a pan-ethnic solidarity among native-born Latinos and migrants from Latin America in the United States. Hence, many—but certainly not all—US citizen Puerto Ricans and second- and third-generation Chicanos share a sense of solidarity with recently arrived Latino migrants.

It is precisely at this nexus between the state and civil society, history and the present, where the battle over immigration is being fought. Indeed, at all the sites of state power, there is a struggle rooted in a nexus with civil society for ideological leadership over the direction of the state's repressive apparatuses and for the rights and benefits of racialized migrants vis-à-vis the state. This state–civil society nexus is present at nearly every level of governance, from debates over immigration legislation in Congress, to the approval of local anti-migrant ordinances, to providing military aid to El Salvador to police deportees, to the tightening of possibilities for asylum in immigration court. At nearly every instance in which there is an effort to expand the repressive field of the state, there are groups operating in civil society that ultimately seek to make Latinos and other racial minorities the legal objects of state violence. Conversely, there are also groups, albeit less powerful ones, that seek to resist or ameliorate state violence against those perpetually suspected of being detainable and deportable.

The Organic Crisis of North American Capitalism and Race Relations

Although this study is focused on the conjuncture between 2001 and 2012, a Gramscian method of analysis requires us to study the day-to-day struggle between the Latino migrant activists and the homeland security state as part of a deeper historical process.[39] As alluded to earlier, Latino migrant activism and migration control did not start on September 11, 2001. To understand the conjuncture under study, it must be contextualized by what I call the organic crisis of North American capitalism and race relations, which has emerged over the last thirty years.

This crisis is marked by the transition between the Fordist model of development in which capital and labor relations were organized within a nation-state system to a post-Fordist model of development and the emergence of a truly global capitalist economy, or what scholars call globalization. Along the lines of William I. Robinson, I view globalization as the latest phase in the evolution of the five hundred-year-old process of capital accumulation in which new forms of production and finance displace older ones across the globe.[40] This reorganization of production is at the heart of global migration over the last three decades in which, according to the United Nations, there were over 214 million migrants living across the globe in 2010.[41]

Globalization is the primary dynamic driving migration from Latin America and the Caribbean, which have become the largest migrant-sending regions to the United States in the world. This migration relationship came about through the dual process of economic restructuring in the United States and in Latin America and the Caribbean. The reorganization of production has led to the deindustrialization of the United States and the relocation of production, in search of greater profits, to the Global South. In Mexico and Central America, states adopted structural adjustment programs backed by the World Bank and International Monetary Fund that were aimed specifically at transitioning national economies based on an import-substitution industrialization model into export-led models at the service of global capital. In the process of making this transition from a national system of production to a global one, millions of people in rural Latin America and the Caribbean faced massive unemployment, forcing them to either migrate or live in misery. Economically displaced people, and those displaced by war, migrated either to the overpopulated urban centers of Latin America or to El Norte.

The reorganization of production in El Norte gave rise to a post-Fordist economy, which is characterized by deindustrialization and the ascendancy of a massive service sector. The service sector, in turn, is dependent on a highly flexible labor force, which is made up of unskilled, nonunionized migrant workers. The reorganization of production has set the material conditions for the massive displacement of millions of Latin Americans into the US labor market and for the emergence of a transnational model of society and economy. This set of social and economic relations is the product of the nearly thirty years of neoliberal restructuring that began in the 1970s. The transnational economy is composed of previously separate national economies, like those of the United States, Mexico, and Central American countries, which are integrated via remittances, trade, labor supplies, and a series of binding free trade agreements. Thus, rather than being an anomaly or self-propelling force based simply on social networks, migrant labor is a central component of the integrated global economy of the Americas.

Globalization and the emergence of the transnational model of society and economy under asymmetrical geopolitical relations between the United States and Latin America set the groundwork for the massive influx of Latinos into the country over the last thirty years. Almost immediately following the 1982 debt crisis, labor migration from Mexico to the United States began to increase. The pace of labor migration accelerated with the introduction of a series of neoliberal reforms in Mexico, including when it signed the General Agreement Trade and Tariffs in 1986. Moreover, the rate of labor migration from Mexico to the United States intensified with the deepening of the neoliberal model with the signing of the North American Free Trade Agreement. In fact, between 1990 and 1995, Mexico was the country with the largest number of emigrants in the world. According to Raúl Delgado Wise, from 1990 to 1995, Mexico lost an average of 400,000 people per year.[42] Moreover, from 2000 to 2005, the Mexican annual exodus grew to 560,000 per year.[43] These numbers held steady until the global recession of 2008.

Although Mexican migration to the United States in the aftermath of the North American Free Trade Agreement surpasses that of any other part of Latin America, one must also take note of the sheer magnitude of the number of Latin American and Caribbean people displaced by neoliberal policies, too. With the ascendancy of neoliberalism, many Central Americans continued to migrate to the United States despite the end of the civil wars of the 1980s. Salvadorans, the largest of the Central American groups, now represent the third-largest Latino group in the United States after Mexicans and Puerto Ricans, respectively.[44] The 1990s also witnessed an increase in mass migration from South American nations. The first modest wave of South American migration took place in the 1970s. Before this wave, the relatively few South American migrants living in the United States were primarily middle-class professionals who came on work visas. With the onslaught of neoliberal reforms in South America in the 1990s, however, there has been a dramatic increase in South American migrants arriving to the United States. For instance, the number of South Americans living in the United States went from 1,035,602 in 1990 to 1,847,811 in 2000.[45] The two decades of mass migration from Latin America to the United States are the product of the transition from nation-based economic systems to a global capitalist system.

The organic crisis of North American capitalism marked by a shift from the Fordist model of production to a global economy occurred during a shift in racial politics. Scholars like Howard Winant, Eduardo Bonilla-Silva, and others note that after the civil rights movement, racial politics shifted from an openly racist discourse to an ostensibly race-neutral one.[46] This post-racial discourse, sometimes reffered to as colorbliness, argues that racism is no longer a major impediment for racial minorities. This shift has set the foundation for post–civil rights race relations. Thus, rather than using such terms as "subhuman," "genetically inferior," "wetbacks," or "spics," the contemporary discourse that is used in multiple sites of state power and civil society racializes Latinos through the process of criminalization. Although apparently race-neutral, criminalization attributes historical stereotypes about Mexican male criminality to all Latino groups in the North American imaginary, an imaginary that is shaped by two hundred years of conflict and colonization.[47] This characterization explains how many Central Americans and Ecuadorans, for instance, are often suspected of being undocumented Mexicans, with deadly consequences in the most extreme cases, such as the young Ecuadoran father of two who was killed by a group of teens who wanted to go "Mexican hunting."[48] As I demonstrate in the chapters to come, post–civil rights racism and globalization are two sides of the same organic crisis that has defined the terrain of struggle in which Latino activists and the migrant rights movement operates.

Reform Without Justice: A Chapter Road Map

The chapters in this book should be read as case studies in which the specific configurations of the anti-migrant bloc exert their hegemony over migration control in multiple sites of state power at the local, federal, and transnational levels of governance. The chapters are also meant to illustrate how immigration reformers and the oppositional faction of the Latino migrant movement could either sustain or challenge the hegemony of the dominant bloc. For instance, chapters 1, 3, and 4 are primarily focused on illustrating how dominant groups wield hegemony at distinct levels of governance, such as the US Congress, the

Riverside County Board of Supervisors, and US foreign policy institutions. These studies are not meant to be an exhaustive list of the institutions in which hegemony is exerted; there are many more sites that could easily be included, such as the US Supreme Court, academia, popular culture, etc. Regardless of the site, hegemony is always contested; thus chapters 2 and 6 focus on the struggles of Latino migrant activists and the migrant rights movement to resist and miti-gate migration control policies and practices. The chapters take place at two dis-tinct geographic and historical junctures: chapter 2 centers on the 2006 migrant marches in Los Angeles under the Bush administration, and chapter 6 looks at the migrant mobilizations in Washington, D.C., and in New York City under the Obama administration in 2010.

In chapter 1, I explain how the anti-migrant bloc congealed in the aftermath of 9/11 and how it sought to expand the police power of the homeland secu-rity state in the 109th Congress. Through the use of critical discourse analysis, I show how the Republican-dominated House of Representatives of the 109th Congress sought to expand the repressive capabilities of the state by passing the Border Protection, Antiterrorism, and Illegal Immigration Control Act (HR 4437), the most repressive immigration legislation considered in a hundred years. I examine the passage of HR 4437 on December 16, 2005, by contextual-izing the debate over the bill through the discourse of the "war on terror" and by exploiting historical stereotypes that associate migrants, and Mexicans in partic-ular, with crime. I also show how the leadership of the Democratic Party, as well as immigration reformers in civil society, adopted many of the policy proposals and the discourse of their Republican counterparts in the House floor debate over HR 4437 despite their opposition to the bill.

While it may seem that the hegemony of the power bloc is a dominant force, it is not totalizing and stagnant. It was momentarily challenged by Latino migrant activists during the 2006 mega-marches. Chapter 2 is written from the front lines of the Latino migrant struggle in Greater Los Angeles. I argue that the mega-marches were a counterhegemonic act that momentarily broke the hegemony of the anti-migrant bloc by briefly shifting the national debate on immigration reform and advancing policy proposals that went beyond the bounds of the acceptable policy proposals. I show how Latino migrant activ-ists in Los Angeles helped their allies around the country galvanize a national movement powerful enough to prevent HR 4437 from becoming law. I also illustrate how despite their ability to mobilize millions, the marches were not enough to stop the subsequent onslaught of anti-migrant policies at multiple levels of governance. I also draw upon field research and interviews with a range of leaders of the 2006 mega-marches that emerged in opposition to HR 4437 in Greater Los Angeles, including labor organizers, community organizers,

Mexican and Central American leaders, male and female leaders, and youth and student leaders.

In chapter 3, I illustrate how in the immediate aftermath of the mega-marches, federal authorities and the Riverside County Board of Supervisors implemented migration control policies at the local level that adversely affected Latino communities in inland southern California. The county has recently experienced a dramatic demographic shift from being an Anglo-majority county in the 1990s to almost having a Latino majority in 2010. Through critical discourse analysis of the Riverside County Board of Supervisors' meetings and interviews with Latino migrant activists from the region, I show how the Riverside County government implemented a pilot program to conduct deportations of migrants from its jails and how Latino migrant activists sought to challenge this policy after the 2006 mega-marches. I also illustrate how anti-migrant hegemony in Riverside County serves to conceal the impact of global capitalism and its dependency on Latino labor in the region.

To illustrate the complexity and transnational dimensions of what the movement is facing, in chapter 4, I focus on the geopolitics of the war on terror and deportation in El Salvador. Indeed, I explain how the discursive continuum among gangs, migration, and terrorism has been used by forces located within the state–civil society nexus in the United States and El Salvador to forge a transnational system of migration control with disastrous human rights consequences for deportees. To develop this argument, I draw upon testimony of the US military's Southern Command before the 109th Congress, policy briefs by the Heritage Foundation, and interviews with policy makers and deportees in El Salvador.

As a way to highlight the agency of Latino migrant activists and the resiliency of the state in the face of pressures from below, chapter 5 draws on interviews with Latino migrant rights activists and policy makers in Washington, D.C., and in New York City during the first term of President Obama. Looking at migrant activists' responses to New York senator Charles Schumer's blueprint for CIR in 2010, I examine how some groups within the movement (the oppositional forces) resist hegemonic proposals and how others lend them active support (immigration reformers).

To conclude, in chapter 6, I question the celebratory accounts of Latino political power in light of the 2012 election and the emergence of a new class of Latino politicians that includes Cuban American senators Marco Rubio, Ted Cruz, and Mel Melendez, among others. I also interrogate the Border Security, Economic Opportunity, and Immigration Modernization Act (S. 744) subsequently considered by the Gang of Eight in the US Senate. I advance the thesis that this proposal, and most like it, would under the best circumstances bestow

citizenship upon only a small fraction of the eleven million undocumented people living in the United States, while entrenching the homeland security state for
generations to come. While focusing on the democratic potentiality of Latino
youth and the migrant movement, I advance a vision for building Latino political power and a multiracial working-class coalition for transforming the debate
on US migration control beyond immigration reform and the good immigrant–
bad immigrant binary.

The State–Civil Society Nexus and the Debate over the Border Protection, Antiterrorism, and Illegal Immigration Control Act of 2005

On December 16, 2005, just two weeks before Christmas, the House of Representatives of the 109th Congress, with the aid of its conservative allies in civil society, gave migrants a cruel gift, the Border Protection, Antiterrorism, and Illegal Immigration Control Act (HR 4437). The bill, widely known as the Sensenbrenner bill after the Republican congressman from Wisconsin who introduced it, sought to do the following: make it a felony to be undocumented; expand border-security measures; increase cooperation between federal and local police agencies on immigration-law enforcement; broaden the definition of aggravated felony to include certain misdemeanor charges; and expand the definition of human trafficking to include anyone who transports an undocumented person in an automobile, among other provisions. The bill passed in the House on December 15, 2005.

The Sensenbrenner bill was part of a series of anti-migrant bills in the 109th Congress, which lasted from January 2005 to January 2007. This session was a unique Congress in which a Republican president with Republican majorities in both the House and Senate had the opportunity to advance a partisan legislative agenda. The 109th Congress passed the Real ID Act and the Secure Fence Act, both of which eventually became law, and expanded the power of the homeland security state to police migrants in unique ways.[1] The Real ID Act changed visa laws for temporary workers, introduced national regulations for state-issued identification to prevent states from giving undocumented people driver's licenses, and waived potential barriers to building the border wall, among other provisions. The Secure Fence Act sought to build an additional seven hundred miles of fencing at the US–Mexico border and to increase the amount of money and number of agents dedicated to border enforcement. The bill also sought to expand the use of advanced technology, such as satellites and aerial drones, at the border. Combined, these laws sought to reinforce the homeland security state by mapping out a new terrain of policing that would eventually criminalize Latino migrants and nonmigrants alike.

The Sensenbrenner bill had deep roots in civil society–based nativist organizations and a corps of organic intellectuals who used the post-9/11 security context to help forge the convergence of contradictory groups that would compose the anti-migrant bloc. This bloc of interests was able to wield hegemonic leadership over immigration control issues in the 109th Congress and in other sites of power at the nexus between the state and civil society. The case of the Sensenbrenner bill demonstrates how the narrow ideological discourse of the nativist Right, which was once on the margins of US immigration policy in the early 1980s, was turned into the leading ideological force for passing anti-migrant legislation during the 109th Congress and beyond. Indeed, conservative politicians armed with data and talking points from their civil society allies acted en bloc to create a discourse that criminalized Latino migrants at every opportunity. This discourse limited the parameters of the debate over HR 4437 between the "good immigrant" and "bad immigrant," which ultimately led Democratic members of the House and civil society–based immigration reformers to reproduce the discourse of their conservative counterparts and propose similar policy solutions.

The Nativist Right, Organic Intellectuals, and the War of Position

Perhaps no other force, besides conservative members of the House of Representatives, played a more prominent role in passing HR 4437 than the nativist Right. This sector of the anti-migrant bloc is composed of a constellation of think tanks, intellectuals, grassroots organizations, and politicians operating at the levels of both the state and civil society. The nativist Right shares an ideology in which, as it claims, the rights of native-born Americans should be put before the rights of the foreign born. Yet as we will see in the sections that follow, the nativist faction of the anti-migrant bloc is concerned with much more than people's legal status and birthplace.

Although many groups make up the broad constellation of actors that constitute the nativist right wing and an even broader set of actors are part of the anti-migrant bloc, this chapter focuses on the most influential nativist organizations—the Federation for American Immigration Reform (FAIR) and its affiliate, the Center for Immigration Studies (CIS), their links with the Republican Party, and select fractions of capital. These highly developed and politically sophisticated conservative organizations are at the vanguard of Washington, D.C.'s nativist Right. As Jean Stefancic and Richard Delgado noted, an analysis of FAIR and its affiliate organizations must be placed in the context of the early stages of a broader conservative movement.[2] While liberals and progressives were talking to themselves in academic journals and conferences throughout the 1980s, conservatives were speaking to policy makers and the media. Through foundations and think tanks, they built a political and ideological infrastructure to roll back the gains of the civil rights movement.

The nativist Right cannot be separated from this broader conservative movement and its thirty-year trajectory.[3] Its proponents regrouped after the civil rights movement, organized in the late 1970s, and then began to wage intense culture wars in the 1980s. Funded by billionaires, right-wing foundations, and its own internal funding structure, the conservative movement built a political and ideological infrastructure to shape the political culture of the United States and the globe through a series of public and private institutions such as the Hoover Institute at Stanford University, the Heritage Foundation, the Manhattan Institute, the CATO Institute, the Project for the New American Century, the Center for Strategic Studies, and the American Enterprise Institute, among others. Combined, these institutions fought for an expansion of neoliberal policies throughout the globe and an aggressive US military project and against affirmative action and what they perceived as rabid multiculturalism. Throughout the 1990s and right up to the first year of the twenty-first century, groups like FAIR and CIS aggressively advocated for English to be the official language of the United States and for a crackdown on migrants in places such as California, New York, and Arizona, while their conservative allies in the Heritage Foundation and the Manhattan Institute pushed for zero-tolerance policing in cities.

Following 9/11, a corps of organic intellectuals within the nativist Right and other factions of the broader conservative movement saw the opportunity to make their long-standing agenda on migration control common sense by linking immigration to antiterrorism. Common sense in the Gramscian sense is a contradictory vision of the world that contains not only elements of good sense— that is, some truth—but also elements of folklore and myth. It ultimately reflects the ideas and values of the dominant classes, which make their domination over the working class seem natural and unchangeable. Indeed, Gramsci wrote, "one of the commonest totems is the belief about everything that exists, that it is 'natural' that it should exist, that it could not do otherwise than exist."[4] The common sense of any society, however, does not develop on its own. It is the product of the battle of ideas that takes place in multiple sites of power.

Intellectuals are central to the organization of common sense and to the maintenance of the hegemonic leadership of any group. For Gramsci, there are two types of intellectuals: traditional intellectuals (such as academics, priests, lawyers, and men and women of letters who "put themselves forward as autonomous and independent of the dominant social group") and "organic intellectuals that every new class creates alongside itself and elaborates in its course of development."[5] In fact, the task of any social class seeking to become hegemonic is to elaborate its own corps of organic intellectuals and to assimilate traditional intellectuals. Combined, traditional and organic intellectuals have the power to organize a conception of the world that sustains the hegemony of dominant groups by shaping the common sense of the average person. The nativists and the other sectors of the Right were able to elaborate a corps of organic and traditional intellectuals who were pivotal to passing HR 4437 and to the broader project of building the homeland security state.

Developing the intellectual power necessary to shape a society and prepare it for consenting to authoritarian state practices cannot be reduced to any one essay, book, or intellectual. Nonetheless, the writings of the corps of intellectuals, both organic and traditional, associated with FAIR, CIS, Numbers USA, and the broader conservative movement played a crucial role in creating the conditions that would see the passage of HR 4437 and the forging of the homeland security state. For instance, Mark Krikorian, executive director of CIS, and Dr. Steven Camarota, director of research of CIS, are just two of the leading intellectuals among the corps of intellectuals of the anti-migrant bloc. Both of them have testified before Congress, and they have appeared more often in the leading sectors of the global media on immigration issues than any liberal intellectual or expert.[6] They articulated their vision for US migration control in a CIS document published in November 2001 titled *Immigration and Terrorism: What Is to Be Done?*[7] Pointing out that most of the 9/11 hijackers were immigrants, Krikorian and Camarota argued that the United States must develop a more aggressive migration control strategy as a way to prevent another terrorist attack on the United States.[8] This document was presented in a testimony by Dr. Camarota before Congress in October 2001, just one month after 9/11, and the document was distributed to members of Congress, the Office of the President, the Immigration and Naturalization Service, and other elite sectors of the bureaucracy and major media outlets.

While there are some elements of truth in the argument (e.g., the hijackers were indeed immigrants), the idea that all terrorists are foreigners and that all foreigners are potential terrorists is built on myths. Despite politically correct gestures made by the authors to say that immigrants should not be scapegoated, the discourse in their document builds on racial myths and stereotypes that suggest an intrinsic link between Islam and terrorism. Moreover, by locating the Mexican border as the place from which this supposed terrorist attack will come next, the CIS document constructs a continuum of threats to national security among terrorism, Islam, immigration, and the US–Mexico border. As noted by Katheleen R. Arnold, this type of discourse, advanced by anti-migrant groups in civil society such as the Minutemen and FAIR, supports what she calls prerogative power, "a particular deployment of sovereign power, indicating the act of suspending the law and establishing a less determinate political status of the subjects of this power."[9]

After President Bush's declaration of a war on terror, the nativist Right moved its troops in a disciplined and organized fashion onto the political battlefield with a new zeal, providing critical civil society support for the Real ID Act, the Secure Fence Act, and HR 4437, among other policies at the state and local levels of governance. However, one cannot understand how these laws were passed simply by studying the 109th Congress. Granted, a certain number of votes were required to pass each bill in the exact conjuncture of the 109th Congress. But HR 4437 and other anti-migrant bills should be seen as part of a larger organic transformation in society that was the product of a three-decade-long war of position in American racial politics. "War of position" describes how groups seeking to become hegemonic must struggle over a prolonged period to create the political conditions for implementing their agenda.[10] Since the late 1970s, the nativist Right has engaged in a prolonged cultural-ideological battle in civil society to prepare the political terrain for implementing its agenda at the level of the repressive state apparatus.[11] Using a policy language consistent with the norms of post–civil rights racial discourse, it armed its allies in Congress with a communications and mobilization strategy that framed the drive to build up the repressive capabilities of the state to police Latinos and other suspect groups in ostensibly nonracist terms.[12] Unearthing the roots of these civil society organizations reveals that much more was at stake than people's legal status.

Eugenicist Roots and Anti-Latino Racism

The modern nativist Right started with FAIR, founded in Washington, D.C., in 1979. Since its inception, FAIR has become a fixture on Capitol Hill, where, along with its affiliates, it has helped shape most immigration legislation, and it was an influential lobby when Congress began debating the Simpson-Mazzoli bill, also known as the Immigration Reform and Control Act, in 1986.[13] FAIR's stated goal has always been to keep immigration levels, legal and undocumented, consistent with the "national interest." FAIR's founder, John Tanton, stated, "We felt that the overall volume of legal immigration needed to be looked at from time to time to make sure it was consistent with other national goals."[14] The key part of this statement is the reference to "other national goals." Tanton tries to avoid direct discussion of these goals throughout an oral history conducted by

historian and FAIR founding member Otis L. Graham Jr.—a nativist and former professor emeritus at the University of California Santa Barbara. FAIR takes
great pains to argue that it is simply concerned with immigration policy; it even
claims to be a "pro-immigrant" organization.[15] Yet the origins of FAIR's ideology,
as well as the writings of its founders, suggest that the "other national goals" to
which Tanton was referring include the preservation of whites' racial hegemony
in the face of the demographic growth of those whom FAIR members see as
racially inferior, especially Latinos.

To understand how immigration is fundamentally about race for groups like
FAIR, one must start with the founder of the organization. Tanton subscribes to
a nativist ideology with a deep-seated racial paranoia over Latino demographics
and, in particular, the growth of the Mexican community in the United States.
Tanton came out of the conservationist movement of the 1960s and 1970s but
eventually distanced himself from the movement around 1977 because it did
not "make the conceptual leap" to work on immigration issues.[16] Tanton was on
the board of an organization called Zero Population Growth (ZPG), a group
ideologically nurtured by the neo-Malthusian writings of Paul Ehrlich, whose
influential book *The Population Bomb* argued that economic gains in the third
world were being undermined by overpopulation.[17] Thomas Robert Malthus
argued that population grows exponentially while natural resources grow arith-
metically and that humanity would eventually reach a moment when resources
would deplete and bring civilization to a crash. According to this logic, human-
kind must make efforts to check this population ceiling, either through contra-
ceptive use or by allowing natural checks such as war and disease. Bankrolled by
major foundations, ZPG funded a body of research that called for population
control as the solution for poverty and underdevelopment in Latin America and
Africa. Accordingly, a body of "scholarly literature" was circulated to members
of Congress, who eventually set up a population commission to study the problem. The commission's recommendation, which was later implemented through
groups such as Planned Parenthood, was to encourage "voluntary" sterilization
of women in Latin America and Africa.[18] In states like California, eugenicist policies were responsible for horrific crimes against Mexican American women. For
instance, one recent study has noted Mexican women in California were disproportionately targeted for forced sterilization in the early part of the twentieth
century.[19]

In his interview with Graham, Tanton recalls struggling to get fellow ZPG
board members to see the importance of immigration in relation to ZPG's
concerns over population control. Tanton and other disgruntled ZPG members, including Planned Parenthood employee Sherry Barnes, former chairman of Gulf Oil Sidney Swensrud, and Graham, among others, composed the
first board members of FAIR.[20] Tanton and the other founders subscribed to

a nativist ideology that was rooted in neo-Malthusian and eugenicist thought. For instance, in an interview with *Wall Street Journal* reporter Tucker Carlson, FAIR board member Garrett Hardin expressed fear over "the next generation of breeders…in third-world countries."[21] Carlson noted that for Garrett Hardin, "the problem is not simply that there are too many people in the world, but that there are too many of the wrong kind of people," after Hardin reportedly told him that "it would be better to encourage the breeding of more intelligent people rather than the less intelligent."[22] Hardin is embracing the age-old racist idea that people from Europe are genetically superior and naturally more intelligent than those from Asia, Africa, and Latin America. He sees these latter groups as the "the wrong kind" of people, who must be less intelligent and whom he ascribes an animalistic quality to as "breeders." When Carlson asked former executive director of FAIR Dan Stein about Hardin's comments, Stein retorted, "What is your problem with that? Should we be subsidizing people with low IQs to have as many children as possible, and not subsidizing those with high ones?"[23] Stein defended the ideas of his colleague and advanced the historically inaccurate and racist idea that genetically superior whites are somehow subsidizing less intel- ligent "third-world" people. These views are not limited to Stein and Hardin.

Such views attract a particular type of supporter to FAIR, such as Peter Brimelow, who wrote *Alien Nation*, a book that became a classic in conserva- tive circles and among the nativist Right. Brimelow, a British immigrant himself, wrote, "Suppose I had proposed more immigrants who look like me. So what? As late as the 1950s, somewhere up to nine out of ten Americans looked like me. That is, they were of European stock… And in those days, they had another name for this thing dismissed so contemptuously as the 'racial hegemony of white Americans.' They called it America."[24] The fact that Brimelow is an immigrant of British heritage is not epiphenomenal to his argument. Rather, it reflects the racial politics of the modern nativist Right. When Brimelow raises the question about immigrants who look like him and says "so what," he is candidly acknowl- edging that he and his colleagues have no problem with immigrants who are of Anglo or Western European stock but that they are opposed to immigration from Latin America and third-world regions. There are many more statements from FAIR board members and associates that could be drawn upon to illustrate their neo-Malthusian and eugenicist beliefs.

However, my focus here is on the fundamental assumption built into their worldview and how it relates to Latinos. The founders of the modern nativist Right believed that overpopulation and the overconsumption of resources are a major problem facing mankind and that those causing the crisis are from the third world and those bearing the brunt of the problem are of Western European stock. This belief stems from the historical stereotypes rooted in the colonial beliefs that Latinos, particularly Mexicans, Puerto Ricans, and other people of color, are genetically inferior, hyperfertile, and irresponsible and are consequently pillaging the earth of its natural resources. By contrast, they see themselves as responsible and thus superior Europeans who are burdened with having to manage the globe and its inferior peoples.

When groups from the nativist Right argue that immigration will lead to overpopulation, they really mean that there are too many Latinos, both migrants and native-born, in the United States, and this (according to their view) overpopulation destroys the social fabric and greatness of American society. Such a nativist perspective suffers from historical amnesia built around a fantasy of what scholar Ali Behdad describes as a presumed transhistorical national cohesion.[25] This view, Behdad reminds us, conveniently overlooks the history of hostility toward migrants, genocide against Native Americans, the enslavement of African Americans, and, last but certainly not least, an imperialist war with Mexico.

FAIR's anti-Latino views were explicitly expressed in a memo that was circulated at an annual retreat founded by Tanton. Known as the WITAN (an Old English term for a council of wise men), these retreats were essentially strategy meetings on how to influence the national debate on immigration. A series of memos written by Tanton for the WITAN retreats was leaked to the public. In one of the three memos, Tanton asked the group, "Will the newcomers vote Democratic or Republican, liberal or conservative, and what difference does it make? A lot, if you're one or the other."[26] Here Tanton is concerned with problematic and imaginary relations of force between whites and Latinos. This view is built on the essentialist vision of whites as Republicans and Latinos as Democrats and what he envisions as an almost natural conflict between the two groups.

Tanton also raises the topic of the relationship between population and governance in the WITAN memo. He made the following point, ironically in Spanish: "'Gobernar es popular' translates 'to govern is to populate.' ... In this society where the majority rules, does this hold? Will the present majority peaceably hand over its political power to a group that is simply more fertile?"[27] Once again, Tantan assumes that Latinos and the Euro-American majority could never peacefully coexist and live under the same political community. Rather, he dismisses Latinos as an inferior and hyperfertile horde that is a threat to an imagined Euro-American political community. In another WITAN memo, Tanton raised the following question: "As Whites see their power and control over their lives declining, will they simply go quietly into the night? ... Can homo contraceptivus compete with homo progenitiva if borders aren't controlled?"[28] By "homo contraceptivus," Tanton is referring to a human species of Western European stock that is at a presumed demographic disadvantage with "homo progentiva," a hyperfertile species from Latin America that he sees as undergoing a demographic explosion. Again, the very suggestion that whites and Latinos constitute different species is disturbingly inaccurate and racist in and of itself. Either way, Tanton's words reflect the deep-seated racial paranoia about becoming a white minority in the face of Latino demographic growth that partially drives the nativist faction of the anti-migrant bloc.

Despite the neo-Malthusian and eugenicist origins of their nativist ideology and the explicitly anti-Latino nature of the WITAN memos, CIS vehemently denies that its members or ideology are racist. CIS often touts its "diverse" board of directors, which includes a prominent conservative African American and a Hispanic chair of the board of directors, Peter Nunez, a former federal prosecutor and Reagan appointee based in San Diego.[29] Moreover, in March 2010 it organized a panel and published material in which it brought Carol Swain, a prominent, conservative African American professor, to defend the position that CIS is not a racist organization.[30] Swain, who was invited to defend the ostensibly race-neutral credentials of CIS, took the time to point out that former CNN anchor Lou Dobbs, on whose show she frequently appeared, is not a racist. CIS also hired prominent Pulitzer Prize–winning journalist Jerry Kammer as a senior fellow and has published a document in which it denounces the Southern Poverty Legal Center (SPLC) for what it calls a smear campaign.[31] The document and the panel essentially tried to discredit the SPLC and to distance CIS from Tanton. Besides the narrow and problematic defence of the nativist Right as non racist, the panel and documents associated with it do not confront the racial politics of the enforcement-through-attrition strategy proposed by its fellows, nor do they confront the politics of racial profiling and the mass deportation of Latinos that have resulted because of the policies that they fought to implement. Yet these well-calculated moves to defend the ostensibly race-neutral positions of CIS and its sister organizations must be seen in the context of post–civil rights relations.

Following the civil rights movement, in which Black and Latino activists and other minority groups challenged the openly racist social order, it became increasingly difficult for dominant groups to express racist beliefs and ideology openly in the public sphere. Knowing this, the founders of the modern nativist Right opted for a political war of position in which they would create, over the long run, the ideological and political conditions needed to bring their agenda from the margins of society into the mainstream of contemporary policy debate. A central component of this war of position has been to frame their agenda in ostensibly nonracial terms—the hallmark of post–civil rights racism. For instance, in one of the WITAN memos, Tanton suggested an alternative language to avoid direct reference to race: "Novak's term 'unmeltable ethnics' is probably better than some of the others [terms] that have been suggested.

Similarly, ethnicity is a more acceptable term than race…LANGUAGE IS VERY important here."[32] The context of the memo shows clearly that in referring to "unmeltable ethnics," Tanton is speaking about Latinos, whom he sees as a group that could never assimilate into the American melting pot because they are racially different from people of Western European heritage. This distinction gets to a central concern with the nativist Right that was pointed out by Devin Burghart: "For the essentialists involved in the contemporary nativist movement—men and women like John Tanton, Wayne Lutton, Barbara Coe, and Peter Brimelow—the battle against immigrants is a battle over identity. In their view, non-European immigrants are laying false claim to an American identity that they can never achieve because they lack the essential prerequisite of European ancestry."[33] This issue of identity is why language is so important to people like Tanton and to the nativist Right in general.

When Tanton emphasized that language is important, he was acknowledging that it is better to conceal the racial politics that are at the epicenter of his cause to make it more palatable for an American public that had grown sensitive to issues around race thanks to the civil rights movement. Thus the nativist Right and its corps of intellectuals learned to speak about immigration in such ostensibly nonracial terms as national identity, language, economics, crime, and national security; in other words they learned to use the language of post–civil rights racism.[34] In fact, Tanton understood that this shift in language would be vital to his cause; if it were ever to become mainstream, it needed to be able to win over moderates from the other side of the political spectrum. Tanton once wrote, "The issues we're touching on here must be broached by liberals. The conservatives simply cannot do it without tainting the whole subject."[35] This principle would be indispensible for forging the anti-migrant bloc that would include other factions that do not necessarily share the nativist ideology of Tanton and his colleagues but that embrace similar policies.

Organization and Strategy

Before HR 4437 was introduced on the House floor in December 2005, liberals had begun to couch their concerns about immigration in the terms established by the anti-migrant bloc. Leading members of the Democratic Party and some of the leading national immigrant-advocacy organizations in Washington, D.C., had begun to speak of broken borders, criminal aliens, and, correspondingly, the need to have strong borders and to be tough on crime. Achieving this moral and intellectual leadership over the immigration debate required sophisticated organization and political strategy.

One of FAIR founders' guiding principles in building the infrastructure of the nativist Right was the importance of issue-based organizations that could focus on one issue at a time for the broader nativist movement. Tanton and his allies built three types of organizations: those focused on creating the ideological conditions for implementing their agenda, those directly involved in legal and political battles over immigration, and those devoted to funding and coordinating the activities of the nativist Right.

Based on his convictions that "ideas rule the world" and that "the pen is mightier than the sword," Tanton created CIS in 1985 to focus on producing research that could influence the policy debate on immigration.[36] CIS has full-time fellows who function as organic intellectuals of the nativist Right and produce research and policy analysis that promote its worldview. In addition to maintaining a staff of in-house policy analysts, CIS provides conservative university faculty and researchers across the country who are allied with the anti-migrant bloc with grants and fellowships to produce books, policy analysis, articles, op-eds, and blogs. Numerous CIS fellows have spoken before Congress in immigration hearings held throughout the country. FAIR also created its own publishing operation, the Social Contract Press, which serves as a clearinghouse for books by conservative academics and right-wing public intellectuals who advance the policy agenda of FAIR and its affiliates.

On the political and legal front, FAIR created US English in 1983 to fight bilingual education and promote English as the official language of the United States. In 1989, FAIR also created the Immigration Reform Law Institute (IRLI), which bills itself as "America's only public interest law organization working exclusively to protect the legal rights, privileges, and property of US citizens and their communities from injuries and damages caused by unlawful immigration."[37] Former chief counsel at the IRLI Kris W. Kobach was the intellectual author of legislation such as Arizona's SB 1070. Kobach studied at Harvard University under the mentorship of the late Samuel Huntington and became an adviser to John Ashcroft on legal matters related to immigration.[38] During the 2012 election he became an adviser to former Republican presidential candidate Mitt Romney and is currently the Secretary of State in Kansas and an attorney for the IRLI.[39]

To fund its activities and those of its allies, FAIR also created the American Immigration Control Foundation, which provides funds to the leading nativist organizations and to local anti-migrant projects across the country. For instance, it funded Voices of Citizens Together, the civil society group that put Proposition 187 on the California ballot, and border vigilante groups such as Ranch Rescue and the Minutemen Project.[40] All of these organizations are dedicated to fighting, albeit on different fronts, for the implementation of a migration control strategy known as enforcement through attrition. Outlined in a CIS document written by CIS research fellow Jessica Vaughn, the enforcement-through-attrition strategy "encourages voluntary compliance with immigration laws rather than relying on forced removal."[41] Vaughn proposed that in addition to "securing the border," such an approach also include the following elements: "mandatory workplace verification of immigration status; measures to curb the misuse of social security and IRS identification numbers; partnerships with state and local law enforcement officials; expanded entry-exit recording; increased non-criminal removals; and state and local laws to discourage illegal settlement."[42] In other words, this strategy aims to block the employability of undocumented migrants, advance the localization of federal enforcement through programs such as Immigration and Nationality Act Section 287(g) and Secure Communities, increase the policing of hardworking Latino migrant families (regardless of criminal activity), and encourage the proliferation of state laws like Arizona's SB 1070 and local ordinances that prevent day laborers from finding work and undocumented migrants from renting homes. This ostensibly nonracial strategy translates into the racial harassment and policing of Latino families and other migrants, coercing them into self-deportation.

Having this enforcement-through-attrition agenda implemented in Congress and other sites of state power required a sophisticated mobilization strategy. One such organization advancing this charge was Numbers USA, a nongovernmental organization founded and partially funded by Tanton and his allies. Numbers USA organizes a mobilization system and communication structure designed to have the membership base of nativist groups make phone calls and e-mail prewritten letters to Congress in support of an enforcement-only agenda. Angela Maria Kelley, vice president of immigration policy at the Center for American Progress, a Washington, D.C.–based liberal think tank, said in an interview, "Our opponents have huge lists. They could put in tens of thousands of contacts like that [snaps fingers]—e-mails, texts, faxes, phone calls. They could shut down the phone system! I would always go into Hill offices, and the staffer would come out with a file this big [hand gesture indicating a large file] and then ten pieces of paper and say these are the faxes against immigrants and these are the pro-immigrant [hand gesture indicating a small file]."[43] This anecdote is indicative of the sophisticated letter-writing and phone-banking campaign orchestrated by the nativist faction of the anti-migrant bloc to show mass support for the Sensenbrenner bill and other similar bills. Another part of the mobilization strategy included lobby days in which anti-migrant groups such as the Minutemen and other groups with ties to FAIR, CIS, and Numbers USA and its membership base met with members of Congress to push an enforcement-only agenda.[44]

The base of these organizations comes primarily from working-class and middle-class whites who, under the conditions of neoliberalism, can no longer maintain the privileges that were afforded to them during the Fordist era of production. As sociologist Robyn M. Rodriguez has argued, under such conditions, "there is a resurgence of varieties of xenophobia and nationalism that are

partly...a response to the new kinds of insecurities citizens of different countries around the world experience as a consequence of neoliberalism."[45] If this
sector followed its class interest, it could potentially become a progressive force
that challenges the negative effects of global capitalism. However, this challenge
is unlikely to occur as long as the nativist Right and its allies in the broader conservative movement are essentially mobilizing large sectors of the white working and middle classes through a hypernationalism—or what De Genova has
described as US parochial nationalism—and racism.[46]

Funding and the Anti-Migrant Bloc

Some scholars argue that the leading nativist organizations emulate the fund-
raising tactics of the Christian Right. According to Burghart and Gardiner, many
of their projects are supported by small donations from their members through
direct-mail programs.[47] According to them, roughly a dozen of the leading
anti-migrant organizations have a combined budget of $12 million and a donor
base of over six hundred thousand.[48]

Burghart and Gardiner recognize that Tanton and his supporters also use
traditional sources of funding, such as grants from foundations and philanthro-
pists.[49] This point has been developed by scholars such as Stefanic and Delgado
and others. This body of research has revealed that the leading nativist organizations received grants from the Pioneer Fund, a eugenicist foundation that has
sponsored research that suggests Europeans have a higher IQ than non-European
people, among other racist causes. Like most foundations, it provides support
to academics and think tanks that promote its worldview.[50] Between the early
1980s and the end of the 1990s, the Pioneer Fund provided FAIR with over
$190,000.[51]

While this connection is certainly repulsive, we must understand that the
leading nativist organizations and the elected officials that are politically aligned
with them are factions of a broader anti-migrant bloc that is rooted in powerful transnational corporations and their foundations. One must also understand
how the nativist Right gets much of its funding from entities such as the Pioneer
Fund and the Scaife foundations. The Scaife foundations are run by the Scaife
family, heirs to the Mellon family fortune, and consist of four foundations: the
Sara Scaife Foundation, the Carthage Foundation, the Alleghnny Foundation,
and the Scaife Family Foundation.[52] Richard M. Scaife, who owns and manages
three of the four Scaife foundations, was turned on to the conservative movement during the 1960s and early 1970s. He watched angrily as black and Latino
activists and anti-war protesters challenged the status quo. To counter what he
perceived as an assault on the very system that provided him wealth, power, and
privilege, he began to fund conservative politicians and think tanks to promote

conservative ideas. For instance, he provided a seed grant of over $2 million to the Heritage Foundation and has been a trustee of the organization since its founding in 1974. These foundations fund and essentially organize the corps of organic intellectuals of the nativist and neoconservative Right.[53]

Combined, the Scaife foundations have provided over $1.4 billion to conservative civil society–based organizations to foster conservative ideas around immigration, free trade, and a militaristic US foreign policy, among other issues. Table 1.1 shows that the Scaife foundations have provided funds to the leading nativist organizations such as FAIR, CIS, and Numbers USA and have also funded the leading neoliberal and neoconservative think tanks in the United States, including the Cato Institute, the Heritage Foundation, and the Manhattan Institute, to name just a handful of grantees.

This discussion is not to suggest that the nativists are simply the mouthpiece of a unified and undifferentiated capitalist class, as some might be prone to suggest. Rather, these groups form part of a contradictory (dialectical) relationship of interests. The nativist organizations provide a reactionary but indispensable base of support for corporate factions of the anti-migrant bloc, and the corporate factions provide crucial financial support to the nativist Right, even if these sectors may disagree from time to time over long-term goals and immediate questions around strategy and tactics. Despite the tensions that exist between these factions of the anti-migrant bloc, they facilitated the emergence of a political

Table 1.1 **Select Scaife Foundation Grants**

	Amount of Scaife Foundation grant ($)		
	2001	*2006*	*2011*
Federation for American Immigration Reform	100,000	—	275,000
Center for Immigration Studies	90,000	150,000	125,000
Numbers USA	—	50,000	37,000
Cato Institute	60,000	60,000	40,000
Heritage Foundation	150,000	80,000	1,200,000
Manhattan Institute for Policy Research	90,000	240,000	150,000

Source: Department of Treasury, Internal Revenue Service, 990, Sarah Scaife Foundation, Incorporated, 2001, 2006, and 2012. Available online, http://990finder.foundationcenter. org/990results.aspx?990_type=&fn=Scaife+Foundation&st=&zp=&ei=&fy=&action=Find

and ideological unity that would prove pivotal during the 109th Congress and beyond.

The Nativist Right and the 109th Congress

The 109th Congress provided almost perfect conditions for the nativist Right to advance its enforcement-through-attrition strategy. Vaughn noted in the CIS position paper, "Some of these measures [of the enforcement-through-attrition strategy] are included in HR 4437." With respect to the strategic goal of promoting cooperation between local and federal law enforcement, Vaughn wrote, "the Sensenbrenner bill would advance this strategy by clarifying state and local officers' authority to help enforce immigration laws."[54] Despite not being hard enough on migrants for some members of the House Immigration Reform Caucus (HIRC), who wanted to amend the bill to limit the Fourteenth Amendment to apply only to citizens, the Sensenbrenner bill, as an enforcement-only bill, was a thirty-year dream come true for the nativist Right.

FAIR and the nativist Right knew that in addition to building the ideological groundwork and organizational infrastructure to move their agenda through Congress, they also had to build political capital within the state's juridical apparatus to bring their vision into the mainstream of American politics. For instance, in one of the WITAN memos, Tanton proposed a war of position in which the nativists "infiltrate the judiciary committees." He explained:

> This is a long-range project. We should make every effort to get legislators sympathetic to our point of view appointed to the House and Senate Judiciary Committees, and their immigration subcommittees. Think how much different our prospects would be if someone espousing our ideas had the chairmanship! If we secure the appointment of our people as freshmen members of the committee, we will eventually secure the chairmanship. Remember: we're in this for the long haul.[55]

An increase in committee appointments is indeed the strategic mission that FAIR has pursued since the 1980s. During the 109th Congress, FAIR and its affiliates launched a legislative offensive to pass HR 4437. The HIRC became the epicenter of anti-migrant politics in the 109th Congress. It served as a critical nodal point in the state–civil society nexus between the civil society–based nativist Right and the nativist Republicans in Congress. In a groundbreaking public policy report by the Center for a New Community, researchers exposed the links between nativist organizations and the caucus.[56] The HIRC was founded and headed by Colorado's Sixth District representative, Tom Tancredo, a fanatical nativist (and former middle-school teacher) who had received funds from FAIR and its affiliated organizations. A longtime conservative and appointee to the Reagan White House, Tancredo supported Proposition 187 in California and radical right-wing legislation in Congress before 9/11. For instance, in August 2001, Tancredo introduced HR 2712, a bill that would have put a moratorium on immigration—even legal immigration. Although the bill never passed, it reflected the nativist agenda that Tancredo and his allies had long supported.

Before 9/11, Tancredo and the HIRC were relatively isolated. However, after 9/11 the nativist Right seized the moment to swell the caucus's ranks and push for HR 4437. Tancredo said, "9/11 happened and everything changed. We got sixty members overnight."[57] By the start of the 109th Congress, the HIRC had eighty-two members, including several Democrats, and by January 2006, it had ninety members—one out of five members of the House of Representatives was in its ranks. By 2007, the HIRC had 110 members and played a strategic role in pushing anti-migrant legislation beyond HR 4437, such as the Real ID Act of 2005 and the Secure Fence Act of 2006.

Tancredo, FAIR, and their allies used a variety of tactics to pressure Congress, such as strategically placing former staffers where they could exert influence, developing a mobilization strategy, and holding hearings before the Judiciary Committee. For instance, Numbers USA lobbyists worked for Rep. Tancredo when he was in office, and former FAIR staffers worked for the Judiciary Committee, where they used their connections and influence on behalf of their former employers and the nativist cause. When Tancredo stepped down as head of the HIRC in 2007, Rep. Brian Bilbray, a Republican from San Diego, California, took over the leadership. Before running for Congress, Bilbray was a lobbyist for FAIR.[58] Indeed, with Tancredo and Bilbray at the head of the HIRC for two consecutive terms, the anti-migrant bloc composed of nativist civil society organizations, elected officials operating directly within the state, and funded in large part by billionaire foundations could not have been stronger.

The nativist Right and the corporate factions of the anti-migrant bloc created political action committees (PACs) to fund the HIRC. FAIR used PACs to fund candidates who shared its views. In 2004, for example, Tancredo created the Team America PAC, which supported candidates who shared an agenda identical to that of FAIR and their affiliates and who, upon election, joined the HIRC. Beyond nativist PACs, other committees also shared the goal of providing major donations to the HIRC to help influence it members to support HR 4437 and other anti-migrant bills. For instance, the HIRC received funds from a variety of corporate sources through PACs. According to the Building Democracy Initiative of the Center for a New Community, the top PACs that donated money to the HIRC were the National Beer Wholesalers Association ($833,500), the National Homebuilders Association ($796,500), the National Automobile Dealers Association ($784,500), the National Association of

Realtors ($760,050), the American Bankers Association ($677,050), the National Restaurant Association ($549,371), United Parcel Service Inc. ($533,118), the Credit Union Legislative Action Council ($520,620), and the American Medical Association ($496,000).[59]

The House members who received funds from the PACs were notoriously anti-labor. The Center for a New Community stated, "Although these politicians have often couched their anti-migrant positions in terms of concern about the earning power of native-born Americans, their voting record on labor issues averages a mere six percent. As measured by the American Federation of State, County, and Municipal Employees, eighty-six members of the HIRC scored zero in support of labor."[60] In other words, the nativists found support from fractions of capital that oppose organized labor and that depend on a large flexible undocumented labor force. Indeed, the National Homebuilders Association, the National Automobile Dealers Association, the National Association of Realtors, and the National Restaurant Association represent industries that depend on having a pool of highly flexible, undocumented labor.

These fractions of capital often align themselves with the nativist Right not for the same narrow ideological reasons (i.e., keeping America white) but for material interests. By supporting the nativist Right, these fractions of the anti-migrant bloc are maintaining a large undocumented population that is highly flexible because of their deportability. Capital, resources, and mobilization structures all helped to set the stage for the civil society debate over immigration reform that took place in front of the United States Judiciary Committee.

Judiciary Committee Hearings

Among the tactics that the anti-migrant bloc used to prepare the ideological conditions for passing legislation in the 109th Congress was the holding of Judiciary Committee hearings. Designed to bring the nation's policy experts before Congress to educate representatives on the salience of immigration reform, these hearings provide another concrete example of the nexus between civil society organizations and state actors at the national level. The committee held several dozen hearings during its tenure, at least sixteen of which were directly related to reforming aspects of the immigration system. While civil society organizations from a variety of political persuasions spoke before Congress, nativist right-wing organizations advanced their agenda in a remarkable fashion. Senior staffers from FAIR, CIS, and Numbers USA, among other nativist groups, often spoke alongside leading national law enforcement officers and Department of Homeland Security prosecutors urging Congress to pass legislation that would provide them more police power. High-ranking state personnel—including spokespeople for the Department of Homeland Security,

Immigration and Customs Enforcement, Border Patrol, Department of Justice, and the police departments of Los Angeles and New York City—also play a role as organic intellectuals of the anti-migrant bloc. Through their access to the media and prestige, they are called upon to comment and thus educate Congress and the rest of civil society on threats to national security, usually in support of some type of coercive law or practice. Regardless of their status as objective members of the law enforcement community, they too took part in maintaining the hegemony of the anti-migrant bloc and of the homeland security state in the hearings over HR 4437.

The hearings set the tone for defining immigration as a national security problem in ways that would benefit the anti-migrant bloc and lend support to the solutions it proposed. For instance, in a September 1, 2006, hearing, Michael Cutler, a CIS research fellow and former Immigration and Naturalization Service officer, testified before the Senate Judiciary Committee, urging its members to strengthen the homeland security state and oppose any effort toward legalization, or what the nativist Right calls "amnesty": "Terrorists would not find gaming this system the least bit challenging and our government will have become their unwitting ally, providing them with official identity documents in false names and then, ultimately, providing them with the keys to the kingdom by conferring resident alien status and then, United States citizenship upon those who would destroy our nation and slaughter our citizens. I hope that this doomsday scenario will not be permitted to play out."[61] The CIS fellow constructed a quasi-Christian "doomsday scenario" in which an immigrant would be handed the "keys to the kingdom" to "destroy our nation and slaughter our citizens." This scenario speaks to the binary thinking and almost apocalyptic racial paranoia of the nativist Right.

This type of argument put immigration reformers on the defensive in 2005. Rather than challenge the basic premise that we need more enforcement, immigration reformers began to concede to the argument that more enforcement was necessary. As a case in point, Frank Sharry, the executive director of the National Immigration Forum, one of the oldest migrant rights organizations in Washington, D.C. argued at the House Judiciary Committee meeting on CIR: "And while we certainly need tighter, more targeted, and more effective enforcement as part of a comprehensive overhaul, the fact is that over the last two decades the enforcement-only approach has failed miserably...Instead of enforcement only or enforcement first, we need an enforcement-plus approach."[62] Although Sharry opposed HR 4437, like many immigration reformers, he capitulated to the anti-migrant bloc when he stated that we need an "enforcement-plus approach" in exchange for a path toward regularizing the status of undocumented people. This position was a common one, not limited to Sharry, and led many immigration reformers to applaud President Bush and President Vicente Fox of Mexico for backing the Comprehensive Immigration Reform Act of 2005, commonly known as the Kennedy-McCain bill or S 2611. Sharry stated, "The two presidents imagined a system based on improved border security and widened legal channels." The goal of such a proposal, he explained before the House Judiciary Committee, was to "make the healthy, positive, and predictable movement of workers to available jobs safe, legal, and orderly." Sharry argued that "the president deserves considerable credit for getting this big idea and sticking with it." As did most of the national migrant and Latino advocacy organizations, Sharry then got behind the Kennedy-McCain bill on the grounds that it captured the spirit of the immigration system Bush and Fox negotiated, to bring about what Sharry summarized as "(1) enhanced enforcement to ensure the immigration system is effectively policed; (2) widened legal channels for the future flow of workers and families; and (3) a workable solution for the eleven million undocumented immigrants currently working and living the in the US; and (4) support for the successful integration of newcomers in the communities where they settle."[63] Although the Kennedy-McCain bill, unlike HR 4437, contained a pathway to legalization, it would have resulted in the creation of a more sophisticated and entrenched homeland security state and system of labor control, without challenging the structural causes of migration and without affirming the human rights of migrants.

For all of his good intentions, Sharry conceded, as did the Kennedy-McCain bill, that more enforcement must be part of any legalization package. Just as the good immigrant–bad immigrant binary played out in the civil society debate over HR 4437, it would play out in the debate on the House floor.

The House Debate Over HR 4437

The debate in the House didn't go beyond the discursive parameters already used by the nativist Right and immigration reformers in civil society. The debate that took place on the House floor was preconditioned by the civil society organizations that had created the cultural and ideological conditions that led members of the traditional opposition to adopt a similar discourse and make comparable demands. To study the debate over HR 4437, I systematically studied hundreds of pages of the transcript of the debate and evaluated the language used to support or challenge the bill. This analysis illustrates that the dominant discourse was one that criminalized migrants and that overwhelmingly portrayed them as Mexican.[64]

While there are many examples of this dominant discourse in the debate transcript, I elaborate on representative quotations. The following statements from the bill's sponsor, Congressman James Sensenbrenner, exemplify how the discourse criminalized immigrants: "This legislation, which I introduced with Homeland Security Committee Chairman King...will reestablish respect for our laws by holding violators accountable, including human traffickers, employers who hire illegal aliens, and alien gang members who terrorize communities throughout the country."[65] Rep. Sensenbrenner deployed a common discursive tactic that equates human trafficking and gang activity with terrorism. By doing so, he elevated the issue of undocumented immigration to the level of a national security threat. The following statement from Iowa congressman Steve King is a clear attempt to make this link among national security, the war on terror, and undocumented immigration: "Mr. Speaker, again, it is important for us to bring some stability to this immigration issue. It is a national security issue. This is a national security issue as much as the war on terror is a national security issue...We have a slow-motion terrorist attack going on in the United States that comes across our southern border."[66] In Rep. King's formulation, Mexican immigration to the United States is a "slow motion terrorist attack" and thus requires an expansion of the homeland security state through bills such as HR 4437. Moreover, by equating Mexican immigration with terrorism, he denied Mexicans any sort of humanity and absolved the United States from any responsibility for Mexicans having to the leave their country to the United States. These are but a few examples of how House representatives used a discourse that overwhelmingly criminalized and racialized immigrants throughout the debate over HR 4437.

Racialization is a complex process that attributes racial characteristics to a target group through a variety of both subtle and overt discursive tactics. Republican congresswoman Ginnery Brown-Waite overtly attributed criminality to Mexican immigrants: "Back in November, Homeland Security officials found and deported eighty-five illegal aliens from Mexico. Sixty-three of eighty-five of them had previously committed such crimes as burglary, drug possession, sexual assault, and murder. In September '99, illegal aliens were arrested in a sting operation in my home state of Florida. All of them had violent criminal backgrounds. If these violent criminals could break through our borders, how do we know that terrorist groups have not also?"[67] Rep. Brown-Waite associated Mexicans with illegal aliens, burglary, drug possession, sexual assault, murder, violent criminal backgrounds—in short, undesirables who must be kept out of the nation. In this sense Mexicans stand in for the elusive terrorist threat.

In a similar fashion, Rep. John Carter, a Republican from Texas, continued the criminalization of immigrants by connecting narcotics trafficking, immigration, crime, terrorism, Mexico, Mexicans, and a state of crisis in the country: "These narcoterrorists are so bold, Mr. Chairman, and lawlessness is so pervasive on the border that the narcoterrorists have set up, according to the FBI, at least one narcoterrorist training camp outside of Matamoros, operating in the open, run by the Zetas to train gun runners [and] human smugglers."[68] By advancing the term "narcoterrorist," Rep. Carter clinched narcos in Mexico with the proverbial threat of terrorism. He later went out of his way to make it clear that the targets of legislative actions should, indeed, be Mexican: "Where would the American public define the crisis to be as we deal with people who are coming into this country from other countries? And when I say other countries... predominantly I am addressing today the crossing of our southern border out of Mexico."[69] Rep. Carter made it clear that from his point of view, which he conveniently identifies with that of the politically homogenous "American people," the "crisis" is to be located in Mexico and by default with Mexicans. Such a discourse advanced by this particular faction of the anti-migrant bloc is essentially calling for the use of prerogative power against Mexican migrants.

The Nation of Laws vs. Mexicans

Even though all migrants, regardless of their country of origin, are potential targets of the homeland security state, the focus on Mexicans is no coincidence and exposes the underlying ideological current that permeates the anti-migrant bloc. This ideology poses a binary between the "nation of laws" and criminal Mexicans—the quintessential "illegal aliens," the perennial pariahs. The following statement from Sensenbrenner illustrates this binary opposition in action: "Mr. Chairman, our nation has lost control of its borders, which has resulted in a sharp increase in illegal immigration and has left us vulnerable to infiltration by terrorists and criminals.... Large majorities of Americans support efforts to restore the security of our nation's borders and to assure accountability of those who illegally enter the United States. America is a compassionate nation that welcomes legal immigrants from all corners of the world. But it is also a nation of laws."[70] Like his civil society–based colleagues, he continued to criminalize migrants by evoking an image of the border as a lawless region over which "we" have lost control. He then tried to characterize the vast majority of members of the body politic as being in favor of enforcing the law and actually constructed an image of a nation of laws to be juxtaposed with the image of lawlessness at the border and of the undocumented person.

The concept of a "nation of laws"—which allowed House Republicans to call for an expanded border fence, troops along the US–Mexico border, and greater interior enforcement strategies to defend the "nation of laws" against an enemy— merits careful analysis. Who composes the nation? And from whom does it need protection? From the perspective of the anti-migrant bloc, the nation is composed of white Americans and those willing to assimilate uncompromisingly into their way of life. And the "enemy" is the "alien" who symbolically is presented as foreign, criminal, and most often Mexican.[71] According to the logic of the binary, criminal aliens are terrorists whom the nation of laws must exclude, expel, and police by any means necessary. Setting up the symbolic border between the insider and outsider does two things. First, it rationalizes the organization of state violence against outsiders, especially those "foreign, criminal, and terrorist Mexicans," as the anti-migrant bloc labels us. Second, it neutralizes and silences any criticism of state repression as a threat to the "nation of laws." The following statement from Rep. King illustrates the first point: "We could also electrify this wire with the kind of current heat that would not kill somebody, but it would be a discouragement for them to be fooling around with it. We do that with live-stock all the time."[72] King's proposal suggests that treating undocumented immigrants like animals (livestock) is acceptable behavior in defense of the nation of laws. As sociolinguist Otto Santa Ana has noted, comparing migrants to animals has become a contemporary feature of public discourse on Latinos.[73]

The act of criminalizing Latinos and ascribing to them animalistic character-istics prepares the ideological groundwork for novel forms of violence against them. For instance, Brown-Waite gave the impression that the situation at the border is so out of control that it merits the enactment of prerogative power and therefore justifies extralegal acts of violence against brown bodies: "Everyday citizens have had to virtually consider taking matters into their own hands."[74] It is important to note that these statements were made at a time when the Minutemen Project and other paramilitary anti-migrant organizations operating along various parts of the US–Mexico border were in full force.

While Rep. Brown-Waite did not condone the Minutemen Project, Rep. King did. He went as far as talking about his involvement with the Minutemen Project. "Americans are being personally impacted piece by piece," he said. "They are standing up and saying what can I do within the jurisdiction that I have, within the resources that I have? How can I step in and fix this? ... And the Minutemen, I had the privilege to go down to the border and help get that project started."[75] To illustrate how the anti-migrant bloc has factions both at the level of the state and civil society, Rep. King proudly claimed to be one of the founders of the Minutemen Project and lauded the civic-patriotism of its members.

The discourse of Reps. King, Senssenbrenner, Grown-Waite, and many more must be conceptualized as part of a broader hegemonic discourse that permeates the homeland security state, not just in Congress but in other sites of state power and in the integral state that also includes civil society. In this respect these rep-resentatives are a special strata of organic intellectuals of the anti-migrant bloc because they are elected officials who, by virtue of their direct influence over the 109th Congress, had the power to expand the repressive field of the state. They exerted their influence on the state not just by casting a vote for a bill that eventually died in the Senate but through cultivating a new moral and intellectual leadership that allows for undocumented people and anyone to be exposed to the prerogative power of the homeland security state. From their point of view, it is perfectly fine for those suspected of being undocumented, such as Mexicans, to be equated with terrorists, treated like animals to be shocked with electric wire, and hunted by paramilitary organizations. Regardless of their intentions, their discourse had implications beyond HR 4437; they were creating a new consciousness in civil society that allows for growth and reproduction of the homeland security state and the myth of a postracial society.

The ultimate power of this discourse is that it constructed a binary opposition between the nation of laws and the criminal alien. Moreover, it gained ascendancy among some of the most influential House Democrats, and it silenced many members of the Congressional Hispanic Caucus. Thus the traditional opposition conceded the discursive terrain—and with it, the moral and intellectual leadership—needed to effectively challenge the position advanced by the anti-migrant bloc.

The majority of Democrats rejected only the most draconian aspects of the original bill submitted by the Republican leadership, such as the clauses that would have turned millions of undocumented people into felons and criminalized those that work with them. Few among them, however, challenged the racist nature and origins of the Sensenbrenner bill, nor did they object to the human tragedy of people separated through deportation or of the thousands of people who have died at the border. Still fewer were those who addressed the structural foundation for mass migration over the last thirty years—US-led global capitalism. On the contrary, the majority of House Democrats went out of their way to make it clear that they could be just as tough as Republicans on "illegal immigrants." For instance, Rep. Gene Green, a Democrat from Texas, who was purportedly sympathetic to migrants, read a banner written by children, mostly Mexican, from his district on the House floor asking for immigration reform. Indeed, Green voted against HR 4437 but while also exhorting his colleagues that "we need . . . increased border security, more detention beds to prevent catch and release, requiring applicants to go through criminal background checks, to learn English, and also pay a penalty."[76] Rep. Green failed to realize or care that the children and their family members whom he was invoking would be targeted by the new border security system to fill those detention beds that he was so kindly endorsing.

Rep. Green seemed to be following the party line. The following statement from House minority leader Nancy Pelosi best illustrates the Democratic Party's thinking on immigration reform: "Broken borders—that is an oxymoron, something we cannot tolerate. Borders, by their nature, are our definition as a nation and our protection as a country. Broken borders, they do not exist.

We cannot tolerate them. Democrats also support enforcing laws, current laws, against those who came here illegally, and those who hire illegal immigrants. Democrats have led the way to meet our urgent homeland security needs as well. Not only at our borders but in all aspects."[77] Here Pelosi argued that the nation is defined by borders, not a shared political community built around ideas such as justice and solidarity. Moreover, rather than defend civil liberties and the rights of migrants, which include the right to work, she reaffirmed on the House floor that the Democratic Party supports "enforcing laws" and that it has historically and consistently sided with "our homeland security needs," a subtle discursive formation that indicates an insider who must be protected from the outsider. In other words, Pelosi bought in to the good immigrant–bad immigrant binary and posited a policy scenario in which the nation of laws must be protected from those criminal aliens. The only difference between Pelosi and her Republican counterparts in this case was over tactics; whereas Republicans wanted to pass HR 4437 to deport people, Pelosi was assuring them that the homeland security state was strong enough to get the job done without passing the bill.

Pelosi was not alone in this binary thinking. Rep. Sheila Jackson Lee, one of the more progressive Democrats in Congress and a member of the House Judiciary Committee, argued, "We have laws on the books to prosecute these individuals. We have laws on the books to prevent them from coming into the United States."[78] Moreover, Rep. Jackson Lee stated: "It is all a question of resources. How do we use our resources? In this bill, we do not have sufficient dollars for prosecutors, for court systems, for detention systems and for jails.... We should be focusing today on comprehensive immigration reform."[79] Much like Rep. Pelosi, Rep. Jackson Lee did not challenge the fundamental premise behind the racist enforcement-through-attrition strategy at the heart of HR 4437; instead she reaffirmed that "we have laws on the books" to get the job done, and she reduced the rights of undocumented workers vis-à-vis the homeland security state to questions of resource allocation.

These statements, taken from a sample of hundreds of similar remarks by House Democrats, reflect how the Democratic Party failed to challenge the underlying logic and presuppositions that sustained HR 4437. Although most Democratic members of the House voted against HR 4437, and many such as Rep. Jackson Lee found the bill repulsive, very few challenged the racist nature of the bill or of the forces that backed it. This challenge did not happen because they are unsympathetic or anti-migrant per se, but rather because they had lost the ideological and discursive battle over the politics of migration control in civil society long before the Sensenbrenner bill came to the House floor.

As Gramsci notes in his writings, hegemony is never a complete and totalizing force. As we will see in the next chapter, a massive civil society–based migrant rights movement emerged to challenge the bill. Moreover, within

Congress some Democrats and members of the Congressional Hispanic Caucus attempted to fundamentally challenge HR 4437. For instance, Rep. Raúl Grijalva lamented, "HR 4437 is unrealistic, it is based on fear, and it is financially irresponsible and even unconstitutional at times. It joins rank with the Chinese Exclusion Act and the Depression-era repatriation of US citizens to Mexico."[80] Grijalva rejected the binary of the anti-migrant bloc and relegated HR 4437 to a long list of shameful state practices against racial minorities done in the name of the law. Following Rep. Grijalva, Rep. Charles Gonzalez added, "First of all, let us get it straight, this is not about border protection, and it is not about anti-terrorism. But instead, that bill has been hijacked and now is a vehicle used to promote ineffective and hypocritical so-called illegal immigration control."[81] In this speech, Rep. Gonzalez rejected the bill on principle, broke with the pragmatism of post–civil rights racial politics, and exposed the bill's authors' use of antiterrorism discourse to push through a hypocritical enforcement agenda.

Remarkably, most members of the Congressional Hispanic Caucus did not even attempt to counter the Republican discourse. In fact, out of the caucus's twenty-one members of the 109th Congress, only eleven—slightly more than half—appear as making remarks in the Congressional Record in the documents that were consulted in this study.[82] Hispanic Democrats in the House, including Xavier Becerra and then caucus chair Grace Napolitano, voted against HR 4437, and they likely quietly lobbied their colleagues to vote against it also. However, as some rights organizations have correctly pointed out, a champion for Latinos or migrant rights never emerged from the Southern California Mexican American congressional delegation. House Democrats from this region of the state came under intense criticism from local immigration groups in Los Angeles for not being vocal enough against the Sensenbrenner bill, despite being in safe districts.[83] Among the Latinos in Congress, it was the Puerto Rican representatives from Chicago and New York, Rep. Luis Gutierrez, Rep. Nydia Velázquez, and Rep. José Serrano, who were among the most vocal and active members of Congress against the Sensenbrenner bill. This list of primary advocates is ironic given that Puerto Ricans are US citizens.

The post-9/11 security climate created an atmosphere in which eight House Democrats voted for HR 4437, and politicians seeking election reached out to voters by appealing to insecurities about terrorism and immigration. In fact, several Democratic Party candidates running for the Senate in the November 2006 elections reproduced the same anti-migrant discourse of their Republican counterparts while on the campaign trail. For example, the campaign materials of Arizona Democrat Jim Pederson declared, "Illegal immigration is endangering our security, putting a huge burden on our communities' schools and hospitals." In Missouri, Democrat Claire McCaskill advocated for building a border fence, and in Montana, Democrat Matt McKenna stated he was against "amnesty" for "illegal immigrants."[84]

The Democratic Party's leadership failed to forcibly challenge HR 4437 as a bill that would have led to novel forms of policing against Latino communities and other groups treated as perpetual suspects. On the contrary, during the debate the Democrats and their allies, with few exceptions, reinforced and naturalized the idea that state violence against undocumented people is an acceptable practice in the nation of laws. Unwittingly, they reinforced post–civil rights racial ideology by deliberately avoiding open discussion about race and racism in the House debate in the name of pragmatism—a code word for conforming to the powerful cultural-ideological norms of Washington, D.C., politics. It may be the case that most House Democrats voted against the bill and that many found the bill repugnantly racist, but in the name of pragmatism, they chose not to challenge the bill for what it was: the brainchild of a racist anti-migrant bloc. Rather, the Democrats and their allies tried to show that they are just as tough on immigrants as, and in some cases tougher than, their Republican counterparts.

*　　*　　*

The debate over HR 4437 in Washington, D.C., was lost in civil society long before the bill was even introduced on the House floor. The bill was the legislative fruit of the nativist Right's thirty-year war of position in which a corps of organic intellectuals such as Tanton, Brimelow, Stein, Graham, Hardin, Camarota, Vaughn, and Kobach formed not just in universities but in the nativist movement alongside traditional intellectuals such as Samuel Huntington. This corps sought to perfect their vision of a society built around an Anglo-American polity and culture protected by a security apparatus that could "cleanse" the United States of twelve million undocumented people, that were in the United States in 2006, through force or attrition. The Sensenbrenner bill was just one part of the enforcement-through-attrition strategy to be implemented in various sites of power of the homeland security state.

The bill passed in December 2005, facilitated by an anti-migrant bloc that took advantage of the post-9/11 political context and used the moment to play its hand in the House of Representatives of the 109th Congress. Indeed, the anti-migrant bloc had direct ties to the HIRC and the nearly 110 members of the House of Representatives that helped pass HR 4437. The anti-migrant bloc was able to advance its agenda in the 109th Congress with a discourse that clinched together crime, immigration, Mexicans, and terrorism while concealing its neo-Malthusian and eugenicist views about Latinos.

Although the focus on this chapter has been on the 109th Congress, anti-migrant hegemony cannot be reduced to a single site of power. It exists in multiple sites of power, including the Supreme Court, the presidency, the Department of Homeland Security, and in the integral state—that complex superstructure of relationships, including those considered part of the private realm of civil society, that has characterized modern capitalist societies. Nonetheless, HR 4437 helped to set the terms of the debate on immigration reform and policy well beyond the 109th Congress. From that point forward, almost all legislation at the local, national, and transnational levels would have to include aspects of the enforcement-through-attrition agenda of the nativist Right and its corporate allies in the anti-migrant bloc, even when proposed by liberals and backed by immigration reformers.

The terms of the debate were steered away from addressing the root causes of migration or the human and civil rights of Latinos, most of whom are suspected of being undocumented because of their physical features and culture. Rather, the debate was constructed around a good immigrant–bad immigrant binary that assumed that there are some immigrants who may "pass" and others who must be policed and cleansed from the nation. For those who subscribe to this binary, the massive security apparatus of the homeland security state has become common sense, part of a natural and accepted conception of the world that appears unchangeable. From this perspective, the best immigration reformers can do is save the good immigrant who may pass while rendering deportable those bad immigrants who cannot pass. Thus, immigration reformers and their allied House Democrats subscribe to an "enforcement plus" solution rather than questioning the legitimacy of the homeland security state and its use of racial profiling and state violence to enforce the "law."

As noted by political scientist Chris Zepeda-Millán, as problematic as HR 4437 may have been, it served as a catalyst for a civil society–based Latino migrant movement.[85] In the next chapter, we will see how Latino migrant activism, born not in Washington, D.C., but in the barrios of the United States, was capable of momentarily challenging the hegemony of the anti-migrant bloc and preventing the Sensenbrenner bill from becoming law in the spring of 2006.

The 2006 Mega-Marches in Greater Los Angeles: A Counterhegemonic Moment and the Limits of Mass Mobilization

> You may think that we don't have rights, but we have rights. And that's OK because *la raza* is coming at you like a tsunami and you can't stop us![1]

The above words were shouted by a Chicano day laborer and Vietnam veteran during a clash at a day laborer site in the parking lot of a San Bernardino, California, Home Depot, where a group calling itself Save Our State, with ties to the Federation of American Immigration Reform (FAIR) and neo-Nazi skinheads, was protesting the presence of the *jornaleros* (day laborers).[2] The day laborer's words were almost prophetic coming just months before the mega-marches, a series of mass mobilizations that took place across the country in the spring of 2006 to oppose the Border Protection, Antiterrorism, and Illegal Immigration Control Act of 2005 (HR 4437). As discussed in the previous chapter, this bill would have turned undocumented migrants into felons and further militarized the US–Mexico border and interior enforcement policies and practices. Moreover, it would have criminalized any individual or organization that provides services to undocumented migrants.

In response, millions of Latinos—migrant and US born, documented and undocumented—and their allies took to the streets of almost every major US metropolitan area and nearly one hundred small towns to repudiate HR 4437 and to advocate for a humane and just immigration bill. Beyond the immediate issue of HR 4437, most migrants and their allies took to the streets to protest the anti-migrant policies, practices, and sentiments that have plagued migrant communities and nonmigrant Latinos in the United States for the past two decades.

Most of the political science scholarship on the mega-marches has focused on empirical questions such as the role of the mass media in the historic mobilizations.[3] A notable recent study, by political scientist Chris Zepeda-Millán, draws upon more traditional social movement literature to examine the dramatic increase after the marches in anti-migrant ordinances and raids in migrant communities by DHS.[4] Theoretically driven scholarship on the marches, however, is scarce.[5] Two exceptions come from anthropologist Leo Chavez and political theorist Cristina Beltrán. Chavez argues that protesters were citizen subjects calling for inclusion into the American polity. Beltrán argues that the marches are a uniquely twenty-first-century phenomenon that should not be conceptualized as directly linked to older Latino social movements. Still, there is little theoretical work in the field of Latino politics to date that explores the roots, dynamics, and impact of the mega-marches from a structuralist perspective.

This chapter tackles the development and significance of the mega-marches in the Greater Los Angeles Area (the series of actions on March 25, April 10, April 15, and May 1, 2006, along with student walkouts and actions throughout the last week of March) as a case study. While the focus is on Greater Los Angeles, I also briefly discuss the marches in the national and transnational context of Latino migrant activism and the migrant rights movement. I am interested in unearthing how the mega-marches were a radical moment that illustrated the organic capacity of the Latino migrant working class. Indeed, the marches were built upon three generations of Latino activism and social movement organizing that briefly but effectively challenged the efforts of the anti-migrant bloc to build a more powerful and omnipresent homeland security state through HR 4437. This action was a moment of a profoundly democratic and transformative potential. The marches provide clues for those interested in advancing an oppositional migrant politics that makes demands beyond those normally considered acceptable policy proposals (and thus confined to the good immigrant–bad immigrant binary).

To achieve this goal, I draw upon Antonio Gramsci's notion of organic intellectuals in a slightly different way than presented in the previous chapter, where I speak about the organic and traditional intellectuals of the anti-migrant bloc. In this chapter the focus is on the corps of Latino organic intellectuals who made the marches possible. Gramsci argued that it is precisely the task of organic intellectuals formed outside the traditional sites of intellectual production to grapple with the common sense of ordinary people and raise their consciousness to a more critical level. In fact, Gramsci argues that although it may seem absurd that a factory worker or peasant could become an intellectual, it was precisely the task of radicals to raise the consciousness of the working class and turn them into a fighting force. To be sure, he argued that the only way to counter the hegemonic leadership of the dominant classes in the state and in civil society was by cultivating organic intellectuals of the working class. While Gramsci did not use the term *counterhegemony* in his own writings, I am using it to distinguish the political and ideological leadership of Latino migrant activists from the hegemony of the anti-migrant bloc.

From this perspective I argue that the 2006 mega-marches were a counter-hegemonic moment: for the first time since the rise of the war on terror and the homeland security state, Latino migrant activists and their allies were able to briefly counter the hegemonic leadership of the anti-migrant bloc. Indeed, a relatively small corps of Latino organic intellectuals was capable of articulating a message that could resonate with the common sense—or in this case, "good sense"—of millions of migrants and their allies who heeded the call to take to the streets to protest HR 4437 in the spring of 2006. These Latino migrant activists motivated a shift in the national debate on immigration that helped to prevent HR 4437 from becoming law. Before the marches immigration reformers would either embrace or capitulate to elements of the enforcement-through-attrition agenda of the anti-migrant bloc in exchange for the legalization of some migrants. Yet during the spring of 2006, oppositional Latino migrant activists were boldly able to go beyond the usual demands of immigration reformers and break with the good immigrant–bad immigrant binary to demand the full legalization of twelve million undocumented workers. They also demanded an end to militarized state migration control in the halls of Congress. Moreover, rather than stick to the same safe and acceptable policy solutions built on the assumption that the "immigration problem" could be "fixed," Latino migrant activists called into question the driving force behind the mass migration of people from Latin America over the last thirty years, namely US-backed neo-liberal globalization.

The counterhegemonic moment did not emerge spontaneously or because of the media or new technologies, as some scholars have suggested. Rather it was organized by a group of Latino organic intellectuals whose ideas formed through unique genealogies of struggle. This genealogy refers to a historically and geographically specific knowledge and style of organizing that emerges from diverse moments of struggle of Latinos in the United States, Latin America, and elsewhere.[6] Each genealogy—whether the Chicano movement of the 1960s and 1970s, the struggle against the repressive measures in the Simpson–Mazzoli bill or the Central American peace movement of the 1980s, the Proposition 187 generation of the 1990s, or others—provided a body of knowledge that contributed to the development of the 2006 mega-marches. To be sure, these genealogies of struggle allowed for Latino organic intellectuals to draw upon their experience and informal education as organizers with deep ties to the Mexican and Central American working class to articulate a message that would resonate with the base of migrants in Greater Los Angeles.

By mobilizing a great mass of Mexican and Central American migrants, Latino migrant activists were able to build the political capital necessary to build a historic coalition that I term the Latino social bloc. This bloc combined both oppositional forces and immigration reformers into a short-lived multisectoral coalition of forces that emerged in the spring of 2006 to challenge HR 4437. It united a socially diverse constellation of actors—men and women, documented and undocumented—who hailed from a variety of national backgrounds and social sectors. It comprised workers, students, indigenous groups, clergy, media personalities, and groups such as hometown associations, unions, community-based nonprofit organizations, and leftist parties.[7]

Although the mega-marches constituted a counterhegemonic moment, they should not be mistaken for a sustainable and successful counterhegemonic project that could completely turn the tide against the anti-migrant bloc and lead society toward a radical democracy where there is a sustainable and transformative justice for all migrant workers. Rather, the Latino social bloc disintegrated almost as quickly as it congealed, owing to a familiar set of contradictions plaguing social movements: divisions over the substantive content of the legislative proposals being considered in Congress, internal class and ideological differences, co-optation by traditional political parties, lack of political clarity, lack of resources, and good old-fashioned *caciquismo*.[8] Most important, however, the Latino social bloc was not able to maintain the momentum needed to mount a sustained challenge to draconian migration control policies. As noted by Zepeda-Millán, the movement nationally may have contributed to the defeat of HR 4437, but it prompted a backlash against migrants that the organizers of the 2006 marches were not ready to confront.[9] Indeed, I argue that the organizers of the Latino social bloc underestimated the capacity of the anti-migrant bloc to shift its strategy in the aftermath of the mega-marches from one set on passing a single bill in Congress to one pushing for a barrage of anti-migrant policies and practices at the federal and local level. At the federal level, the state deployed National Guard troops to the US–Mexico border, expanded the border wall, increased military aid to Mexico to control the flow of Central American migrants attempting to enter the United States through Mexico, and began implanting new technologies of governance for migration control such as Secure Communities and E-Verify (further discussed in chapters 4 and 5). At the same time, state and local governments oversaw a proliferation of anti-migrant bills and ordinances.[10]

In Gramscian terms, the Latino social bloc was able to win the war of maneuver—that is, a frontal attack—against HR 4437 becoming the law of the land, but it failed to win the war of position—that is, long-lasting struggle in the trenches—against the anti-migrant bloc operating at the level of the state and civil society. Not withstanding the disintegration of the Latino social bloc, when all accounts are settled, the mega-marches represent a monumental feat in the history of social movements in the United States, one that we can only begin to appreciate. Although this chapter examines the conditions that led to the mega-marches and the collapse of the Latino social bloc, I am not arguing that Latino migrant activism and the broader migrant rights movement was defeated, nor am I suggesting that a new social bloc cannot rise again. Rather, I am critically explaining what happened to the particular constellation of forces that made the mega-marches in the Greater Los Angeles area possible. In the chapters to follow, we will consider other contestations within the broader movement and the ongoing attempts to advance the migrant rights struggle in Washington, D.C., and New York City.

This chapter is based on twelve semi-structured interviews with key leaders of some of the organizations in the Greater Los Angeles area comprising the Latino social bloc. Although hundreds of organizations played a role in the marches, I chose individuals from these organizations for several reasons. First, during the course of my participant observation, I observed that these individuals played a leading role within the Latino social bloc during the mega-marches. Second, they represent the different sectors that helped make the marches materialize, including labor, community-based organizations, hometown associations, leftist political parties, Mexicans and Central Americans, youth, students, and veterans. Finally, I chose some of these individuals to illustrate the complex relationship between gender and organizing and to avoid the mistakes of previous studies on the Chicano movement, which often omitted the contributions of women. As we will see, women played a leading role in organizing for the mega-marches.

Individuals interviewed for this chapter were Arturo Carmona, then the executive director of the Council of Mexican Federations in North America; Angelica Salas of the Coalition for Humane Immigrant Rights of Los Angeles; Isaura Rivera, leader of the Frente Continental, which during the marches represented organizations from five Central American nations; Juan José Gutiérrez, executive director of Latino Movement USA; Gloria Saucedo, executive director of the Hermandad Mexicana Nacional of the San Fernando Valley; Nativo Lopez, director of Hermandad Mexicana Latinoamericana and president of the Mexican American Political Association; Mario Martínez, field organizer for Hermandad Mexicana Latinoamericana; Manuel Roman of UNITE HERE Local 11; Victor Narro of the UCLA Downtown Labor Center; Rosalio Muñoz of the *People's Weekly World*; Esther Portillo of the Salvadoran American National Association; and Ron Gochez, member of Unión del Barrio, the Raza Graduate Student Association, and the Coordinadora Estudiantil de la Raza during the mega-marches. I also drew on an extensive published interview with Jesse Díaz and Javier Rodríguez, the two spokespeople of the March 25 Coalition, one of the leading coalitions for making the marches materialize.[11] While the focus is on activists in Greater Los Angeles, I also briefly draw upon interviews conducted with advocates from the national migrant organizations in Washington, D.C., including Ali Noorani of the National Immigration Forum and Angie Kelly of the Center for American Progress to illustrate the dialectic between the movement in California and the broader migrant rights movement. This chapter is also based on my participation in and observation of movement activities: I spent hundreds of hours in community strategizing sessions, press conferences, meetings, and summits before, during, and after the mega-marches of 2006.

Genealogies of Struggle and Roots of the Latino Social Bloc

Various genealogies of struggle set the ideological groundwork and organizational infrastructure that allowed the corps of Latino migrant activists in Greater Los Angeles to congeal around a national campaign to defeat HR 4437. Political theorist Albert Ponce correctly points out that contemporary migrant resistance movements are linked to a broader history of Mexican and Latino resistance to colonialism, dating back to 1848.[12] While this assessment is fundamentally true, for the sake of understanding the organizations that were part of the conjuncture from 2001 to 2012, I focus on the Chicano movement of the 1960s and 1970s; the Central American peace movement, especially the sanctuary movement of the 1980s; and the brief period of Mexican and Latino migrant activism in California during the early and mid-1990s.[13] These genealogies served as political schools, so to speak, for the formation of the organic intellectuals who helped to organize the mega-marches.[14]

The Chicano movement of the 1960s and 1970s provided the Latino social bloc with its nuclei of leadership. In particular, bloc leaders (including Javier Rodríguez, Nativo Lopez, Armando Navarro, and Carlos Montes) came from two organizations, Centro de Acción Social Autónoma (CASA) and the Brown Berets.[15] That a substantial part of the bloc came from CASA is no coincidence: the organization was founded by Bert Corona, a true organic intellectual in his own right, whose approach to organizing and forming leaders influenced a generation of activists who would eventually become major players in Los Angeles and, indeed, national politics.[16] A Mexican activist from El Paso, Texas, Corona came to Los Angeles, where he founded CASA and began training a host of cadres to do what many of the Chicano movement organizations before them could not do well: organize Mexican migrant workers.[17] CASA emphasized the need for autonomous social action, a form of mass-based organization that could be free to act without constraints put on them by political parties or other forms of external power. Corona created CASA to begin working with undocumented workers around 1969 and advanced the idea that Mexicans were one people on two sides of the US–Mexico border. Indeed, he "waged an ideological battle that focused on the contributions of Mexican immigrants in the United States," according to Lopez.[18] Among those influenced by CASA was Rudy Lozano, whose family went on to create Centro Sin Fronteras in Chicago; the Centro, in turn, became the epicenter of the migrant rights movement in Chicago and a leading organization in the Chicago Mega-Marcha on March 10. Even Rosalio Muñoz, who was never a CASA member but played a leading role in organizing the mega-marches, admitted that Corona's method of organizing Mexican migrants had an important impact on him during his years as head of the Chicano Moratorium Committee in the early 1970s.

Although the Chicano movement and the legacy of Corona in particular set the foundation for the emergence of the Latino social bloc, other genealogies of Latino struggle had an important impact on its development. Indeed, in the 1980s Central American activists influenced a generation of Chicano and Latino labor and community organizations across the United States at a time when most scholars agreed that the Chicano movement was over. Central American migrants, mostly from Guatemala and El Salvador entered the United States en masse in the 1980s as refugees.[19] Many of the refugees had organizational, leadership, and political skills that they brought with them from Central America. These Central American leaders played a critical role in challenging US foreign policy and in fighting for the legalization provisions in the Immigration Reform and Control Act of 1986.[20] Throughout the 1980s, many Central American activists were entering the labor movement and developing community-based organizations that provided desperately needed services for Central American asylum-seekers and migrant workers. The resources and knowledge acquired during the fight for a pathway toward legalization in the Immigration Reform and Control Act and the overall struggle for the rights of Central American refugees were vital to the formation of the Latino social bloc. Moreover, many of the individuals and leaders who made the Latino social bloc viable came directly from the Central American activist community. Central American leadership also had a tremendous impact on Mexican American activists. For instance, Isaura Rivera, leader of the Frente Continental, although Mexican, came from Central American community organizations, as did Angela Sambrano, a Chicana organizer who at the time of the mega-marches was executive director of the Central American Resource Center of Los Angeles. Other key leaders from the Latino social bloc, such as Javier Rodríguez, Gloria Saucedo, and Juan José Gutiérrez, also gained invaluable experience in the 1980s struggle for amnesty for Central American refugees and other migrants.

The third important set of leaders came from what I term the Proposition 187 generation. This cohort of young Latino leaders came of age politically in the struggle against Proposition 187, a 1994 California state ballot initiative that would have banned undocumented people from state health and educational services. In response, Chicano students and community activists launched a series of walkouts and protests.[21] These actions coincided with a period of growing student militancy over demands for Chicano studies programs at UCLA and at high schools throughout Southern California.[22] The Proposition 187 generation provided an indispensable source of battle-tested leadership and organizational skills in conducting walkouts, running voter registration drives, and organizing labor and communities. Key leaders from the Proposition 187 generation participated in a series of meetings and conferences that led to the mega-marches, and many more became teachers and youth organizers who were able to draw upon a recent history of activism to reach out to young people from San Diego to Los Angeles and from Long Beach to Oxnard. Proposition 187 generation leaders include Mario Martínez, field organizer for Hermandad Mexicana Latinoamericana; Arturo Carmona of the Council of Mexican Federations in North America; Ron Gochez, one of the founders of the Coordinadora Estudiantil de la Raza; and Esther Portillo, one of the leading Salvadoran women organizers who worked with the March 25 Coalition during the height of the marches. This sector of organizers and leaders brought the energy to do the grueling legwork needed to pull off the mega-marches and to reach out to the youth sector, which played a critical role in the spring of 2006.

Clearly, there is a degree of overlap across these three traditions, and some of the leading activists could be said to come from more than one genealogy. For instance, Esther Portillo came from a Salvadoran organization with its roots in the 1980s, but she came of age politically after Proposition 187. Others, such as Javier Rodríguez, were active during the Chicano movement during the 1980s and during the fight against Proposition 187.[23]

Beyond the constellation of movement leaders, a central condition that allowed for the mega-marches to materialize was the lack of credibility of the Democratic Party with the oppositional sectors of the movement. Scholars such as Armando Navarro, Robert Smith, and Paul Frymer remind us that the Democratic Party has proven to be a stubborn vehicle for advancing a working-class black and Latino agenda.[24]

Congealing of the Latino Social Bloc

The Latino social bloc was formed by a cadre of organic intellectuals who were able to mobilize Mexican and Central American migrant workers and their allied classes and second-generation working- and middle-class Latinos and other migrant communities. As in all social movements, groups with competing and contradictory views jockeyed for leadership, but despite tendencies among some movement leaders to claim ownership over the movement, no single group or individual leader could take credit for its congealing. Rather, the congealing of the bloc was a product of the organizational experience and political knowledge acquired by three generations of activists and the structural and demographic transformations brought about by thirty years of neoliberal globalization and intensifying anti-Latino racism.

Many meetings, conferences, actions, battles, and failures took place for the bloc to congeal. With that said, there is no doubt that the core set of organic intellectuals hailed from the oppositional sector and that they were responsible for integrating the immigration reformers into the bloc. Central to the formation of the Latino social bloc were two summits that took place in Southern California: La Tierra Es de Todos (The Land Belongs to Everyone) Summit held in Riverside in March of 2005 and the Beyond the Minutemen Summit held at the UCLA Downtown Labor Center in December 2005. These summits, organized by grassroots organizations before HR 4437 had captured the attention of the migrant rights movement nationally, were designed to forge a coalition to confront the Minutemen and to address a growing anti-Latino migrant climate. After the passage of HR 4437 on December 16, 2005, many of the grassroots groups active in the summits began to meet with some traditional community-based migrant rights organizations. Calling themselves La Placita Working Group, in January 2006 they started holding meetings in the basement of Nuestra Señora de Los Angeles Church. The organizations that comprised La Placita Working Group would become the heart of the mega-marches. Gloria Saucedo, executive director of Hermandad Mexicana Nacional, indicated, "At the beginning there were just a few of us; soon, however, the meetings would be attended by hundreds of people and dozens of organizations."[25] La Placita Working Group would become the main forum for organizing the first major mobilization on March 25, 2006. It is in the Placita meetings that most (although not all) movement organizations convened and publicly debated strategy and tactics.

Perhaps no other conference was more pivotal in congealing the Latino social bloc, however, than the Mexicano/Latino Leadership Summit held in the Riverside Convention Center, attended by over 550 migrant activists.[26] The Summit was organized by the National Alliance for Human Rights, an oppositional organization led by political scientist and veteran organizer Armando Navarro. The National Alliance for Human Rights summit was the first to convene with the explicit purpose of building a new movement at a national level to defeat HR 4437. Out of this conference came an agreement on a set of demands and actions that would be adopted by organizations across the United States. Without these efforts by grassroots organizations to agree upon dates and actions, the Latino social bloc could not have emerged, and the mega-marches would not have materialized.

Moreover, the National Alliance for Human Rights summit successfully brought together multiple sectors of the movement across the nation and with leaders from Mexico and Central America. In attendance were activists from all over California and from Arizona, New Mexico, and Chicago, including those who convened La Tierra Es de Todos Summit, the organizers of the Beyond the Minutemen Summit, community-based organizations, labor unions such as the Service Employees International Union and the United Farm Workers (UFW), and student and international organizations. The summit drew up explicit plans to transnationalize the movement by having a series of delegations of movement leaders meet with members of prominent social movements around Latin America. Delegations were sent to Mexico City to meet with Mexican presidential candidate Andrés Manuel López Obrador and the Popular Assembly of the Peoples of Oaxaca. Activists also agreed to gain support from Central American social movements.

By the summit's end, most groups were on board for the first action on March 25, 2006; these groups, primarily oppositional, comprised the heart of the Latino social bloc. Although traditional nonprofit and labor organizations such as the Coalition for Humane Immigrant Rights of Los Angeles, the Central American Resources Center, and the UFW played an important role within the Latino social bloc (and were represented at the summit), they did not provide the leadership for the mega-marches to materialize. Rather, they were skeptical of focusing all of their energy on big marches and emphasized using traditional lobbying and advocacy tactics.[27]

Indeed, organized labor, although a major sector of the Latino social bloc, remained divided and ambiguous about its support of the mega-marches. The base of UNITE HERE Local 11, Justice for Janitors, actively participated in the marches, and rank-and-file members and some union organizers attended the aforementioned meetings leading to the mega-marches. Nevertheless, the labor bureaucracy never fully committed to moving its base and union machinery to make the mega-marches happen. The UFW, meanwhile, along with the Catholic Church, organized an alternative action on Sunday, March 26, 2006, which would culminate with a mass in honor of the late César Chávez, but the majority of groups did not congeal around this plan.

The Archdiocese of Los Angeles, however, did provide support for the mega-marches in other ways, playing a critical role in bringing legitimacy to the first planned march. The Nuestra Señora de Los Angeles Church lent its basement for the meetings of La Placita Working Group, and Cardinal Mahony brought attention to HR 4437 when he publicly told reporters that the Church would not comply with federal laws that would criminalize their parishes and that it would be calling for Catholics to peacefully protest against the proposed bill. As Victor Narro and Rosalio Muñoz both noted, without the support of the Church at the beginning, the mass media probably would not have felt it was safe enough to promote the protest action on March 25, 2006.[28]

Another key sector of the Latino social bloc was the youth and student sector. It is important to distinguish between youth and student organizations; the former tends to be community based and the latter, campus based. The majority of youths who participated in the protest activities were not directly part of the student organizations to come out of the Chicano movement. There were also large contingents of youths that did not belong to any organization. Among the student groups, various chapters of Movimiento Estudiantil Chicano de Aztlán (MEChA) sporadically played a supportive role during the mega-marches, especially during the student march that took place on April 15, 2006. Since 1969 MEChA was in the vanguard of Chicano student organizing in Southern California; it provided political direction, and a regional organizational structure. However, MEChA as a regional organization did not assume its traditional role as the vanguard of the student movement in Greater Los Angeles.[29] While there are important exceptions, over-bureaucratization and lack of political clarity prevented the Los Angeles–area chapters of MEChA from taking on their historic role as the vanguard of the student movement during the mega-marches. The vacuum in the traditional student leadership structure was filled by alternative student and youth organizations, including the Raza Graduate Student Association of UCLA, the youth and student component of the organization Act Now to Stop War and End Racism (ANSWER), and youths from the International Socialist Organization (ISO). The ISO and ANSWER, along with select MEChA chapters, played a major role in organizing a youth and student march of roughly 15,000 participants that took place on April 15, 2006. The Raza Graduate Student Association worked to forge the Coordinadora Estudiantil de la Raza, a coalition of student organizations spreading from Oxnard to San Diego, that would eventually play a major role in the mega-marches and in the Southern California student movement. Although these groups did not always agree, they had two things in common. First, they did not receive funds from any major foundation or university. Second, combined, they formed the core of oppositional youth and student organizations within in the Latino social bloc.

Last but not least, the Spanish-language media provided a vital resource for disseminating the call to mobilize.[30] Organizers of the mega-marches reached out to Ricardo "El Mandril" Sánchez of La Que Buena 105.5 FM, who on March 15, 2006, put out a call to other radio personalities in the Los Angeles area. Sánchez reportedly announced, "*Si estamos pidiendo que la gente se una a una marcha, por qué los locutores no ponemos el ejemplo y nos unimos a esta causa?*" (If we are asking people to unite to be part of a march, why don't we disc jockeys unite for the cause?).[31] El Mandril's call was met by the two leading personalities on Spanish-speaking radio, Eddie "El Piolín" Sotelo of La Nueva 101.9 FM and Renán "El Cucuy" Almendárez Coello of the La Raza 97.9 FM. After these leading personalities began to support the first action on March 25, 2006, other radio personalities followed suit, and by the beginning of the first march, over twenty-five radio stations had begun supporting the first mega-marcha, including Tijuana radio stations Radio "W" 690 AM and La Formula.[32] In addition to the radio personalities, Spanish-language television networks such as Univisión, Telemundo, and Azteca América played a critical role in disseminating the word about the protests, especially the first major action on March 25, 2006.

The Counterhegemonic Moment

The Latino social bloc's thunderous rejection of HR 4437 disrupted the increasingly intolerant and punitive national discourse on migration control. This counterhegemonic moment extended in the Greater Los Angeles area across a series of mass mobilizations, which were amplified by regional, national, and transnational actions. In the following discussion, I describe a series of marches and actions organized, or inspired by, the Latino social bloc that took place in the spring of 2006. In particular, I focus on March 25 mega-marcha, the student walkouts of March 27–31, the April 10 national day of action, and the Great American Boycott of May 1. I write about these actions with an eye toward understanding how these mobilizations helped to prevent HR 4437 from becoming law and changing the national discourse to consider briefly the legalization of the twelve million undocumented migrants in the United States in 2006.

March 25, 2006: The *first* of the Los Angeles mega-marches

Based on the turnout at the March 10 protest in Chicago, which was attended by 100,000 to 300,000 people, organizers knew that the Los Angeles protest scheduled for March 25 would be well attended.[33] None, however, expected the march to galvanize over half a million workers, families, and youths. Indeed, the permit secured for the protest was written for 5,000 protesters to convene on Olympic and Broadway and to travel north en route to city hall. In the few days before the March, Victor Narro indicated that he had to call the LAPD to ask them to increase the number of expected protesters to 50,000. Organizers had no idea that hundreds of thousands would take to the streets.

That Saturday morning, countless workers and their children, overwhelmingly of Mexican and Central American origin, could be seen walking to the convening points on Olympic and Broadway from South Central Los Angeles and across the bridge that connects downtown to East Los Angeles. The march was so large that protesters took three parallel streets as they marched north toward city hall.[34] Unlike most Los Angeles protests, which tend to attract the usual set of hardcore activists that I recognized from years of participant observation, this action was overwhelmingly dominated by families and working-class migrants. Victor Narro, who was one of the first organizers present on the day of the march, related how surprised he was by the massive turnout:

> I remember waking up with a weary feeling about the march. As I caught the train to Olympic and Broadway from the labor center [located in MacArthur Park], I noticed all kinds of people dressed in white huddled in the park. I saw masses of people dressed in white and with signs heading to downtown on the buses and trains. Since I had filed the permit, the LAPD called to tell me that there was no way they could provide security for so many people. They told me that they can only provide security for 50,000 people. By 7 A.M. it was clear that there were more than 50,000 people ready to march. Most of the organizers had not even got there. Some had not even woken up yet. I had to quickly recruit people to do crowd control. I remember asking random people to help with security as they got off the bus and training them on the spot.[35]

The success of the March 25 demonstration gave the organizers an unprecedented level of social capital to galvanize the nation on both sides of the immigration debate. As expected, the anti-migrant pundits focused on the Mexican flags of many protesters as proof of their unwillingness to assimilate. Moreover, these pundits characterized marchers as gang members and thugs, even though the marches were peaceful. Migrants and their allies across the United States viewed March 10 in Chicago and March 25 in Los Angeles as a national call to action. The first to take heed in the Greater Los Angeles area were Latino youth and students.

March 27–March 31, 2006: A week of youth and student resistance

Perhaps nothing symbolizes the momentum created by the first major march more than the student walkouts that took place on March 27, 2006, in the Greater Los Angeles area. As in the Chicano movement of the 1960s, youth from the barrios represented the bulk of protesters and evoked the greatest fears in the state.[36] What particularly scared the authorities was that barrio youth were unpredictable and seemingly outside the formal control of any organization. Indeed, they did not always participate within the protest framework that liberal Latino organizations wanted them to adopt. On the contrary, they represented the most militant and volatile sector within the movement. In fact, most youth heard of the walkout through text messages and through the Internet message system MySpace. For instance, on April 15, 2006, a short-lived student wing of the March 25 Coalition called for a student protest. The protest was organized with the explicit vision of channeling the energy of the walkouts into an organized and sanctioned student march and discouraging more walkouts.[37] While it was certainly a successful, large march, it was dwarfed by the size and scope of the student walkouts.

During the student protests tens of thousands of young people walked out of their classrooms and took to the streets of major Latino cities and regions. In Los Angeles, student protesters descended onto the busy 101 Freeway near downtown.[38] In Montebello, students raised the Mexican flag above an upside-down US flag, and in Riverside, Latino students walked out from several area high schools and convened at Riverside City Hall for a rally.[39] Students in Long Beach coordinated walkouts in which even middle school and elementary school children took to the streets. The most organized set of walkouts during the general week of youth and student resistance occurred in San Diego and Oxnard. On March 28, 2006, thousands of students in San Diego walked out of school and convened at the historic Chicano Park, where they heard speakers and watched Aztec dancers perform.

Perhaps no other action represents the rawness of the student and youth sector than the walkouts that took place in Santa Ana, California, on Monday, March 27. Santa Ana is a unique city; in the 1960s it was a mostly white suburb but became a major site of international migration from Mexico in the 1970s and 1980s, quickly becoming a Mexican enclave in the notoriously Anglo and Republican stronghold of Orange County. Today, Santa Ana is a city with one of the highest concentrations of Mexican-born residents in the United States, and it is the cultural and demographic hub of the Mexican community in Orange County.

In the immediate aftermath of the massive protest on March 25, tens of thousands of youths walked out of nearly every high school in Santa Ana and took over the busy thoroughfare of Bristol, whose mini-malls are the shopping and cruising destination for Chicano youth. Youth in the area engaged in protests that resulted in a twelve-hour standoff with the Santa Ana Police Department. Santa Ana police went on tactical alert on Monday March 27. Between four and five hundred police officers from the city of Santa Ana, sheriffs from Orange County, and police from surrounding counties and cities occupied Bristol. Like a scene from a war zone, police had full riot gear, "nonlethal" weapons, armored vehicles, and contingents of officers mounted on horseback. The Santa Ana Police Department on Civic Center Drive and Broadway had a barricade with officers in riot gear surrounding it with crowd-control weapons and armored vehicles, as if protesters were going to take over police headquarters.[40]

During the protests, dozens of people were arrested, and prisoners in Orange County jails were put on lockdown. Among those arrested, several were deported. Jailed protesters also reported that Orange County sheriffs abused them for their protest activities and threatened to kill one of the protesters. For example, Mario Martínez, a day-laborer organizer at the time, recalled the physical and verbal abuse he faced while in police custody:

> I had my genitals grabbed and my arms pulled behind me while a deputy attempted to interrogate me; he had me bent over with my head against the wall and my arms twisted behind me asking if I was American or Mexican.... The deputy made gestures of bashing in my face with his fist and told me...that Mexicans are pieces of shit, they hate us, fuck Mexicans.... The demeanor was racist and hateful.[41]

The type of violence described by Martinez toward Mexican and Latino activists and community members by law enforcement has become all too familiar in Santa Ana and in Orange County. But what makes this a particularly disturbing moment is that the Santa Ana Police Department and Orange County Sheriffs—the local repressive apparatus of the homeland security state—were taking retaliatory action against what they perceived to be unruly and unassimilated protesters (hence the question hurled at Martinez about his nationality).

Meanwhile in Los Angeles on day two of the walkouts (March 28), between 5,000 and 7,000 high school students converged on city hall after spending the day staging militant protests against the draconian legislation.[42] Mayor Antonio Villaraigosa gave students a patronizing speech about practicing their First Amendment rights, then asked them to go home and attend school the next day. According to Ron Gochez, who was present at this action,[43] students heckled the mayor and began to chant typical movement slogans such as "*Aquí estamos y no nos vamos*" (We are here and we will not leave); "*Somos un pueblo sin fronteras*" (We are a people without borders); and "*Esta es mi tierra, esta es mi lucha*" (This is my land, this is my struggle). The more politically savvy student organizations, such as the Raza Graduate Student Association, used the mayor's opposition and media presence at the action to call for the formation of a Southern California student coordinating committee, which would eventually become the first general meeting of the Coordinadora Estudiantil de la Raza.[44]

April 10, 2006: Local fissures on the national day of action

After the week of student walkouts, the next major action to take place in the Los Angeles area was the April 10 protest, which was part of a national day of action. Nationally, the day of action was a dramatic success, with hundreds of cities taking part; over 50,000 people took to the streets in Chicago and over 200,000 in New York City. In Phoenix, Arizona, activists organized the largest protest in the state's history, with over 100,000 taking part. Ironically, however, in Los Angeles, which along with Chicago was one of the epicenters for the movement nationally, the April 10 action was relatively small, with approximately 5,000 to 10,000 protesters.[45] According to Victor Narro, the April 10 protest was never meant to be a large march but rather a rally and a media bite to get the Somos America coalition's position out.[46] Somos America was a coalition of immigration reformers that opposed HR 4437 and that was willing to support the Kennedy-McCain bill. Others such as Nativo Lopez would argue that the low turnout—despite the tremendous amount of resources and connections that immigration reformers who spearheaded the action had with the media, unions, and Democratic Party establishment in Los Angeles—was symptomatic of major problems with the Somos America coalition, namely, they did not have a program that would resonate with the common sense of migrant workers to mobilize hundreds of thousands to downtown Los Angeles.[47]

As immigration reformers within the Latino social bloc were organizing for April 10, the opposition sector announced its plans for the Great American Boycott, a national mobilization in which people were asked not to attend work or school in protest to HR 4437 and to demand the legalization of the eleven to twelve million undocumented workers in the United States. The announcement coupled with the powerful but controversial student walkouts led the immigration reformers to break publicly with the Latino social bloc over the boycott.[48] For instance, Cardinal Mahony issued a statement opposing the boycott, saying, "Personally, I believe that we can make the May 1 a win-win day here in Southern California: go to work, go to school and then join thousands of us at a major rally afterwards."[49] Similarly, Angelica Salas, director of the Coalition for Humane Immigrant Rights of Los Angeles, argued that a boycott would backfire and create a backlash against migrant communities; on Telemundo and other Spanish-language media, Angela Sambrano of the Central American Resource Center called on potential migrant protesters to go to school and to work.

What was occurring in Los Angeles was also occurring at a national level. For example, the vice president of the National Council of La Raza, Cecilia Muñoz, took an anti-boycott stance. In an ironic historical twist, the UFW, which had called for a national boycott of grapes in the 1980s and 1990s, did not support the Great American Boycott. As expected by most activists, President Bush came out against the boycott, as did Senator Mel Martínez, Republican from Florida, who went on record in the national media, stating, "Boycotts, walkouts, or protests are not going to get this done.... This is an issue that isn't going to get fixed on the streets. It's going to take thoughtful action by Congress."[50] Mayor Villaraigosa, who in the 1970s worked with CASA, the very organization that provided a key source of leadership for the Latino social bloc, came out against the boycott along with other national Hispanic figures.

May 1: The Great American Boycott

Despite efforts by immigration reformers to dissuade people from participating, the Great American Boycott was a monumental event in the Greater Los Angeles area, nationally and transnationally. As immigration reformers of the bloc backed away from the boycott, new groups began to support it. For instance, the Frente Continental and the Coordinadora Estudiantil de la Raza attempted to counter church and union leaders' call to ignore the boycott by holding a press conference to express their support. At the press conference, they expressed their support for the action by having religious leaders from smaller churches stand with them and by invoking the image of César Chavez. They argued that if Chavez would have been alive he would have supported the Great American Boycott. In a separate press conference held on April 25, 2006, the Coordinadora Estudiantil de la Raza, which ironically had been meeting in the basement of Nuestra Señora de Los Angeles (a historic Catholic church in Los Angeles), held a press conference on April 25, just before the May Day action. Church administrators responded by banning the group of mostly high school students from using its basement and prohibited them from having the press conference on the premises. After being forced off church grounds, the students held their press conference across the street from La Placita, despite harassment by church officials and what organizers perceived as undercover police agents.

May 1, 2006, International Workers Day, was the date set for the Great American Boycott. The action on this date represented the apex of the counterhegemonic moment at the local, national, and transnational levels. Locally, Los Angeles witnessed a massive protest, in which at least 400,000 marched to city hall on Monday morning, and 500,000 marched along the city's Wilshire Corridor that evening.[51] The entire port of Los Angeles came to a standstill when the truckers and port workers refused to work. Workers also shut down the garment and produce sectors, two of the largest industries in the Los Angeles area. Nearly 20,000 students throughout Southern California did not attend school. Most of the hotel and restaurant sectors faced shortages for the day. One *Los Angeles Times* article read, "Dolls from China, DVD players from Japan and shirts from Malaysia piled up the ports. Lettuce wasn't picked in Blythe and strawberries languished in Oxnard." The article also quoted the president of the Economic Roundtable, Daniel Flaming: "This was a reality check.... You can't wish away these workers, they are rooted in the community."[52] Nearly 90 percent of the 10,000 truckers who work at the port of Los Angeles did not report to work, and Los Angeles schools experienced a 27% drop in attendance. One Los Angeles news report featured a story titled "Boycott Turns Panorama City Mall into a Ghost Town."[53] In the agricultural sector, farms from the Central Valley to the Imperial Valley and back to northern California came to a halt. In fact, according to the UFW spokesperson, the protests in the agricultural sector were the largest in California's history, overshadowing the grape boycotts of the 1970s.[54]

May Day actions were coordinated throughout the entire country. Chicago was the site of another of the largest protests, with about 300,000 demonstrators marching downtown.[55] Across the country, schools with a large Latino population experienced a 10% to 33% drop in student attendance.[56] In New York City, thousands of people turned out to form eight human chains throughout Manhattan, Brooklyn, Queens, and the Bronx symbolizing their opposition to HR 4437. The day's actions culminated in a rally in front of the Federal Building in downtown's federal district. In San Francisco, 55,000 took to the streets chanting and waving flags, and most businesses in the Mission District closed. San José experienced a large protest of at least 30,000 people.[57]

On the transnational level, there was a wave of solidarity actions across Mexico and Central America. In Mexico, activists urged citizens not to buy anything "gringo" on May 1, and while Mexican politicians aligned with the Partido Revolucionario Institucional and the Partido Acción Nacional walked a delicate and hypocritical tightrope as they tried to appear supportive of migrant rights but not too critical of the United States, grassroots activists and the members of the Partido de la Revolución Democrática handed out pro-boycott flyers in solidarity with "los mexicanos del otro lado" (Mexicans on the other side). Moreover, in Ciudad Juárez, Monsignor Renato Ascencio called on Catholics in northern Mexico to support the boycott, arguing, "Los mexicanos que vivimos de este lado nos debemos solidarizar con los inmigrantes, como lo estan haciendo los guatemaltecos, nicaraguenses, y otros paises de Centroamerica" (The Mexicans who live on this side should show solidarity with the immigrants, just as are people in Guatemala, Nicaragua, and other Central American countries).[58] Other bishops in the border communities of Tijuana, Tecate, Mexicali, Nuevo Laredo, Reynosa, and Piedras Negras supported the actions, as did the Consejo Coordinador Empresarial de Ciudad Juárez (Business Council Coordinator of the City of Juarez) and the Cámara de Comercio de Tijuana (Chamber of Commerce of Tijuana).[59] Groups like the Council of Mexican Federations in North America also held binational press conferences, where activists in Los Angeles and Chicago would inform major Mexican newspapers such as La Reforma and La Jornada about the demands of protesters.[60] Activists in Tijuana blocked the US–Mexico border for hours before being removed by the Mexican police. And in El Salvador and Guatemala, youth and labor organizations also held solidarity actions.

Beyond the number of people who attended these protests and scope of the mega-marches, there are several reasons why they should be conceived of as a counterhegemonic moment. First, the boycott and demonstrations of May 1, 2006, exemplify what Gramsci called an organic crisis, in which a constellation of strategic political forces led by organic intellectuals emerges to defy the traditional political institutions of power. These organic intellectuals were able to articulate a simple message around full rights for workers that resonated with the masses of Latino migrant workers who heeded the call to support the boycott and to take to the streets. The crisis is further manifested in the refusal of millions of Latino migrant workers and their allies across the nation to heed the call to ignore the boycott made by elected officials and immigration reformers. The call made by elected officials, the Catholic Church, unions, and some of the nonprofits did not resonate with the common sense of the masses of the migrant workers and their allies, who flooded the streets of Los Angeles, the nation, and the transnational cities in Mexico and Central America that are connected to the global city region of Greater Los Angeles.

The second reason why the mega-marches were a counterhegemonic moment relates to the unity that Gramsci describes in his writings on the philosophy of praxis. The unity achieved between organic intellectuals and the masses of Latino migrant workers of the Latino social bloc allowed for them to gain moral and intellectual leadership on the issue of immigration reform in the public and political sphere for a brief moment. An indicator of this achievement could be seen in the brief shift in the national discourse on migration control. The national discourse went from one in which members of the dominant Anglo-American society would speak about migrants as criminals, gang members, diseases, and a burden to the economy to one in which major newspapers momentarily featured positive headlines.[61] For instance, the May 2 front-page headline of the Los Angeles Times read, "Marchers Fill LA's Streets: Next Converting the Energy of Protest to Political Clout," and other articles were titled "When I See This I See

Strength," "Migrants Demonstrate Peaceful Power," and "Throngs Show Their Potent Role in the Economy."[62] These stories invoke images of political agency and often focused on specific life histories, presenting readers with the names, occupations, and current struggles of migrant workers. For instance, the front page of that same issue of the *Los Angeles Times* had a picture of Max Amenero, a Peruvian migrant who came to the United States when he was sixteen and contracted polio and now sits in a wheelchair. Hundreds of similar stories that humanized migrants were written all over the nation.

Furthermore, the mega-marches were a counterhegemonic moment because the Latino social bloc was able to make powerful corporate and state interests concede to support the boycott. Protesters were also able to win concessions from local governments and multinational corporations. The first concession came from the California State Senate, where Gil Cedillo and Gloria Romero sponsored a resolution to endorse the May 1 boycott. Then, in the weeks leading up to the May 1 protest, it became evident that powerful multinational corporations would concede to giving workers the day off, in some cases with pay. For instance, Tyson Food Inc., Purdue Farms, and Swift Inc.—three of the largest meat and poultry plants in the United States—granted workers the day off.[63] The marches had a similar impact nationally. For instance, the New York City Hispanic Chamber of Commerce heeded the call for the boycott. "We are calling it a day of solidarity with migrants," said Eduardo Giraldo, chairman of the New York Statewide Coalition of Hispanic Chambers of Commerce. "We are asking for compassion from the employers towards the employees."[64]

Finally, the Latino social bloc was able to expand the scope of policy proposals seriously considered in the 109th Congress. Not until after the first action on March 25 did the Senate gain the courage to vote on S 2611, a less punitive bill which would have included a limited path toward citizenship for about half of the twelve million people undocumented living in the United States at that time. The late Senator Edward Kennedy made the following statements on the Senate floor just four days after the March 25 protest: "Those who have peacefully demonstrated their dedication to justice and comprehensive immigration reform should not be relegated back into the shadows....I had hoped we would recognize the lawful, heartfelt protests of millions against the harsh House-passed criminalization measures.... Criminalizing that status was punitive and wrong....These policies, which were included in the House-passed bill and supported there by congressional Republicans, understandably sparked nationwide protests."[65] As the words of the late senator indicate, the mega-marches gave the Democrats the ability to argue against HR 4437 and propose an alternative bill, one that although not entirely supported by all sectors of the Latino social bloc—especially the oppositional sector—was able to prevent the Sensenbrenner bill from becoming law. Even some of the leading immigration reformers in Washington, D.C., conceded that had it not been for the mega-marches, HR 4437 may not have been defeated. For instance, Angela Maria Kelly of the Center for American Progress remarked:

> As the marches were just rolling through the country members [of Congress] started showing up and we got the bill moving—the Kennedy-McCain bill. It came out with four Republicans and all of the Democrats supporting it. And that is what sustained us, we actually had pulled the bill off the floor and thought it was dead. We got the bill off the floor with twenty-four Republicans supporting the Kennedy-McCain bill. But what got people there were people on the streets. I have never seen such a direct line of how people could force lawmakers to act. It was beautiful![66]

As the words of Kelly suggest, the marches created the pressure on the Democratic Party to propose an alternative bill and essentially prevent HR 4437 from passing in the Senate. The Kennedy-McCain bill, or S 2611, as problematic as it may have been to some sectors of the Latino social bloc, helped dig the grave for HR 4437. Efforts to move forward with the Kennedy-McCain bill had been abandoned until the mega-marches put the pressure on Senate to act. Indeed, had it not been for the congealing of the Latino social bloc and its ability to galvanize a movement across the United States, in small towns and major cities and in Mexico and Central America, a Senate version of HR 4437, the legislative baby of the anti-migrant bloc, would have passed in both houses and been sent to President Bush. Paradoxically, this victory for the Latino social bloc was also its undoing.

Disintegration of the Latino Social Bloc

Despite the ascendency of the Latino social bloc, the counterhegemonic moment was lost almost as fast as the bloc congealed. A defining characteristic of hegemony, according to Gramsci, is that when the political leadership of dominant groups is threatened, they reassert their leadership through a delicate balance of co-optation and repression. In Greater Los Angeles, the bloc was disintegrated through a similar balance of forces.

After the success of the half-million march on March 25, 2006, and the raw acts of resistance that took place in Santa Ana on March 27 and in the immediate aftermath of the May 1 boycott, the Latino social bloc began to disintegrate rapidly. As described by Kelly, Congress saw that the masses of Latino migrant workers and their allies would not go quietly into the night and began to move forward with the Kennedy-McCain bill (S 2611). The new bill removed the most draconian aspects of HR 4437, including turning all undocumented migrants into felons and criminalizing those who provide services to undocumented migrants as aiding and abetting the crime of "illegal entry"—but it still divided Latino migrant activists and the migrant rights movement. With this bill on the table, the tensions between the oppositional groups and immigration reformers deepened the fissures in the Latino social bloc. The Catholic Church, labor unions, and moderate nonprofit organizations completely broke with the oppositional side of the bloc and adopted the position of the Somos America coalition, which was taking the lead of Congressman Luis Gutiérrez of Chicago and backing the Kennedy-McCain bill. Angelica Salas, the executive director of the Coalition for Humane Immigrant Rights of Los Angeles, expresses the views of immigration reformers: "We felt that this was our best chance to be able to bring all the different sectors and different parties on board to be able to fight for this reform."[67] From the perspective of Salas and other immigration reformers in Los Angeles, 2006 was a watershed moment but also a missed opportunity. For instance, Ali Noorani, director of the National Immigration Forum, reflecting on the 2006 marches and the proposed Kennedy-McCain bill, which did not pass in the Senate, said "I do think we missed an opportunity. I think as a result there has been a lot of pain and suffering… That was a big mistake on our part."[68] The position put forth by Salas and Noorani, both of whom were part of the Somos America coalition, was representative of the position put out by immigration reformers in Los Angeles and across the country in 2006.

Oppositional forces such as the March 25 Coalition and other groups such as the Frente Continental and the Coordinadora Estudiantil de la Raza argued that the Kennedy-McCain bill betrayed the spirit of the million or so activists who took to the streets on March 25, 2006. They held this position because the bill would have provided a punitive and complex path toward legalization for some migrants in exchange for more border security and interior enforcement. Other national groups, such as the National Network for Immigrant and Refugee Rights, also denounced Somos America and the Democratic Party establishment for essentially riding the wave of protest to push through an immigration bill that would have resulted in a punitive and unreasonably long legalization process in addition to the continued militarization of the border and interior enforcement efforts.

The power of hegemony lies precisely in its ability to make groups believe that the current state of affairs is natural and fixed. Many of the well-intentioned immigration reformers failed to see beyond the limits of the Somos America strategy. In other words, they accepted the terms of the debate in Congress that essentially called for legalization in exchange for more enforcement without having the vision and power to propose a more just immigration reform bill.

The oppositional forces of the Latino social bloc demanded an immediate and unconditional legalization for the twelve million undocumented workers in the United States and committed to struggle against the forces of global capitalism that displace workers in Latin America. However, they did not have a concrete strategy on how to get what they wanted and they were marginalized from the Beltway policy discussions occurring in Washington, D.C.

Immigration reformers being led out of Washington, D.C.–based civil-society organizations such as the Center for Community Change and Service Employees International Union (SEIU) had a plan and strategy to push the Kennedy–Mcain Bill and to court Latino voters. Nativo Lopez reflected on how this plan occurred.

> The Democratic Party apparatus and the party activists didn't see it early in the year, but after March 10 in Chicago and March 25 in Los Angeles...[they] began providing infrastructure and logistical support and messaging throughout the country. Through liberal foundations all of a sudden money started appearing to organizations that had been involved. By May 1 we started hearing this "Today We March, Tomorrow We Vote" slogan. It surfaced from the We Are America Coalition. They saw how the movement could be channeled toward an electoral push. The party started pushing the movement in this direction, and that is OK because ultimately we defeated Sensenbrenner...But we ultimately didn't get the kind of immigration reform that we wanted in 2006, but neither did the right wing. [69]

Lopez was partially right, and he was wrong. The movement defeated HR 4437 and the Democratic Party was able to court the Latino vote and channel the movement into electoral politics, but the anti-migrant bloc got to build up the homeland security state by passing the Secure Fence Act of 2006 and by expanding enforcement efforts in other parts of the country.[70]

The second reason why a large sector of the Latino social bloc disintegrated is material. One should recall that the first HR 4437 was so draconian that it would have converted twelve million undocumented workers into felons and criminalized anyone who works with them. Thus, the unions, nonprofits, the Catholic Church, and even the Congressional Hispanic Caucus were not going to be able to work with a large part of their constituencies. These major institutional players were at risk financially by HR 4437, which would have cost them through fines, legal battles, loss of donations, or dues in some cases. Nonetheless, once these draconian elements were dropped from the negotiating table, the Latino social bloc began to disintegrate further, as immigration reformers flocked to the congressional negotiating table under the leadership of the Democratic Party in favor of the Kennedy-McCain bill. Immigration reformers made these decisions because they thought this bill was the best bill that they could possibly get.

Labor had to oppose the boycott for practical reasons. Manuel Roman of UNITE HERE Local 11 during the marches explained, "There's absolutely no fucking way because any tacit support...by any union, saying we support the May 1 [boycott], right, would be in direct violation of pretty much every existing union contract in this country."[71] The union did not support the boycott to avoid breaking its contracts. The union's refusal to support the boycott created a tension in which the base of the union wanted to attend the May 1 boycott, but the union leadership was opposed to participating in the boycott and instead organized an afterwork/school march along with other immigration reformers for the evening of May 1. Roman noted, "Our members, our housekeepers, our cooks, *our meseros* [waiters], who were coming and saying, 'So what's up?' you know, 'are we going to take out our picket signs or are we going to take our banners?'" Although Roman and several local union leaders and rank-and-file members attended the May 1 boycott "on their own," as he emphasized in our interview, he admitted that officially the Los Angeles County Federation of Labor "didn't use the machinery, you know, we didn't, and anyone who tells otherwise is lying!"[72] Nativo Lopez of the Mexican American Political Association contends that labor, especially the UFW, opposed the boycott and supported the Kennedy-McCain bill because it contained a guest-worker program for which the farmworkers' union would have won millions of dollars in contracts.[73]

As Gramsci pointed out, however, co-optation is just one face of hegemony. In fact, he wrote that "the apparatus of state coercive power which 'legally' enforces discipline on those groups who do not 'consent' either actively or passively" is always reserved for "moments of crisis of command and direction when spontaneous consent has failed."[74] Indeed, much like the Chicano movement before it, the Latino social bloc was unraveled and disrupted by state coercion. Organizers reported being followed, receiving threatening phone calls, having their pictures taken, and facing direct physical abuse by law enforcement.[75] Perhaps the most visible incident occurred a year after of the Great American Boycott, on May 1, 2007, during the notorious MacArthur Park incident. As the world watched, the LAPD attacked thousands of protesters for nearly thirty minutes. Police fired tear gas and rubber bullets into crowds of peaceful protesters who included women and children and members of the television media. Regardless of the official intentions, the repression, which was televised all over the world, sent a chilling message to the base of supporters of the migrant rights social movement: participating in protest activities could be met with state violence.

In August 2007 federal agents captured Chicago activist Elvira Arellano in Los Angeles. Arellano, the mother of a US citizen child, Saul Arellano, had become an icon of the migrant rights movement in 2006 when she, in an act of resistance against a federal judge's orders, refused her deportation and sought sanctuary inside a Chicago church.[76] Arellano left her sanctuary and traveled to Los Angeles, evading authorities from the DHS and ICE. Nonetheless, she was captured by authorities in Los Angeles as she traveled with some of the leaders of the 2006 mega-marches to speak at a rally. Another incident of state repression occurred on April 19, 2007, when DHS and ICE officials used force to break up organizational efforts to protest the further militarization of the US–Mexico border at the No Borders Camp in San Diego. In the brutal attack, Border Patrol agents used pepper spray on a group of peaceful protesters as they conducted a binational protest against the US–Mexico border wall in San Ysidro. The intensification of state repression aimed at Latino migrant communities and at the migrant social movement should not be viewed as simple, isolated acts of state violence. Rather, it should be conceptualized as a shift in hegemony, which relied on consensual domination before the mega-marches, to one that still used co-optation, but that also used state violence, deportation, and the threat of force.

Notwithstanding the severity and brutality of these actions, the disintegration of the Latino social bloc cannot be explained simply by state repression. State repression can destroy movements, but it can also inject a sense of urgency and vigor that allows movements to take the struggle to the next level. Social movement leaders must anticipate and have a strategy for responding to state repression and infiltration. Well-prepared organizers can turn tragic incidents of state repression and intimidation on their heads, as was the case in Little Village in Chicago. In a classic display of how organized communities can respond to repression, a mass protest took place in the Latino community of Little Village after the ICE conducted a raid in a busy shopping mall as a reprisal for the 2006 marches.

In addition to state repression, a set of internal contradictions facilitated the disintegration of the Latino social bloc. First, there were serious divisions within the oppositional faction of the Latino social bloc. Moreover, there was often a battle among charismatic personalities for leadership. As Chicana feminist scholars have pointed out, these divisions have been a historic problem among men in the Chicano movement.[77] The Latino social bloc was no exception. Male leaders often had dramatic macho power struggles for leadership over the movement. The main problem was with a few key male leaders who used authoritarian tactics that alienated many potential allies. There were often divisions over who would get credit for the mega-marches, who would be the spokesperson of the movement, and in some cases, who could participate in the meetings. A notable difference between the male and female leadership is that most of the women belonged to well-established organizations with a mass base, democratic structure, and a system of accountability, whereas the main nuclei of the male leadership, with few exceptions, did not. But personality conflicts, gender dynamics, and possible infiltration that divided the Latino social bloc cannot fully account for its demise; such problems are, unfortunately, part of the reality of building social movements in the United States. A challenge for forging a new social bloc is building the necessary organizational sophistication and internal democratic structures to deal with these internal problems while building a sustainable and effective social movement.

The Counterhegemonic Moment and the Limits of Mass Mobilization

This chapter argues that the 2006 mega-marches in Greater Los Angeles materialized through the work of organic intellectuals who were able to organize a broad coalition of forces into what I term the Latino social bloc. The bloc was built on the culmination of three generations of Chicano and Central American political organizing, as well as the militancy of the Proposition 187 generation. These genealogies of struggle served as a sort of school for the formation of organic intellectuals or Latino migrant organizers who were educated in political strategy and tactics and understood the nature of the conjuncture at hand. Unlike a typical coalition or united front, the Latino social bloc was able to lead diverse and at times contradictory factions of the Latino migrant movement and its allies to overcome their immediate interests in support of the mega-marches. The result was the defeat of a draconian immigration reform bill that was the brain child and legislative baby of the anti-migrant bloc in Congress during the spring of 2006. The mega-marches also resulted in a brief shift in the national discourse on migration control from one that criminalized migrants to one that humanized them and placed legalization on the congressional negotiating table and in the national psyche. The mega-marches stand as an unprecedented benchmark in Latino migrant politics and social movements more broadly. Indeed, as Gramsci writes about Red Sunday in Italy, when tens of thousands of workers took over the factories, "For the workers, one day like this is worth ten years of normal activity."[78] The same could be said about the mega-marches, for they illustrated that Latino social movements could transcend traditional local coalition politics and defeat draconian legislation in Congress. They also illustrate that these movements can potentially mobilize millions of migrants and their supporters in the United States and transnationally. In the words of organizer Esther Portillo, "One of the lessons that the mega-marches has showed us is that using traditional lobbying, brokering, and advocacy is not enough. These tactics alone have failed. The people affected by these issues have to take the streets and make demands."[79]

Portillo is not suggesting a complete abandonment of traditional tactics but rather emphasizing that unless a mass movement to create the political pressure on state leaders emerges, such tactics alone are bound to fail.

Despite the historical magnitude of the marches and their immediate impact on HR 4437, one must note that there are serious limits to mass mobilization as a sole tactic for creating sustainable social change. Indeed, the 2006 marches in Greater Los Angeles were just a few among many contestations between the migrant rights movement and the anti-migrant bloc for intellectual and ideological leadership over the direction of state migration control and the rights of migrants. Indeed, perhaps one of the greatest shortcomings of the Latino social bloc was that it was ill prepared for the success of the mega-marches. Bloc leaders did not have the foresight and capacity to organize a significant portion of the millions of people who came to the mass mobilization into a sustainable, long-term organizational structure. Without cultivating this type of mass-based power in civil society, oppositional forces within the migrant rights movement and its allies will not have the capacity to meet their more far-reaching demands for social justice.

Latino migrant activists and organizers in 2006 did not foresee the resiliency of the anti-migrant bloc that was operating in distinct sites of state power and in civil society. These forces shifted their approach from a top-down strategy of a sweeping "immigration reform" bill to implementing their enforcement-through-attrition agenda through a piecemeal strategy. Concretely, this shift was manifested in a barrage of migration-control policies in multiple sites of power. For instance, just six months after the Great American Boycott, President Bush signed the Secure Fence Act of 2006, a bill for expanding the border wall by 700 miles and adding additional security personnel and measures for border enforcement. Following the marches, raids into migrant communities and work sites dramatically increased, more National Guard troops were deployed to the border, and local anti-migrant ordinances and repressive practices aimed at Latino communities proliferated, at times aimed directly at organizers from the Latino social bloc. In the following chapter, I illustrate the impact of local migration control on the Latino communities of Riverside, California, and elaborate on the challenges that such policies have for the Latino migrant movement more broadly.

Race, Domestic Globalization, and Migration Control in Riverside County

287(g) in our community is basically SB 1070, like the one they have in Arizona.

—Emilio Amaya[1]

Since the 2006 marches, the Latino migrant activists and their allies have been unable to roll back the barrage of anti-migrant policies and practices implemented at the local, state, and federal levels. Alarmed by the massive turnout in streets across the United States, the anti-migrant forces operating at the nexus between the state and civil society stepped up their push for state and local governments to control the flow of migrants.[2] The number of anti-migrant bills at the state level doubled between 2006 and 2007.[3] In 2007, there were 1,562 immigration-related bills in all of the fifty states. A total of 240 bills became law in forty-six states. In addition to legislation at the state level, local ordinances have also become popular among municipal and city governments from Hazelton, Pennsylvania, to Farmers Branch, Texas, to Escondido and Costa Mesa, California, and many other localities across the country.[4] Indeed, local governments have attempted to regulate migrants through a variety of measures, including barring undocumented migrants from renting homes, revoking the business licenses of employers that hire undocumented workers, and banning and shutting down day-labor centers.

Clearly, not all local and municipal governments' policies conform to this trend. Major cities such as San Francisco and New York City have—at least symbolically—declared themselves sanctuaries for migrants in the face of federal ICE raids. Moreover, small cities in California such as Southgate, Huntington Park, and Coachella have provided city services to migrants regardless of their legal status. Nonetheless, the vast majority of local policies covered by the media following the mega-marches have been those designed to discourage migrants from settling in communities or to expand the power of local police officials to cooperate with federal immigration authorities. Most important, however, the decision of local and municipal governments to regulate the flow of migrants, or integrate them, is the product of the relations of force between groups with competing interests and visions over the direction of the local governing apparatus and the rights of migrants vis-à-vis the state.

To illuminate how such struggles take place, in this chapter I look at migration control in Riverside County, California, and Latino migrant activists' efforts to mitigate the human rights consequences of the county's draconian policing practices. To conduct this analysis, I examined the proceedings of a meeting of the Riverside County Board of Supervisors and conducted interviews with Latino migrant rights activists in the region. The Riverside County Board of Supervisors governs the County of Riverside, and, next to the state of California and the federal government, it is the most powerful governmental institution in the area. The County Board "enacts ordinances and resolutions, adopts the annual budget, approves contracts appropriates funds, determines land use zoning for the unincorporated area, [and] appoints certain County officers and members of various boards and commission," among other duties.[5] As the following discussion shows, the county government represents the convergence of corporate interests linked to the emergence of a global capitalist economy and reactionary conservative forces in civil society.

I also draw upon interviews with leading Latino migrant activists who work in Inland Empire, a region of Southern California comprised of Riverside and San Bernardino counties. Organizers and activists interviewed for this chapter include those from the National Day Laborers Network, San Bernardino Community Service Center, and religious organizations including the Archdiocese of San Bernardino. My observations and interpretation of the material are also guided by my own auto-ethnographic knowledge from growing up most of my youth in the community of Mira Loma, located in the western part of the county.

Riverside County, located one hour from the city of Los Angeles, is one of the largest counties in the United States. It experienced a rapid demographic transformation during the 1990s that has accelerated in the early twenty-first century.[6] There are now nearly two million Latinos in the Inland Empire, a region of over four million people, and, in fact, Latinos are expected to become the majority by 2015.[7] It is an area that has dramatically transformed from a rural backwater of Southern California to an extension of the Los Angeles greater metropolitan region and thus a critical nodal point in the infrastructure of global capitalism.

While the Inland Empire area of Southern California is growing overall demographically, Latinos—migrant, as well as second- and third-generation—constitute the largest group driving the growth. The majority of the Latino population in Riverside County is Mexican, reflecting both the indisputable fact that the county was once part of Mexico and the long history of Mexican labor in the region's agricultural sectors.[8] There is also a relatively small but emerging Salvadoran and Guatemalan community. Salvadorans are spread throughout the county, and the Guatemalan community is overwhelmingly concentrated in the neighborhood of Casa Blanca, where thousands of indigenous Q'anjob'al Mayans reside. Given these conditions, Riverside County is a prime locality to study the policing of migrants and Latino migrant politics under the conditions produced by global capitalism and post–civil rights race relations.[9]

Following the mega-marches Riverside County's municipal government was one of the first in the nation, and the second in Southern California, to sign a Memorandum of Understanding (MOU) with DHS.[10] The MOU in Riverside County was made possible by section 287(g) of the Illegal Immigration Reform and Immigrant Responsibility Act of 1996 (IIRIRA), which was signed by President Clinton two years after signing NAFTA. Section 287(g) of IIRIRA provides in part that the federal government

> may enter into a written agreement with a state, or any political subdivi-
> sion of a state, pursuant to which an officer or employee of the state or
> subdivision, who is determined . . . to be qualified to perform a function
> of immigration officer in relation to the investigation, apprehension, or
> detention of aliens in the United States (including the transportation of
> such aliens across states lines to a detention center), may carry out such
> function at the expense of the state or political subdivision and to the
> extent consistent with state and local law.[11]

The agreement made in the MOU grants local law enforcement agencies the power to enforce federal immigration law, although local police forces were not granted such power previously. Although police and sheriff departments have had the authority to implement such a MOU since 1996, it was not until after 9/11 that this provision of IIRIRA was implemented nationally. The Department of Justice's Office of Legal Counsel issued a memorandum to the attorney general in 1989 concluding that unauthorized presence in the United States is not a crime[12]—thereby implying that local authorities do not have the authority to enforce immigration law. In 2002, Attorney General John Ashcroft issued a new memorandum stating that the 1989 memo was flawed.[13] According to the new memo, states have an "inherent authority" to enforce immigration law. This statement essentially opened the door for local governments to embrace section 287(g) of IIRIRA.

On a national level, the implementation of 287(g) was part of the formation of the homeland security state. This process involved the integration of the Immigration and Naturalization Service under the newly formed DHS in 2003. Indeed, the implementation of the 287(g) throughout the United States cannot be separated from the goals of the anti-migrant bloc and their effort to implement the enforcement-through-attrition strategy. Indeed this strategy was outlined in Operation Endgame, a ten-year strategic plan that calls for the deepening of interagency cooperation between the DHS-ICE and local law enforcement agencies to implement an enforcement-through-attrition strategy.[14]

As part of this strategy, the federal government advanced a series of initiatives to expand its capacity for enforcement from the traditional zone of the US–Mexico border into the interior. One of these new forms of interior enforcement was made possible by the MOU between the DHS-ICE and municipal governments to implement the 287(g) program by authorizing police and sheriff agencies to be trained to enforce federal immigration law. During 2006, the first year that the program was implemented in Riverside County, ICE trained eight deputies from the sheriff's department and referred 71% of the roughly 196 inmates that it screened in an average month for deportation.[15] In the two years following the 2006 mega-marches, the 287(g) program was expanded to seventy-one local law enforcement agencies in twenty-six states.[16] ICE reports that since the program was implemented, it has trained 1,190 officers to enforce immigration law and has identified more than 173,000 deportable individuals.[17]

The MOU was implemented under the premise that there is a natural connection among crime, migrants, terrorism, and threats to public safety. Ironically, however, at the time that local governments and state agencies were signing the MOU, crime had been declining nationally. According to a study conducted by the Public Policy Institute of California, even in migrant-receiving states such as California, immigrants are less likely to commit crimes than US citizens are, and cities experiencing an increase in their immigrant populations have seen a net drop in crime.[18] Nonetheless, the county governments of Los Angeles, Orange, San Bernardino, Riverside, and Ventura have all signed the MOU. The findings made by the Public Policy Institute of California suggest that no positive correlation exists between an increase in the immigrant population and crime in California cities. Despite the declining crime rate, the Riverside County Board of Supervisors approved and justified passing the MOU as an ostensibly race-neutral policy that would curtail crime in the county.

The Local Anti-Migrant Bloc

There was nothing inevitable about the implementation of the MOU in Riverside County. If oppositional Latino groups and their allies had possessed the political power necessary, they might have, in theory, pressured the county's Board of Supervisors not to participate in the 287(g) program. Local governments do not implement policies on their own; rather, policies are passed when a group harnesses the power of the state to implement its agenda, prevailing over subordinate groups that may also be competing for control over the institutions of governance.

Those governing are not the enlightened statesmen of the polity whom they are assumed to be in classic pluralist theory. They are individuals who are rooted in racialized class relations. In other words, they are governing in a society in which race and class greatly affect the distribution of resources, rights, and privilege. Under such conditions, it is critical for dominant groups to create the conditions for the social reproduction of racialized class relations by bringing together different social bases into a constellation of force in both the state and in civil society. In the context of Riverside County, this coalition could only happen through the formation of a regional or local bloc of interests comprised of capital, elected and appointed officials, and civil society–based organizations that seek to ensure that Riverside County continue its regional transformation from a rural backwater of Southern California to part of the Los Angeles global city region and hence a critical nodal point in the global capitalist economy.

I conceptualize this regional constellation of forces in Riverside County as a local anti-migrant bloc. Indeed, it is a highly heterogeneous and contradictory set of actors that includes elected and appointed officials who are linked to the most lucrative fractions of capital in the region and a reactionary base of conservative whites and a handful of Republican Latinos. Elected officials and state personnel who work with the county, such as the Board of Supervisors and the Sheriff Department, act as organic intellectuals for the bloc as they seek to win ideological consent for the dual system of justice and for the development model they have imposed on the region. The language that they use to criminalize Latinos in the region is one that resonates with the common sense of supporters among a large sector of the working- and middle-class whites who no longer have the same standard of living afforded to them under the Fordist mode of production. Thus, the Riverside County anti-migrant bloc brings together corporate and socially conservative Republican interests under a ruling coalition at multiple levels of governance, including but not limited to the Riverside County Board of Supervisors, city governments, school boards, and a variety of civil society–based organizations. It has a corporate faction that actively promotes the interests of corporate capital in the county by imposing a neoliberal development model in

which the state is supposed to attract investors by subsidizing their use of water
and power and their development of roads and by lifting any social and environmental regulations considered barriers to development. However, it is also a
racial bloc. Since its inception, it has been led by a faction of male Anglo leaders
who have historically relied on reactionary whites as a base of support and legitimacy while politically marginalizing the county's working-class Latino communities. For instance, while the county is 46% Latino, the Riverside County Board
of Supervisors is entirely composed of white men.

The anti-migrant bloc is the premier socioeconomic and political force in the
region, and it operates without major rivals. Despite the region's demographic
trends, the bloc will be a feature of governance in Riverside County for some
time to come, unless progressive forces in the Inland Empire region can build a
class-based alliance between the region's different ethnic and racial groups with
the political capacity to challenge its hegemony. To begin, a recent study by the
Public Policy Institute of California on the future of the Inland Empire pre-
dicts, "By 2015, whites will account for only 35 percent of adults in the population but will make up almost half (48 percent) of registered voters. By contrast,
Latinos will make up almost half of the adults (48 percent) but only 33 percent
of the registered voters."[19] The same report also indicates that Latinos already
compose the majority of the region's workforce and that wages and educational
levels are significantly lower in the region than in the rest of the state.[20]

While the federal government provided in 2002 the impetus for enforcing
the program nationally, the Riverside County Board of Supervisors was all too
ready to comply with enforcement on April 11, 2006, just one day after the
National Day of Action for Immigrant Justice and a few weeks after the first major
march in Los Angeles on March 25. Indeed, the board laid down the ideological groundwork for implementing the MOU by criminalizing the Latino communities of Riverside County: during the hearing to implement the MOU, they
constantly associated crime, Mexicans, and threats with the public safety of the
"good" citizens of Riverside County. Criminalizing Latinos, by using racial profiling and specialized draconian police practices that specifically target Latino
communities, deepens the county's dual system of justice, and it further blurs
the lines between local and federal police systems. Riverside's dual system of
justice, in turn, provides the local anti-migrant bloc with an apparatus to regulate
the spatial boundaries between its necessary barrios of Latino workers and its
newly built, luxurious centers of middle-class suburban leisure.[21] Most important, however, criminalization allows the bloc in Riverside County to appeal to
its working- and middle-class white social base while concealing the fact that the
development model that it has imposed on the region is what is driving Latino
labor into the county.

Globalization and Demographic Change in Riverside County

One must locate the development model in Riverside County in the context of neoliberal globalization. Globalization has led to the transformation of regions as far away from each other as northern Mexico, El Salvador, and Southern California as they become integrated into a transnational model of society and economy. Although theoretical explanations of how globalization is uprooting communities in regions across North America may seem abstract, these changes can be viewed in the concrete transformation of communities across Riverside County.

Riverside County is one of the largest counties in the United States; it is also a county of great inequality. As Figure 3.1 shows, its eastern part includes the affluent resort cities of Palm Springs, Palm Desert, Indian Wells, La Quinta, and Rancho Mirage. These communities are located next to low-income areas including Coachella, Indio, and Cathedral City, which are populated overwhelmingly by Mexican and Central American laborers and their families. The western end of the county is home to racially diverse working-class communities, where Mexicans and Central Americans live alongside a shrinking population of poor and working-class whites. This division of socioeconomic classes is the case in parts of Riverside and Corona and in the formally unincorporated areas of Rubidoux, Mira Loma, and Norco. These working-class communities are separated from one another by newly built middle-class suburbs such as Eastvale, Indian Hills, and Corona Hills. These distinct regions are targets of the Board of Supervisors' "redevelopment" zones and its efforts to regulate migrant flows in a region that has been marked by racial strife and repression for generations.

The development of Riverside County reflects that of the rest of the Southwest, which functions as an important region in the world capitalist system.[22] Like many communities of the Southwest, the area known as Riverside County has been a site of racial conflict and state repression for over two hundred years. Before colonization, indigenous groups such as the Gabrielino, Cahuilla-Luiseno, and Serrano inhabited what is now prime real estate, from coastal Southern California to the Los Angeles and Santa Ana river basins.[23] In the late eighteenth century, the Spanish crown set up a mission system with the dual goal of Christianizing indigenous people and coercing their labor. The mission system marked the beginning of a long pattern of suffering and injustice for nonwhites in what would become Riverside County. After the war of 1848 and the onslaught of the Gold Rush, Anglo colonial forces launched an offensive with the goal of destroying the local indigenous groups. Southern California Indians resisted until they were largely confined to reservations located in the most uninhabitable parts of eastern Riverside County. Ironically, these areas

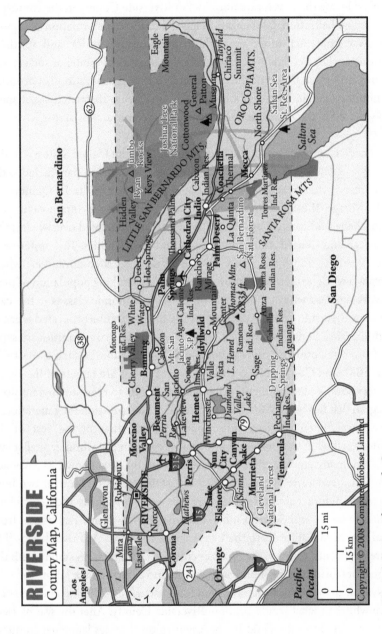

Figure 3.1 Map of Riverside County.

have become the site of a multibillion-dollar casino and resort industry in the twenty-first century.

After being colonized and incorporated into the Anglo-American capitalist economy, Riverside County became known for its vineyards, citrus orchards, large dairies, and rich agricultural valleys, where lettuce and grapes, among other products, are grown. Although official histories of the area often celebrate the orchards and vineyards, such as the Cantu-Galleano Ranch, which was founded by Italian immigrants, these histories often omit the fact that regional development was dependent on Mexican labor. From its inception, Riverside County has relied on Mexican and indigenous land/labor. *Mexicanos* composed the majority of the labor force in the vineyards, citrus orchards, and dairies throughout most of the twentieth century.[24] This history played out partially because of the arrival of a large base of Mexican workers who were fleeing the Mexican Revolution and who settled in the communities of Casa Blanca, Corona, Eastside Riverside, and in small pockets of the unincorporated ranchos in Rubidoux and Mira Loma.

During the Fordist era of production (World War II to the late 1970s), the rise of the aerospace industry brought three military bases and companies, including Kaiser Steel to the region, and well-paid, unionized Anglo-American workers became the majority in Riverside County. In the 1950s, the area saw the building of the Rubidoux Drive-In, and boutiques and hotels predominated along Mission Boulevard, which connects Rubidoux with a bridge over the Santa Ana River to the city of Riverside. Moreover, after the Watts Rebellion of 1965, Riverside County, like the rest of the Inland Empire, became a choice destination for whites fleeing the Los Angeles area. By the 1970s, it was known as a hotbed of racism and was home to a large base of the KKK and to outlaw biker gangs such as the Hells Angels.[25] During this era, the Mexican population was a numerical minority, confined to small, isolated barrios.

However, as Raymond Rocco reminds us, globalization can lead to the transformation of once-Anglo-majority areas into Latino communities in places like southeastern Los Angeles County.[26] While not as rapid or complete as the transition that occurred in southeast Los Angeles, economic restructuring has led to a transformation of Riverside County. The closing of military bases and the decline of the aerospace industry meant that the once mostly Anglo working-class communities saw their employment opportunities shrink. This loss of high-paying jobs set the material basis for the white flight that gradually began in some parts of the county in the late 1980s and accelerated in the 1990s, as Mexican, Central American, and African American families from the surrounding counties moved inland in greater numbers. By the 1990s, many whites had moved to the newly built southwestern suburbs of Murrieta, Temecula, and Lake Elsinore.[27] Throughout the first decade of the twenty-first century, many whites left the county altogether as Latino and African American families, displaced by gen-trification and in search of affordable housing, left Los Angeles for the Inland Empire.[28] In what has become an ironic and perhaps irreversible cycle, by 2010 the city of Riverside had lost nearly thirty thousand whites, and the only cities in the county to gain whites were located in the southeastern suburban cities near San Diego County, which have become hotbeds for anti-migrant racism and human rights abuses.[29]

The demographic transformation in Riverside County is a reflection of the demographic changes occurring throughout the Inland Empire. The latest cen-sus data reveal that Latinos in Riverside County made up 45.5% of the popu-lation in 2010, whereas in 2000 they composed just 36.2%. The neighboring county of San Bernardino has experienced a similar demographic change, with Latinos composing 49.2% of the population in 2010 versus 39.2% in 2000.[30]

The demographic transformation occurred for two interrelated reasons. First, the implementation of a neoliberal economic model in Mexico set the conditions for the displacement of millions of workers in the 1990s.[31] In fact, in the 1990s the United States would see the dramatic influx of post-NAFTA migrants from Mexico. Second, NAFTA was accompanied by the rapid restruc-turing of Southern California's Fordist economy to a post-Fordist economy highly dependent on flexible labor. In such conditions, transnational corpora-tions rely heavily on nonunionized, part-time, subcontracted labor and on the use of just-in-time delivery systems made possible by the logistics revolution.[32] The ascendency of neoliberalism in Mexico and economic restructuring in the United States are in fact part of the same process involving the reorganiza-tion of capitalist production around the globe from nation-based systems of production and trade to a transnational system of production, trade, finance, and labor.

Riverside County is no exception to what social scientist Raúl Delgado Wise calls the dialectic between development and migration.[33] For instance, in the aftermath of the General Agreement on Trade and Tariffs in 1986 and later NAFTA in 1994, the community of Mira Loma, located in the far western tip of the county, along with parts of neighboring Ontario, Fontana, and Rancho Cucamonga became one of the primary nodal points of the post-Fordist econ-omy in the United States. Because Mira Loma is no more than two days away from nearly 85% of the population in the western United States, it became a strategic inland port for the transnational corporations that do business there.[34] Inland ports are designed to store overflow cargo from saturated seaports and to serve as forwarding locations for moving cargo into strategic routes. The inland port became a central part of North America's post-NAFTA capitalist infrastruc-ture. Currently there are several inland ports along the United States' main com-mercial highways.

As a result of the influx of capital into the region, the Mira Loma port, which has further grown to absorb the overflow from the Long Beach port, has the dubious privilege of being one the largest inland ports in the United States. The formally unincorporated community of Mira Loma, which is just one part of the distribution network that cuts through the Inland Empire, is currently home to some of the largest warehouses for the most powerful transnational corporations, including Walmart, Union Pacific, General Motors, Hyundai, FedEx, and UPS, to name a few.[35] Mira Loma is also home to the largest automobile distribution center in the world. Research shows that the air pollution created by these industries is so bad that if Mira Loma were its own country, it would have the world's fourth-worst air quality, rivaled only by that of Bangkok, Manila, Mexico City, and New Delhi. And much like their third-world counterparts, the people bearing the brunt of the environmental damage are predominantly working-class people of color.[36]

The transition of Riverside County from a Fordist economy to a post-Fordist hub of global capital was made possible by the combination of factors such as acces to cheap land and the County Board of Supervisor's laissez-faire treatment of the logistics industry. Edna Bonacich has written that part of the reason for the growth of giant distribution centers in the Inland Empire is that regional government allowed major corporations set up shop with little to no interference. This process contributed to the political and material conditions for the demographic transformation of the region. As Latino urban scholars have observed, one of the notable characteristics of the flexible labor practices in Southern California is the highly racialized labor force.[37] Latino labor is an essential feature of the system of flexible labor practices in Riverside County. For instance, at least 50% of the thousands of warehouse workers for the world's largest corporations doing business in Mira Loma are migrant and second-generation Latinos.[38]

Latino labor is also essential to the most lucrative industries in the eastern part of the county, where Mexican and Central American communities are concentrated in agriculture, construction, hospitality, and service. In eastern Riverside County, Latinos have long been the majority in cities like Coachella and Indio, but the whole region has experienced an overall growth of its Latino population over the last two decades that parallels the growth of the casino and resort industries.

It is precisely at this junction in the world capitalist system that Riverside County has become a battleground for both corporate capital and migration control. Indeed, this scene is the landscape in which the anti-migrant bloc implements public policy to "deal" with the immigrants that it depends on as part of its development model. This tumultuous and contradictory landscape has put the local anti-migrant bloc of Riverside County in a predicament. They are dependent on both reactionary Anglo Republican voters and a domestic flexible labor force composed of Mexican and Central American workers to attract the industries that have turned their rural backyard of vineyards, orchards, fields, and dairies into a critical nodal point of the global capitalist system. This system puts pressure on the anti-migrant bloc in Riverside County to come up with ways of balancing its contradictory need to secure a flexible Latino labor force and maintain its hegemony among a political base of reactionary white voters.

The Riverside County Board Meeting

On April 11, 2006, the Riverside County Board of Supervisors publicly discussed and approved agenda item 3.23, a proposal to implement the MOU enforcing 287(g) in the county. Throughout the discussion, the board completely evaded the subjects of why Latinos are attracted to the region and the proposed policy's legal and human rights impact. The meeting was a reminder that the ability to define the boundaries of public debate is an artifact of power.

The meeting began with a Christian prayer, which, ironically, praised American democratic values of freedom and liberty and pointed out the authoritarian and undemocratic character of other nations throughout the world. After the prayer, the meeting proceeded with public comments; there were two speakers, one for and the other against the MOU. The board completely ignored the comments made in opposition to the bill. There was no substantive debate among the supervisors about the fundamental problems or merits of the MOU. Rather, the deliberation seemed more like a dialogue among the Board of Supervisors, the Riverside County Sheriff's Department (RSD), the Riverside Police Department (RPD), DHS, and the FBI that, in effect, naturalized the need to implement the MOU. The RSD representative, Neil Lingle, went before the board to state, "This request is simply for training to ask your board to approve to eventually augment and enhance our ability to send these criminal illegal aliens back to their country of origins."[39] There was no debate as to the nature of the policy—no discussion of whether migrant communities were actually criminally engaged, how the policy would impact communities, or the fundamental consequences of blurring the lines between federal and local law enforcement.

The only "issue" brought up by the board concerned the costs of the program and reimbursement from the federal government. For instance, Supervisor John Tavaglione of the Second District asked the RSD representative to tell him the net cost of sustaining the MOU over a one-year period. After the RSD representative indicated that the net cost of the program for the county would be over $5 million per year, for which it would be reimbursed only $1.2 million, Supervisor Tavaglione made the following point:

> [The MOU is] a loss for us obviously. And the reason I bring that up is because I support this. I wholeheartedly support this. I think it's the right thing to do. This is no different than training any of our deputies or police officers in drug recognition, gang recognition. We put them to special training to identify certain levels of criminal behavior. This is just another level to help us deal with the system much more efficiently. I am very happy that you brought this forward; I think it's the right thing to do, and I will support this wholeheartedly.[40]

Supervisor Tavaglione makes clear that he "wholeheartedly" supports the construction of this new apparatus of state violence for racial profiling as a sound and rational public policy option. Moreover, he equates criminal activity, such as selling drugs or belonging to a gang, with the status of undocumented workers, when in fact the courts have been clear that being in the United States without documents is only an administrative violation, not a criminal offense. We will return to this issue later. For now, however, we will evaluate how other members of the board pushed for the MOU.

The following excerpt from the record reveals Supervisor Stone's logic in supporting the MOU:

> I believe that we are in this position we are in this country today, not because we didn't have the laws on the books. We did not enforce the laws that we have today.... In plain English, I fully support to identify and to return illegal aliens, especially those that commit crimes, back to Mexico. My concern is that we are just extending the revolving door back to the border. They are going to be coming back in.... Will [the federal government] be proactive in ensuring that we keep these dangerous criminals off our streets?[41]

Supervisor Stone describes undocumented workers as "illegal aliens"—the most basic and consistent form of criminalizing migrant workers. Second, in what was perhaps a Freudian slip that violates the rules of post–civil rights race relations, he makes it clear, in "plain English" in fact, that the county board is concerned with immigration coming from Mexico and the "revolving door" at the border, implying that many migrants are returning after being deported and thus perpetuating the stereotype of lawlessness on the border.

Supervisor Wilson immediately sought to cover up Supervisor Stone's remarks with the following cumbersome comment:

There is going to be equal opportunity in deportation. That is deportation to Mexico, to Canada, deportations to whatever country you came from if you commit a serious illegal act in the county of Riverside. And I think that will send a deterrent effect out to all the communities in Riverside, to immigrant communities, to cities, to counties. It's not something we are doing in the streets, it's something we are doing after people are in the jails after there is a higher probability of conviction, or after conviction?.[42]

The words of Supervisor Wilson reflect the way that the county board supports anti-migrant policies brought to its floor without having full knowledge of what is at stake. It is clear that Supervisor Wilson did not care to know how the MOU would actually be implemented. The fact remains that the sheriff deputies conduct immigration interviews with any "suspected" undocumented person in its county jails regardless of whether he or she is actually convicted. Despite not being clear on the policy, Supervisor Wilson restated his unequivocal support for the MOU in the name of public safety:

> In addition to the monetary savings that's a very important issue.... Beyond that the overriding thing is the general effect on public safety in the county I think will be enhanced. The word will go out. People will think twice about committing these offenses that will not only land them in jail but actually will cause them to be deported to their country of origin, wherever that may be.[43]

The board never addressed the nature or potential consequences of the type of policing model that it wanted to support. On the contrary, a blind willingness to continue expanding RSD's police powers to deport "dangerous criminals" was the central theme throughout the discussion of agenda item 3.23. For instance, the following statement from RSD representative Neil Lingle summed up what the county purported would be the benefit of the MOU:

> What this program really does for us is that it ensures safer communities. Anytime that we have an opportunity to take criminals off the street, it is going to fit very nicely into our crime prevention strategy in the county. It opens up opportunities for federal databases to check the status of people that we do not have the ability to access right now.... There are seven different databases that the fed[eral] gov[ernment] has to determine alienage, and we don't have that right now.... The bottom line is that it is going to prevent the victimization of innocent people.[44]

Throughout the board's deliberation on the MOU, the issue of protecting the nation and its presumably innocent citizens was consistently brought to the floor. For example, in the following remarks, Supervisor Stone and Neil Lingle go as far as to advocate a preemptive police strategy to go after the infamous transnational Salvadoran gang, the Mara Salvatrucha. Supervisor Stone states:

> I hope we can get ahead of the ballgame here. I read about the highly sophisticated international gang members such as Mara Salvatrucha; they are actually coming back and forth, back and forth, almost redoubling their strength, knowledge, and organization. That hasn't reached our county yet, but it may. . . . It's an extremely grave issue that affects many metro police and sheriff departments in our county. Do you [the RSD] see that as an emerging issue that you have to be concerned about?

Neil Lingle, representative of the RSD, responds to Supervisor Stone's question:

> It goes to the insightfulness of your board to support our gang task force. What we are experiencing here is a manifestation of our own growth. I don't think it's a matter of if, but when these things will come to Riverside County. The hope we hold is that we will be able to positively influence our future.[45]

These excerpts from the April 11, 2006, meeting of the Riverside County Board of Supervisors reveal how local policy makers associate undocumented migrants with crime, gangs, Mexicans, and terrorism. The board's discourse doesn't just make this association—it naturalizes it, thereby making the need for draconian police policies appear self-evident. Equally as critical, the criminalization of Riverside County's Latino communities obscures the real causes driving Latino migrant labor to the region, and it conceals that the real impact of the MOU will be the separation of families.

As the county board presented it, the "debate" on the MOU was about the program's cost, and the subjects of the policy were criminals from Mexico and Salvadoran gang members. The board's discussion in effect absolved them from advocating a development model that depends on flexible migrant labor. Rather than being an anomaly or just a bad policy, the discourse that we find in the halls of the Riverside County board is reproduced in multiple sites of state power and in hundreds of county boards throughout the country. For now, however, we will briefly explore how the MOU affects the Latino communities of Riverside County.

Dual System of Justice

The discursive link between crime, migrants, and Latinos sets the ideological conditions for implementing the MOU enacting 287(g) authority in Riverside County. This authority, in turn, provides the institutional and juridical framework for the consolidation of a dual system of justice in the county. Indeed, in Riverside County there is a system of justice for whites that functions like the justice systems in most democratic societies. For the Mexican and Central American communities of the Inland Empire, however, there is a prosecutorial system made possible by the homeland security state that works more like a national security system than a civilian police system in a democratic society.[46]

This dual system of justice is perhaps most pronounced at the intersection of the immigration and the criminal justice systems. For whites, there is a separation of federal and local police institutions unless a warrant is issued by a federal judge. Latino communities are often subject to racial profiling by city, county, and federal authorities that work together on a regular basis. Whites are presumed innocent until proven guilty in a court of law. Latinos are presumed to be undocumented until they prove otherwise. Whites found guilty for committing a crime are given regular sentences. Latinos convicted of a crime are regularly assigned harsh sentences. Moreover, when undocumented Latinos have contact with any law enforcement agency in Riverside County, they are likely to be deported—even if they have not been convicted of a crime.

Indeed the 287(g) agreement in Riverside County is a preconviction agreement, meaning that any contact with law enforcement, regardless of whether a crime is committed, could result in deportation. According to Emilio Amaya, executive director of the San Bernardino Community Service Center, the impact of the 287(g) agreement has been devastating:

> After reviewing the data, about 80 percent of the people who are transferred to ICE under 287(g) are people who are stopped for traffic infractions or minor convictions such as DUIs. These are allegations, not even convictions, and they are going to be transferred to ICE, which basically means that they are going to be put into deportation proceedings. And that is a big difference when compared to other places such as [Los Angeles] County, which is post-conviction, meaning that most people don't get [ICE] detainers until they get convicted. In Riverside it is regardless of [conviction].[47]

The dual system of justice often has severe consequences for the county's Mexican and Central American communities. For instance, Amaya relates what happened to an undocumented Latina mother from Riverside in March 2010 when she called the police to report domestic abuse.

> Even though she was a victim of domestic violence, the family court judge in Riverside got upset with her and called the Border Patrol. So she was arrested by the Border Patrol at the family court and transferred to ICE. We filed a U visa because she was a victim of a crime, but that illustrates the fact that when you have something like 287(g), not just police officers but anybody else that deals with immigrants and criminal justice issues feels empowered to enforce immigration law.[48]

As pointed out by Amaya, the 287(g) program creates a situation in which law enforcement officers, whether the RSD or the RDP, feel empowered to enforce immigration law. For instance, Daniel Guzmán, a community organizer and member of the Rapid Response Network (a migrant rights group that documents human rights abuses in the Inland Empire), relates the following firsthand account of a joint police and Border Patrol operation that took place on Madison Avenue in the Riverside neighborhood of Casa Blanca:

> In February of 2009 we got rapid calls, "Hurry, hurry, they are arresting day laborers. . . . It's a huge operation." I immediately see what they meant. Two officers running after a man with a hood over his head. Basically they were going to question and arrest him. Tapping hurryingly on his shoulder the man turns around and they see a black face. They laugh and chuckle, and wave to the man and turn around. Seconds later, there were throngs of patrol cars with day laborers in those patrol cars. The Riverside police had mounted a huge undertaking to "clean up the neighborhood"—that was the phrase that was used. I then saw patrol cars backing up the policemen and the bicycle policemen. They were stopping a young man who was simply riding a bicycle on the sidewalk, and they themselves were on bicycles! As if he was a drug criminal they ran at him and they stopped him. They demanded identification. The young man simply puts his bike down. They surround him. They forced him to sit on the floor so they can look at his ID. The young man is very calm and gives it to him. They leave to catch other people. There was lots of videos caught of officers going around asking people for their ID simply because they were standing on the sidewalk. Standing on the sidewalk, that is not a violation, but for them it was.[49]

The words of Guzmán illustrate how Latinos are profiled and then subject to a dual system of justice in Riverside County. Indeed, when the police officers saw

that the man on the bike was African American, they let him go. Had he been
Mexican or Guatemalan, he would have been subject to a series of questions and
forced to prove that he was in the United States legally until proven otherwise.[50]
Moreover, no law makes it illegal to stand on a sidewalk. However, Mexican and
Central American day laborers are de facto suspected of being undocumented,
and standing on the sidewalk becomes grounds for local and federal police to
cooperate and to profile and interrogate them. The fact that riding a bike or
standing on the sidewalk could result in such police action for Latinos and not
whites is a prime example of the dual system of justice that has emerged in local
communities under the homeland security state.

While an operation consisting of arresting day laborers for the simple act of
looking for work is deplorable enough, the 287(g) agreement created the insidious climate in which the police felt empowered to hand over those captured in
the raid to the Border Patrol. According to Guzmán, the Border Patrol was "in
cahoots" with the RDP. In an interview recounting what had occurred on that
day, the Riverside chief of police told reporters that the Border Patrol was called
in to help them "translate." During the operation that day, roughly thirty people
were captured, jailed, and deported.[51] This event is not an isolated incident.

In the city of Temecula, located in the southeastern tip of Riverside County,
there have been many incidents of police abuse against Latino communities. Temecula is home to an immigration checkpoint along Interstate 15. The
checkpoint is a regular site of racial profiling and harsh interrogation that many
Southern California Latinos—regardless of legal status—dread crossing when
traveling between the Inland Empire and San Diego County. Beyond the checkpoint, local rights groups report that Temecula's Latino communities face harassment from the Temecula Police Department and RSD deputies, who regularly
cooperate with ICE and immigration officials. In one case, the police handed
over the only witness to a homicide to immigration authorities for deportation.[52]
A local migrant rights activist, Estella, relates the details of another incident:

> A young man from Temecula was walking on the street when the police
> stopped him just because of the way he looked—Mexican or Latino
> with dark hair. The cop asked him, what are you doing on the street?
> The young man answered, I am walking home. The cop asked him,
> Where is your house? The young man answered, In those apartments.
> The cop asked, Do you have identification? Yes, said the young man and
> showed him. The police officer said, This is not a United States iden-
> tification. Do you have identification? No, he told him. Do you have
> immigration papers? You know you can't be here, you are illegal! I am
> going to arrest you. This was the Temecula police! He took him all the

way to Murrieta, another city where the immigration is at. And there he turned him in to immigration.[53]

The incident reported by Estella is just one documented case in the city of Temecula. It should be kept in mind that cases that are brought to the attention of activists represent only a few of many similar occurrences that have taken place throughout the county since the MOU was implemented.

The MOU is just one component of the dual system of justice. It is neither the beginning nor the end of this racialized system of migration control. Rather, it represents a deepening of the injustices facing Latino communities in places like Riverside County that have a long history of violence against communities of color. Latino male youths are but the latest targets of this racialized violence. For instance, in 2005 and 2006, Riverside County sheriff deputies were involved in more fatal shootings than their counterparts in Los Angeles County, where the population is twice that of Riverside.[54] While 287(g) provides a mechanism for novel forms of policing Mexican and Central American migrants, law enforcement in the region has a long history of using violence against communities of color. Indeed, police violence against Latinos, blacks, and Native Americans in Riverside County has been all too familiar in the 1990s and early twenty-first century. For a case in point, in May 1996, the RSD was launched onto the national scene as its deputies chased a van alongside the 60 Freeway in El Monte, California. At the end of the chase, two white male sheriff deputies beat unarmed 28-year-old Elisa Soltero in broad daylight as television news cameras from helicopters above recorded the incident.[55] In 1998, in another high-profile incident, RPD officers fatally shot 19-year-old Tyisha Miller, who was unconscious in a car with a gun on her lap. Miller was shot twelve times by police officers who claimed she reached for the gun, even though lab reports indicated that the gun was never fired.[56]

Violent relations between law enforcement and communities of color were exacerbated with the ascendency of the war on terror. For instance, shortly after the formation of DHS in 2003, a series of raids was launched in Riverside and San Bernardino counties. Border Patrol agents went into busy supermarkets, stopped pedestrians on busy streets, and picked up parents waiting for their children in front of Jurupa Valley High School in Mira Loma.[57]

The raids instilled terror in Mexican communities as children were ripped from the arms of their mothers, and hundreds of families were separated in the first wave of raids that would be systematically implemented throughout the United States in the first decade of the twenty-first century. Such raids were not limited to the Jurupa area. They continued in the Coachella Valley and other parts of Riverside County. In one such raid in 2008 that took place in an unincorporated community near Coachella, the Border Patrol detained parents as they picked up their children from the school bus.[58]

Riverside County has also become the site of federally funded antigang units that disproportionally target Latino communities, with some fatal outcomes. For instance, in 2005, the Jurupa Anti-Gang Task Force fatally shot 26-year-old Robert Mendoza. Mendoza, who was fleeing police on a parole violation, was shot over forty times as his older brother pleaded with police to allow him to coax his brother into surrendering.[59] Police claimed Mendoza had brandished a firearm, yet family members and witnesses insisted that Mendoza was carrying only his cell phone. In 2007, RSD deputies were involved in the fatal shooting of three Saboba tribe members in a one-month period.[60] As in the cases of the fatal shootings of Miller and Mendoza, the law enforcement agency, in this instance the RSD, claimed that its officers felt that their lives were in danger. Tribal leaders, however, echo the criticism put forth by the Miller and Mendoza families: officers shot first and asked questions later.

Resisting the Dual System of Justice

In Riverside County, as in other areas of the United States facing programs like 287(g), activist voices have emerged to challenge these new forms of anti-migrant policies and practices. Since its inception, the MOU has met with resistance. For instance, in the hall of the Riverside County Board of Supervisors, which was filled with a crowd of sheriff deputies and DHS-ICE agents, community organizer Esther Portillo voiced this powerful critique:

> I work in Riverside, specifically in the Mira Loma Glen Avon area. In the past what has happened is RSD is not only identifying and racial profiling people that are driving and asking them for their immigration papers.... These laws that you are approving would be violating the civil rights of people.... It hasn't been the "criminals," the "gang members" [affected], it has been the community, it has been the workers that are building all these new buildings here in Riverside.[61]

The words of this local activist went against the grain of the terms of the debate in several ways. First, she situated her critique from the perspective of the communities affected rather than law enforcement. Second, she refused to use any criminalizing terms, such as "illegal alien" or "criminals," to talk about the communities affected. On the contrary, she explicitly challenged the notion that those who will be affected by the MOU are criminals. Third, she affirmed that the people affected are workers, who have civil rights and who are part and parcel of the community and labor market. Finally, she explicitly challenged the County Board of Supervisors' and the RSD's practices of racial profiling.

Despite the valiant efforts of this organizer, the reality is that in 2006 the resources available to organize around immigration issues in Riverside were nonexistent, thus there was not enough community pressure at the April 6 meeting to make the board vote against 287(g). Portillo describes how only four organizers from the Center for Community Action and Environmental Justice were present the day the county voted to implement the MOU.

> The meeting was jam-packed with the FBI, police, sheriffs—a lot of sheriffs. It was standing room only. I don't think people understood the severity of 287(g) at that point. Some had an idea, but they did not foresee what was going to happen in the future. Even with community pressure present, the Riverside Board of Supervisors is made up of mostly conservative white males.[62]

The words of Portillo are a testament to the need for Latino migrant activists in the Inland Empire to build a more sophisticated organizational infrastructure and mobilization strategy. After taking busloads of activists to downtown Los Angeles for the mega-marches, Riverside County–based organizations could not mobilize effectively against the signing of the MOU that was implemented almost a month before the May 1, 2006, Great American Boycott.

It was not until the aftermath of the 287(g) program that organizers began to reactivate coalitions and to create new organizations to fight the agreement, ICE raids, and other forms of cooperation between the police and Border Patrol. The two main coalitions founded to challenge the 287(g) agreement and work to defend the rights of migrants were the Justice for Immigrants Coalition of the Inland Empire and the Rapid Response Network. Founded in 2008, the Justice for Immigrants Coalition is composed of community-based organizations such as the San Bernardino Community Service Center, Libreria del Pueblo, the Pomona Economic Development Center, the Day Laborers' Council of the Inland Empire, Warehouse Workers United, Laborers International Union of North America, and religious organizations such as the Archdiocese of San Bernardino.[63] The Rapid Response Network was founded the next year to provide a quick response to immigration raids and abuses in the Inland Empire.

Together these two groups have mobilized against the cooperation between local law enforcement agencies and ICE. In February 2009, the social justice community in Riverside turned out in large numbers to protest cooperation between police and immigration authorities. Daniel Guzmán vividly recounts, "Everybody joined in less than two weeks later. We did a huge march, closing down some of the main streets in downtown Riverside all the way to the Border Patrol office. It was a five-mile walk in the middle of heavy rain. And people did not stop. They just wanted to keep on going, even people with babies—it was that important."[64]

Mobilizations have provided some important victories for the Mexican and Central American migrant communities of Riverside and San Bernardino counties. In some cases, activists have been able to prevent deportations resulting from the cooperation between local law enforcement and federal immigration authorities. With respect to the MOU itself, the Justice for Immigrants Coalition and the Rapid Response Network have been able to meet with local and federal law enforcement agencies and get them to abide by the MOU. They have ensured that officers read people their rights and that they implement 287(g) within the regulations that are stipulated in the actual MOU. For instance, the MOU states that local law enforcement agencies in Riverside County can hold people for only forty-eight hours for ICE to pick them up for deportation. After the forty-eight hours, the sheriffs are supposed to release the individual, according to the agreement. In practice, however, sheriffs were holding individuals for up to five days to facilitate their deportation.[65] Thanks to the work of the coalition and network, this practice has ceased, or at least has been seriously curtailed. In some cases, with the leadership of Emilio Amaya of the San Bernardino Community Service Center, they were able to have some people released after forty-eight hours.[66]

There have been other small-scale victories. Amaya pointed out that in some cases, county workers who are not lawyers were advising undocumented migrant workers to sign their own deportation orders. To rectify this practice, the Justice for Immigrants Coalition has conducted workshops for county workers instructing them to refrain from providing potentially misleading or erroneous legal advice. Other small-scale victories have occurred in Temecula; for instance Estela states that they have been organizing actions and stopping some deportations.[67]

Despite the saliency of these immediate victories for those facing deportation, demanding that migrants be read their rights or that police authorities implement the MOU correctly reinforces the state's power to use racial profiling and to enact legal violence against Riverside County's Mexican and Central American communities. The Rapid Response Network and the Justice for Immigrants Coalition are part of larger network of immigration reformers across the country that would like to see the MOU dissolved. However, they are up against the power of the state and a politically active civil society that supports programs like 287(g). Notwithstanding the oppositional currents within these coalitions, in the face of this reality, organizers and activists mentioned here cannot realistically put a stop to the systematic and daily deportations that take place every morning from the Robert Presley Detention Center. Nor can they realistically stop the Border Patrol's systematic and daily harassment of Mexicans and Central Americans at immigration checkpoints and throughout the county as a part of the so-called roving patrols conducted by immigration authorities. Given the asymmetrical relation of force among Latino migrant activists, the anti-migrant bloc, and the homeland security state, it is near impossible for activists to effectively defend the rights of migrants throughout the entire county without building up their political power and their internal organizational capacity.

For the Mexican and Central American migrant communities of Riverside County, there are no short cuts to finding justice. Amaya critically points out:

> The long-term goal is to stop the cooperation between local immigration enforcement, but we understood that it was going to be very difficult to have the politicians do something about it [287(g)]. Most of them like it, and most of them see anyone here without documents as a criminal regardless. The long-term goal is to stop cooperation with ICE in the two counties [Riverside and San Bernardino counties]. It takes a lot of political will for the county to stop this practice, but we don't have this at the time. We have to do our work.[68]

Indeed, there is much work to be done in Riverside County to find a sustainable and transformative justice for migrants and their families. The gloomy reality is that the dual system of justice that exists in Riverside County is one that exists in many communities throughout the United States where the forces of global capital and economic restructuring have created the conditions for local right-wing politicians and police agencies to cooperate with the homeland security state, with deadly consequences for local communities of color.

*   *   *

The MOU between the Riverside County Board of Supervisors and the DHS cannot be viewed in a vacuum. The structural forces that have led to the transformation of Riverside County are the same forces that have led to the demographic transformation of communities throughout the United States. These are the same structures that help explain the large migrant population in Georgia, Nebraska, Kansas, and other states. In these areas powerful transnational corporations such as Swift and Company, which own meat processing plants, employ tens of thousands of migrant workers and their second-generation offspring, while local and federal authorities attempt to repress Latino migrant workers. In fact, although Riverside County is in Southern California and now shares many characteristics with nearby Los Angeles County, it also has much in common with the small rural regions in the midwestern, northeastern, and southern United States that are contradictorily dependent on nonunionized migrant labor and a mostly white political base.[69]

Global capitalism has created the conditions in which Latino communities are emerging throughout the United States. Yet it is precisely in regions outside the main metropolitan centers of political power where the Latino migrant movement must be strengthened. A few activists and nonprofit organizations can always resist draconian immigration policies. But resistance in and of itself is not the same as launching an effective oppositional politics capable of winning sustainable and transformative social justice victories against programs like 287(g). Latino migrant rights activists do not have the organizational and political infrastructure in place to launch an effective oppositional politics in Riverside County. Until the Latino migrant movement can build the necessary resources for securing social justice victories for communities like Riverside County across the country, there will be no justice for migrants and their families.

4

The Geopolitics of the Homeland Security State and Deportation in El Salvador

> The people who get deported are treated like the worst criminals that there could possibly be in the world.
> —Mirna Perla, Supreme Court Judge of El Salvador[1]

Reporters swarmed the press conference in December 2005 held in downtown Los Angeles as Alex Sanchez of the organization Homies Unidos stood in front of the microphone and did what many immigration reformers in Washington, D.C., were too scared to do: he denounced ICE raids perpetrated in the name of the war on gangs and war on terror, and he called attention to the plight of deportees in Central America. Sanchez, a former gang member turned community organizer and violence prevention worker, along with family members of deportees and a group of community allies, were denouncing Operation Community Shield, a campaign headed by DHS-ICE in partnership with local law enforcement agencies to ostensibly remove alleged gang members from the streets through detention and deportation. DHS-ICE argued that such raids were designed to go after transnational gangs and claimed that the raids were a major success in what was becoming a coordinated effort between federal law enforcement agencies in the United States and its partner nations in Mexico and Central America.

I vividly recall Sanchez eloquently explaining to a reporter from the Spanish-language media after the press conference that while there may have been some gang members caught in those raids, the raids were the opening of a Pandora's box that would eventually be used to detain, incarcerate, and deport scores of deportable Latinos, that is, both undocumented migrants and those with some type of noncitizen legal status, such as those with a visa or those with

Legal Permanent Resident status. Unfortunately, Sanchez was correct. From its inception in 2005 through September 2009, 8,575 criminal arrests were made under Operation Community Shield. There were also 10,350 administrative deportations carried out under the program.[2] In essence, a significant number of people who could not be tried for any crime were deported for being undocumented under a program designed ostensibly to go after the most dangerous criminals.

Operation Community Shield was part of a trend in which the homeland security state claimed to be concerned with gang members, drug dealers, and human smugglers and ended up deporting thousands of people, who were treated like the collateral damage of US bombs in Iraq. Since then the homeland security state has evolved into a more sophisticated and efficient deportation regime through a variety of programs that have resulted in the expulsion of over one million people between 2009 and 2011 alone. The vast majority of these people did not have violent criminal records or were deported for petty crimes, even as state authorities claimed to be looking for dangerous criminals.

At the December protest, Homies Unidos was denouncing policies that anthropologist Elana Zilberg describes as part of a neoliberal security scape. In this scape, neoliberalism and transnational police practices, instituted in the name of antiterrorism, represent a continuation of US-sponsored violence in El Salvador that dates back to the Cold War.[3] Building upon and departing from Zilberg's succinct analysis of a very complex problem, I argue that governments in the United States and El Salvador used the new security paradigm of the global war on terror to export US migration-control policies into the Mesoamerican region, with torturous and, at times, disproportionate and deadly consequences for young, male deportees because of their imputed gang identity. By "imputed gang identity," I am referring to how young Latino men are policed and suspected of being in, or affiliated with, a gang regardless of having actual gang membership or affiliations.

As in other sites of state power discussed in the previous chapters, I illustrate how the state does not act on its own as if it were a monolithic and homogenous institution but through a bloc of actors that operate at the nexus between the state and civil society. They work to create the ideological conditions for the expansion of the state's coercive powers to police migrants and deportees domestically and globally. In this case, one of the civil society actors is the Heritage Foundation, a think tank that has historically brought together leading nativists including the late Samuel Huntington and neoliberal intellectuals with policy makers and media agencies to advance a conservative social-political agenda domestically and in the foreign policy arena. Like its nativist counterparts FAIR and CIS did with respect to interior enforcement in the United States, the Heritage Foundation helped to create the hysteria over transnational gangs and to push for the expansion of draconian police practices domestically and transnationally. Indeed, this constellation of actors in the US government and the Heritage Foundation also pushed for deepening the neoliberal development model into the Mesoamerican region, with devastating consequences for the human rights of deportees arriving in El Salvador from the United States. This imputed transnational gang identity assigned to Latino youth and the transnational system of migration control can not be separated from the broader process involving changes to the modern state under the conditions of globalization and transnationalism.

Scholars have noted that globalization has fundamentally challenged our understanding of the state.[4] While there are many approaches to understanding the state and globalization, I share much in common with the global capital school that is often identified with the work of scholars William I. Robinson, Bob Jessop, and Leslie Sklair.[5] These scholars contend that the state is neither withering away nor becoming entrenched. Rather, they assert that the state is undergoing transformations to meet the pressures of globalization in two ways. First, the state is yielding many important tasks that were under its exclusive, sovereign domain during the Fordist era to multilateral institutions, such as the United Nations, Organization of American States, and to the regulatory mechanisms created by free trade agreements such as NAFTA and the Dominican Republic–Central American Free Trade Agreement (DR-CAFTA). Second, the global capital school views the emergence of a novel transnational state apparatus emerging from within the nation state. For example, according to Robinson, the transnational state should be conceived of as "an emerging network that comprises transformed and externally integrated national states, together with the supranational economic and political forums, and it is one that has not yet acquired any centralized institutional form."[6] Robinson's conceptualization of the transnational state provides a powerful analytical tool for thinking about the emerging social control network between the homeland security state in the United States and the government of El Salvador's war on gangs.

In this chapter, I analyze the text and talk of political elites such as US diplomats and military leaders in public government documents and of the Heritage Foundation. Studying the discourse of political elites is an important method revealing how dominant social groups exercise their hegemony over allied and subordinate groups in civil society, domestically and transnationally. Indeed, to win consent for building a transnational system of migration control, the US government and its civil society—allies such as the Heritage Foundation— must gain ideological leadership over a transnational civil society in the United States and in El Salvador. In this respect the discourse of US diplomats and think tanks are not just empty words but rather part of a steady discursive narrative that takes on an ideological function in El Salvador. As Gramsci wrote, based on their prestige, intellectuals influence people's everyday, common-sense thinking about politics and society. One cannot underestimate how the words of US diplomats, politicians, and intellectuals are disseminated and used to shape politics in El Salvador.

From this perspective, US diplomats, embassy staff, and scholars at prestigious think tanks take on a role as organic intellectuals in that they condition people's ideological positions on politics and policy to the point that the gang problem and criminal deportees become the rationale for the emergent transnational system of migration control. While elites leave traces of their political ideology in the public record of the traditional institutions of power, marginalized groups such as deportees in El Salvador do not have ready access to think tanks, corporate media outlets, and governmental institutes. Nor do they, as do the State Department and the Heritage Foundation, send their "experts" to testify before Congress to shape US migration and foreign policy. Thus to get access to what deportees are experiencing in El Salvador, we have to turn to ethnographic methods.

Between 2002 and 2009, I interviewed deportees, officials from the government of El Salvador's Human Rights Office, a judge from El Salvador's Supreme Court, members of the National Assembly, nongovernmental human rights organizations, and individuals connected to the criminal justice/public security system in El Salvador. I made my contacts through leaders in the Salvadoran community in Los Angeles.

Scholars have highlighted that El Salvador is a strategic case for understanding the politics of transnationalism.[7] El Salvador's society is embedded in a transnational model of society, economy, and polity that has emerged since the 1980s. The transnational model refers to a set of social, economic, and political relations, the product of nearly thirty years of neoliberal restructuring beginning in the 1970s.[8] The transnational economy is composed of previously separate national economies, like those of the United States and El Salvador, that are integrated via remittances, trade, and labor supplies and locked into place by a series of free trade agreements. This transnational economy is sustained on the backs of millions of Salvadoran families who are overwhelmingly concentrated in the service sector and construction labor markets of the United States.[9]

The Homeland Security State and the Global War on Terror

As part of the same restructuring that occurred in the name of the war on terror, in which the Immigration and Naturalization Service was renamed the United States Citizenship and Immigration Service (USCIS) and was moved to the

DHS, the United States announced what Nicholas De Genova calls "a planetary 'War on Terrorism.'"[10]

As part of this process, the Pentagon began to frame its objectives in Latin America as part of the global war on terror, which cannot be separated from the strategic ambitions of its architects. Former president George W. Bush's foreign policy was devised by a group of advisers, including his brother Jeb Bush, Donald Rumsfeld, Elliot Abrams, Dick Cheney, and Paul Wolfowitz, all of whom signed on to the statement of principles of the Project for a New American Century, a neoconservative think tank that sought to push forth a "Reaganite" foreign policy for the twenty-first century.[11] In such a vision, the United States would be an unrivaled superpower in a unipolar world in which all rivals would be overwhelmed by the grand military power of the United States. When Bush was elected in 2000, this neoconservative group, many of whose members were part of the Reagan administration's interventions in Central America in the 1980s, got the opportunity to apply their grandiose ideas for creating a new American empire as the guiding principles of US foreign policy.[12]

Using the new paradigm of the global war on terror, Bush and the neoconservatives sought to work with their allies in Latin America, especially in El Salvador, to have them endorse the war on terror. Some countries in South America, especially Venezuela, were openly critical of the war on terror from its inception. El Salvador, under the leadership of the National Republican Alliance (ARENA), the leading far-right political party in El Salvador, was all too ready to take advantage of what they viewed as an opportunity to return to the good old days of US military aid and political support. Well rooted in the Washington consensus, in 2001 the ARENA-controlled government gave up its national currency, the colón, and replaced it with the dollar. It also signed an agreement in 1999 that would allow the United States to build a small military base that the US military calls the Forward Operating Location as part of its larger war on drugs in Latin America. By 2002, the ARENA government, under the presidency of Francisco Flores, sent El Batallón Cuscatlán to assist the United States in its Alliance of the Willing, an array of countries that helped to invade Iraq for the second time.[13] The battalion served from 2003 to 2008 in Iraq. El Salvador under the leadership of ARENA was quick to endorse the global war on terror at a critical time, when the Pentagon used the security paradigm to combat what it called transnational threats and to create secure conditions for the flow of capital in the region. Indeed, military and police aid to El Salvador rose from $707,000 in 1996 to $18,646,533 in 2006, at the height of the war on gangs under the ARENA government.[14]

The United States Southern Military Command (SOUTHCOM), which heads all US military operations in Latin America south of Mexico, began to get involved in this emergent system of transnational social control. This institution has a history of coordinating US military intervention and support for repressive regimes in Latin America.[15] In particular, SOUTHCOM played a major role in working with the armed forces of El Salvador during the 1980s. It organized and aided the counterinsurgency model that was used to combat the Farabundo Martí Front for National Liberation and that resulted in the death over 80,000 Salvadorans.[16] SOUTHCOM, formally headquartered in Panama, provided military aid and training to the notoriously brutal government of Efraín Ríos Montt in Guatemala and to the military juntas in El Salvador, Honduras, Colombia, Argentina, Chile, Uruguay, and Brazil.[17] Moreover, SOUTHCOM maintained a close relationship with multiple military regimes in El Salvador from the 1960s to the end of the Civil War in 1992.

After the Cold War, however, SOUTHCOM began to look for a new mission besides fighting Communism. During this period SOUTHCOM underwent a major reorganization. For instance, its headquarters was moved from Panama to Miami, and its Area of Responsibility was expanded to include the air and seaways between the United States and Mexico, which were formally part of the United States Northern Command (Canada, United States, and Mexico). The greatest transformation, however, was the redefinition of its mission. The first of the new enemies or threats that SOUTHCOM would identify after the Cold War were narco-traffickers, which eventually gave rise to the war on drugs. In fact, the war on drugs defined much of US foreign policy toward Latin America between 1989 and 2001, before September 11.

Following 9/11, SOUTHCOM and other sectors of the US foreign policy apparatus began to speak of "transnational threats."[18] Speaking before the 109th Congress—the same Congress that passed the Border Protection, Illegal Immigration, and Anti-Terrorism Act of 2005 (passed in the House of Representatives), the Real ID Act of 2005, and the Secure Fence Act of 2006—General Bantz Craddock, the head of SOUTHCOM, argued that such threats "are not specific to any given country, but really cut across borders and boundaries, across seaways, across the air—and in the end, are threats to the United States as well."[19] General Craddock noted, "The stability and prosperity of the SOUTHCOM's AOR [Area of Responsibility] are threatened by transnational terrorism, narco-terrorism, illicit trafficking, forgery and money laundering, kidnapping, urban gangs, radical movements, natural disasters and mass migration."[20] The very idea of transnational threats problematically lumps migrants alongside terrorism, radical insurgencies, gangs, drug and human smugglers, natural disasters, and radical populism as part of the new constellation of threats to states found within the transnational model of society and economy between the United States and El Salvador.

Scholars have criticized the discursive link that the United States has attempted to make between drugs, insurgencies, and terrorism.[21] However, few have noticed how these categories are subtly and critically being linked to migration. The following quote from SOUTHCOM read before Congress illustrates how this discursive link is made:

> We will put forth a cohesive and coordinated effort, in concert with partner nations to counter: transnational terrorism and crime; illegal narcotics production; illicit trafficking (narcotics, arms and humans); and the proliferation of weapons of mass destruction, their precursors, and delivery systems...when requested by partner nations, we will assist in the reconstructing and training of defense and security forces to combat transnational threats.

As the words of General Craddock suggest, the United States looks for "partner nations" in its global war on terror. Such partners should be willing to combat a seamless continuum of transnational threats that includes terrorists, criminals, drug dealers, and human smugglers as part of the new security scape. The government of El Salvador, under ARENA control in this period, proved to be an eager ally and consented to building a transnational system of migration control with the assistance of its partner to the north.

Beyond General Craddock, Attorney General Alberto Gonzales also helped to advance the expansion of the transnational system of migration control in El Salvador. For instance, Gonzales speaking at the US Embassy in El Salvador about the newly formed transnational Anti-Gang Unit illustrates this point:

> This initiative will enable the United States and our colleagues in Central America to share information and coordinate law enforcement efforts as we work in partnership to target and dismantle violent gangs.... I look forward to working with President Saca and other Central American leaders to fight crime and keep our citizens safe.[22]

These seemingly noble efforts elaborated on by Gonzales to "target and dismantle violent gangs" and "keep citizens safe" solidifies and expands the transnational system of migration control. In fact, these remarks by Gonzales were made at a bilateral meeting in 2007 between the ARENA-controlled government of El Salvador and the US government to sign a binational intelligence-sharing agreement.

Transnational System of Migration Control

The elite discourse of men such as Attorney General Alberto Gonzales and General Craddock does not consist of empty words void of meaning and power. On the contrary, what they have to say, and by virtue of who they are when they say it, advances the consolidation of an emergent transnational system of migration control between the United States and El Salvador. For instance, in 2005, the United States helped finance the creation of a regional Rapid Response Force composed of Central American and Mexican police and military agencies to respond to terrorism and transnational gangs.[23] The FBI also created a special binational task force with offices in the United States and San Salvador to train regional police and military forces in anti-gang strategies/tactics and to coordinate transnational law enforcement efforts. Furthermore, the United States built the International Law Enforcement Academy (ILEA) in El Salvador, which began training Central American and Mexican police and military forces in anti-crime and anti-gang strategies in June 2006.[24] The ILEA will eventually train nearly twice as many Latin American police and military agents per year than does the School of the Americas—now called the Western Hemispheric Institute for Security Cooperation. The curriculum, direction, and personnel for the ILEA come from the US State Department and Department of Defense and is jointly financed by the United States and El Salvador. The authors of curriculum at the ILEA made no reference to the history of training military and police personnel in the region at institutions like the School of the Americas. While state personnel—whether high-ranking members of the military, diplomats, or the former attorney general—take on the function of organic intellectuals of the US government's foreign policy in Central America, the transnationalization of US migration control would be impossible without the support of civil society–based organizations.

The State–Civil Society Nexus

The right-wing civil society–based organization Heritage Foundation is just one of the organizations involved in creating the ideological conditions for the development of the transnational system of migration control. Heritage is part of a broader network of US think tanks and policy organizations that pushed for greater migration control in the United States and for greater police and security cooperation between states in North America. (See chapter 1 for the role of anti-migrant think tanks in supporting HR 4437.) The Heritage Foundation was closely associated with the Reagan administration during the 1980s, publishing reports and documents that provided ideological ammunition and technical support to push through Reagan's neoliberal vision domestically and in the international arena. Even more so than groups like FAIR and CIS, which have also capitalized on the hysteria of transnational gangs to push their domestic migration control agenda, the Heritage Foundation has actively supported the transnationalization of the homeland security state into Mexico and Central America. In a report published in March 2005 by the Heritage Foundation, titled *North American Transnational Youth Gangs, Breaking the Chain of Violence*, research fellows Stephan Johnson and David B. Muhlhausen argued for greater cooperation between local and federal law enforcement agencies to apprehend and deport gang members and for greater transnational cooperation among the United States, Mexico, and Central America to curb the growth and impacts of transnational gangs.

Unlike most academic articles, which are primarily read by a specialized community of scholars and graduate students, the studies by the Heritage Foundation and groups like CIS are used to advance a conservative social agenda in the upper echelons of state power.[25] These documents are usually published and publicized through press releases and, with the help of communications experts, disseminated to the leading national and international media agencies. Many policy reports from the Heritage Foundation and CIS are often presented before Congress in the form of testimony by fellows at each organization. Moreover, like any other Washington, D.C.–based think tank, the Heritage Foundation depends on relationships with members of Congress and an active network of conservative policy and opinion makers. Far from simply producing "objective social science research," these organizations are in the business of advancing research that supports a broader social and political agenda. This agenda cannot be separated from the particular faction of capital to which the Heritage Foundation is linked: sectors of transnational capital that would stand to benefit from DR-CAFTA, such as Exxon Oil. According to Exxon's own website, it gave the foundation $50,000 in 2010.[26] Moreover, the Heritage Foundation has received millions of dollars from the Mellon Scaife Foundation, which has supported both nativist and neoliberal think tanks such as CIS, FAIR, and others, such as the CATO Institute and the American Enterprise Institute.

The Heritage Foundation has long supported neoliberal policies domestically and abroad. The report, which was strategically released during the congressional debate over the DR-CAFTA, was partially designed to address concerns over crime and the controversial free trade agreement, which passed by only one vote. Thus, while recognizing the seriousness of transnational gangs, which were scaring investors in the region, the report called for solutions that would further deepen neoliberalism and the transnational model of society and economy between the United States and Central America. The report called for solutions that would "help to open market economies by supporting foreign projects that foster economic reform, property rights, and the growth of new industry."[27] It urged policy makers to "help to open market economies" and specifically that "the US Congress should approve the Dominican Republic–Central America Free Trade Agreement to help create more job opportunities at home and abroad. Both

US diplomacy and any development assistance must support economic reforms and better governance to provide a foundation for more prosperous societies."[28] Ironically, the report's policy suggestions called for the further expansion of neoliberal policies that have caused thousands of Salvadoran families to seek refuge in the United States. In addition to supporting free trade agreements, the Heritage Foundation called on Congress to adopt policies that would buffer the homeland security state to deport migrants in the United States. For instance, the report called for the US government to "promote stable neighborhoods through collaboration among federal and local law enforcement agencies to minimize characteristics that induce delinquency; reduce illegal immigration through stronger border zone controls to filter out undocumented migrants more effectively and through policies that simplify entry and exit for documented legal workers and visitors."[29] Interestingly the report juxtaposes the protection of "neighborhoods" through policies that will "reduce illegal immigration" through "stronger border zone controls." The policy report also called for the United States to pursue transnational police practices to deal with the problem of transnational gangs. For instance, the report argued that the United States should "cooperate with partner countries by sharing intelligence on gangs, in processing deportees, and by helping them to strengthen their own borders through database sharing and training immigration and customs personnel."

In essence, the report called for the strengthening of the homeland security state within the United States and for a transnationalization of US migration control under the rationale of the war on gangs. It does this by advocating for the expansion of US migration control policies through programs that will result in greater cooperation between local and federal police agencies (in practice, this report translates into programs like 287(g) in Riverside, California, and federal programs such as Secure Communities across the country) and for greater security cooperation among the United States, Mexico, and Central America. In essence, the Heritage Foundation is pushing for an expansion of the homeland security state domestically and as part of US foreign policy while calling for the expansion of neoliberal policies that have led to the mass displacement of Salvadoran families with complete disregard for the human rights of deportees and young people.

Deepening the Neoliberal Model

Neoliberalism in El Salvador was born on the back of the country's civil war. During the middle of the civil war, the United States started to support a faction of neoliberal elites, many trained at elite US universities, to become the dominant economic and political class of El Salvador.[30] This neoliberal faction came to power in 1989 with the presidential victory of Alfredo Cristiani. Cristiani immediately secured loans from the International Monetary Fund and World Bank. As part of his agreement with them, he began a series of privatizations and implemented "austerity" measures by cutting social spending on education, health care, and government aid to the poor and by removing subsidies on basic foods.[31] As in many third world countries that accepted the International Monetary Fund/World Bank/US government model, poverty and greater inequality resulted rather than the promised prosperity. For instance, at the beginning of the civil war in 1980, 68% of the population qualified as poverty stricken. By 1999, the figure had jumped to 80%.[32] The United Nations Human Development Index (HDI) ranks 175 countries based on an aggregate of social conditions such as education, housing, access to health care, mortality rates, and poverty. A country ranked higher on the HDI is presumed to have better living conditions than a country ranked lower. According to the index, El Salvador fell from a ranking of 112 in 1990 to 72 in 1997.[33] This drop represents a serious decline in the social and economic conditions facing the entire population. The neoliberal model further skewed wealth distribution. According to the United Nations Development Fund, in 1992 the richest 20% of the population received 54.5% of the national wealth, whereas the bottom 20% earned 3.2%. Ten years later, in 2002, the richest 20% earned 58.3% of the national wealth whereas the poorest 20% of the population earned 2.4%.[34] Ten years of neoliberal reforms in El Salvador made the richest sectors of society far richer, while the poorest sectors became poorer. This social and economic situation brought about by the US-backed ARENA party's neoliberal policies in combination with the country's demographic profile made gang culture an attractive option for socially excluded youth—not simply deportees from Los Angeles.

Few articles, policy reports, or news reports link these policies with the emergence of gangs. But Salvadoran gangs did not magically appear because deportees from Los Angeles were able to convince youth that being in a gang is "cool," as the State Department, Heritage Foundation, and ARENA government's policies could lead one to believe. Rather, gang life became appealing to socially excluded youth in a system in which millions of family members have been torn apart seeking refuge from the civil war and the deepening social and economic crisis facing Salvadoran families after the peace accords.

The War on Gangs and the Terror of Deportation in El Salvador

While deportation might symbolically banish the brown body from the US body politic, for the majority of young people being deported it was the continuation of a precarious life in which the prospect of being killed, tortured, or arbitrarily arrested by the Salvadoran authorities' new zero-tolerance police model loomed heavily over their daily lives. In June 2003, the same year that the DHS was formed, the government of El Salvador, controlled by the ARENA party, launched Plan Mano Dura under the leadership of Francisco Flores (1999–2003). President Flores's Plan Mano Dura imposed "*la ley anti-mara*" (anti-gang law) that established mandatory minimum sentences for youth convicted of being gang members and made being a gang member punishable with three to six years of imprisonment.[35] The law used an elastic definition of what constitutes a gang member so anyone who "uses tattoos, symbols, or colors, to identify themselves, [and] meets habitually" could be arrested for being a gang member. Reforms to the laws made by the Flores administration made the mere act of associating with a gang member grounds for being convicted under the law. Furthermore, to enforce the law the government utilized joint police and military forces in countergang operations in which security forces rounded up youth in public places such as soccer fields and parks. Joint police and military patrols also conducted checkpoints on busy highways and bus routes in which young men were forced to remove their shirts to be inspected for tattoos.

Super Mano Dura, implemented under the presidency of Antonio Saca, extended the first anti-gang law. Unlike the first Mano Dura, which was a six-month "emergency plan," Super Mano Dura lasted until 2009, the end of President Saca's tenure. Under Saca use of police raids continued in public places, similar to those used in the first campaign. Super Mano Dura also utilized mid-dawn raids, much like their DHS-ICE counterparts in Los Angeles, in which police commandos storm a home, usually between 4:00 and 6:00 AM, and handcuff and interrogate everyone in the household to apprehend suspected gang members. Super Mano Dura also stressed "citizen participation." Yet citizen participation translated into two things, volunteer home registration for search and seizure operations and a government informant program. In the search and seizure operations, state security forces arrive at homes in working-class communities such as Soyapango, Apopa, and Ciudad Delgado and ask people to "voluntarily" permit them to search homes for suspected gang members, drugs, and illegal arms. The stated goal of the measure is to visit as many homes as possible to create a national registry of homes with gang members, illegal firearms, and drugs.

The ARENA government also depended on anonymous tips from citizens to tell them where gang members were staying. Once the government receives a tip of the whereabouts of a suspected gang member, the National Civil Police (PNC), backed by the military, will conduct a "voluntary" home search. The director of the Procurator for the Defense of Human Rights at the time, Beatriz de Carrillo, also denounced the use of secret agents moving within the civilian population in the name of the war on gangs.[36] In the summer of 2005, President Saca deployed 1,000 additional soldiers to patrol the streets of San Salvador as part of his Super Mano Dura policy. Although not officially part of the Super Mano Dura, death squads that were common during the civil war reemerged with the promise to "cleanse" the nation of gang members.[37]

The Terror of Deportation

Given the conditions that emerged from the war on gangs, it is more likely that young male deportees from the United States will face violence and possibly torture or death in El Salvador. For instance, in an interview, Supreme Court Magistrate Mirna Perla notes, "Any person sent here from over there, will surely be killed. Indeed, they will kill him or morally destroy him."[38] What follows are interviews with four deportees, all of whom were legal permanent residents who were deported after their first contact with the criminal justice system as adults. Their experiences highlight the terror of deportation and illustrate the agency that these young men used to survive in El Salvador's post-9/11 security system under the Mano Dura. What Judge Mirna Perla decried was confirmed by Javier and Marcos at Metro Centro, a busy mall in San Salvador. Javier was 27 years old at the time of the interview, and Marcos was about 22 years old. The former had grown up in San Francisco, and the other grew up in Manhattan and spoke English with a thick Manhattan accent. During the interview Javier related the following.

> I went to the US when I was three years old; I got deported when I was 27. I spent most of my life over there. I went to elementary school, middle school; I went to high school, and I worked for KFC. They deported me...over a mistake over identity, over who had the dope and who was around. They took my papers, they took me to El Salvador, I came over here to the penitentiary, twice to jail over here.[39]

Guilt by association is a characteristic of zero-tolerance police tactics in the United States. Under such policies, youth are often criminalized by association, and prosecutors will charge them with possession with intent to sell even though the person may have never possessed the drugs. Indeed, Javier was arrested because his friend had drugs. This minor conviction put him into deportation proceedings and resulted in him being removed to El Salvador. Shortly after arriving in El Salvador, he was one of the 30,000 youth incarcerated under the Mano Dura legislation between 2003 and 2006.[40] He was released from jail because he had no tattoos and could not be charged under the Mano Dura laws. Javier attempted to change his lifestyle, began working in a youth program, and got a second job working for a deputy in the National Assembly. I had heard about threats to activists who worked with deportees and gang youth, so I asked Javier if he had any similar experiences.

J: I got shot once and they broke my arm yesterday.[41] [I noticed that he had obviously been in a physical confrontation. He had a black eye, bruises, and his arm was in a sling.]

A: Yesterday? What happened?

J: I was getting off of my car and some police officer told me to stop and to put my hands against the car. When they asked me who I was, I told them in my wallet you will find my name and everything.... All of a sudden they started hitting me, they whipped me and they hit me with a billy club, and every-thing broke my arm in three places. My ribs are all bruised up.

A: Has this happened to other activists?

J: I know the guy, he was a good person, they took them from their house, and they never came back. They disappeared. Nobody knows where he is at. In *los Estados Unidos* [the United States] or over here in El Salvador, not even the family knows. He just disappeared.

The practice of disappearing individuals that the government of El Salvador or society deems undesirable dates back to the country's civil war, and some would argue to the 1930s. During the civil war, it was common for US-trained death squads and paramilitary forces to take people out of their homes in the middle of the night. Most of the time those picked up would never be seen again alive. This practice reemerged in the context of the war on gangs, and once again the government of El Salvador denies any involvement in extrajudicial violence. Indeed, as many interviewees pointed out, the government often fails to investigate the killing of young people thought to be gang members or deportees. For instance, during interviews with Judge Mirna Perla and with members of the National Assembly, I was told that the police rarely investigate homicides or disappearances involving young people with tattoos. Javier confirmed this.

A: Is there an investigation when a deportee is murdered?

J: The police said they were going to investigate, but when they know you were working with people who have been deported or that are gang members, they don't do anything. And when a guy over here has tattoos, ahha, he is a *marero* [gang member]. We are not going to lose that much. Just put him in a plastic bag and that is about it.[42]

Like many deportees, Javier had a complex theory on why the government was targeting deportees in El Salvador that was rooted in the material reality of the post–civil war political economy.

A: Why do you think this is going on?

J: Most of the guys from the government have security offices. They have *oficinas de seguridad para proteger digamos gente de mercados y ventas. Entonces, a ellos les conviene tener eso* [security firms to protect, let's say, people involved in merchandise and sales, so it is convenient for them to have this]. *Es un* [it's a] business type of thing. Blame it on the dog [the deportee]. Even though he does not have rabies, he is the one that did it![43]

Javier was correct about the booming security business in El Salvador that flourished under the former ARENA government. Indeed, Elana Zilberg points out, the security industry in El Salvador has grown tremendously after the signing of the peace accords in 1992: "Numbering fewer than 10 in 1992…private companies increased to more than 80 in 1995 and 265 in 2001. The number of private security agents more than tripled from 6,000 in 1996 to 18,943 in 2001."[44] Deportees such as Javier describe the critical security situation facing Salvadoran youth. Javier explained:

> There is always going to be death squads to deal directly with people from the street, just like there was the Black Shadow [death squad] during the civil war. But at least that was a war. I mean it was a war. But today, after the peace accords, what is happening is alarming and worrisome at the same time. The future of young people, the way things are going, no one is going to make it to twenty-five years of age.[45]

Javier's words point to the ironic situation facing Salvadoran youth in the aftermath of the peace accords. Indeed, the United Nations held up El Salvador as a democratic model with the best civilian police system in post-conflict society.[46] During the armed conflict it was common for young people to be tortured, killed, or disappeared for being involved with guerrillas. Ironically, however, in the aftermath of the peace accords and since the implementation of Mano Dura policies, it is common for young people suspected of being gang members to be disappeared again. Given this reality, one can see why young people like Javier felt that the ARENA-controlled government is at war with them again.

I asked Marcos if he had anything to add. He was quiet at first and nodded no. I shut off the recorder. A few seconds later he began to describe how it was hard for young people to make it in the United States and in El Salvador. I asked if I could turn on the recorder and he said yes. I proceeded to ask him about his background.

> I was four years old when I went over there. I grew up in Manhattan in Chelsea. I was raised by my mother, grandmother and aunt. At nineteen, I caught a case. I did two years and after two years I got deported. I tried to fight my case. It didn't happen. They gave me a parole date, and when I got to the gate they [DHS-ICE] were already there waiting for me. I had a green card—I was a resident too. They chained me up, and I went to the detention center. They fingerprinted me and put me on the record.[47]

Like many deportees facing their first offence, Marcos pleaded guilty to charges and received a short sentence in criminal court. Like many others, he thought he was going to get out of jail and go home. To his surprise, he was picked up by ICE and deported. In the next vignette, Marcos described the conditions that he faced when he arrived to El Salvador in 2006, the year that El Salvador received over $18 million to fight the war on gangs, more than it ever had since the end of the civil war.

> I was scared, I was shaky. People were telling me you better watch out, El Salvador is real dangerous, you don't talk Spanish—I used to only talk English. When I got out the plane, the cops took me to a room and investigated me. And then some other guy, he was investigating me. What do I expect to do here? Do I plan to sell drugs here, do I have an addiction, and they asked if I have tattoos. They actually made me take off my shirt. They had my picture and they took another picture to update my face to see if I had any changes... I am not even trying to do jail over here, son. This is a hard environment to get accustomed to. I don't have any family over here. All my family is over there. I really don't have nobody to fall on. I have to pick myself up.[48]

Marcos described his fear of being processed by the police, something that all deportees go through. He described the intimidating experience of being processed, in which the Salvadoran authorities have a roster with the names of deportees and the offences for which they are being deported. Although only about one-third of deportees have a criminal record and even fewer are gang members, all deportees are subject to interrogation and run a risk of facing arbitrary detention, a widespread practice in El Salvador that even the Department of State's annual human rights reports have documented.[49]

Chiming in on the discussion between Marcos and me, Javier began to display signs of frustration and despair over his deportation. It uprooted him from his family, which was well established in the San Francisco Bay Area.

> Most of my family has been going over [to the United States] for over a hundred years back. My great grandparents were there, my grandparents were there, my parents were there. I got family that fought in the Vietnam War. My family has been going back and forth, back and forth. My grandmother saw that El Salvador was having problems with the civil war and she said I am going to take you with me. So she took me when I was really young, and I made my life over there. I feel like a fish without water, *a veces desesperado, a veces como con ganas de llorar, y a veces con no saber en que diablo que hacer. Yo no tengo familia aquí, nada de familia* [I feel desperate, sometimes I feel like crying, sometimes I do not know what the hell to do, I do not have family here, no family].[50]

Javier's words remind us that while deportation symbolically banishes the migrant from the body politic of the nation-state, deportation is just the beginning. The stigma of being deported follows the deportee wherever he or she may go. Perhaps the only thing more troubling than the dramatic growth in deportations since the formation of the homeland security state is the tragic fate that an unknown number of deportees have met in their countries of origin. An unknown number of deportees have been killed or tortured upon returning to their place of birth. Those who manage to survive have to live with what scholars David Brotherton and Luis Barrios call the psychological and social stigma of deportation, a concept that they use to describe the sense of deprivation and anguish felt by deportees in the Dominican Republic but that I have also observed with Javier and Marcos.[51] Beyond the issue of social and psychological stigma, deportees like Javier and Marcos live with the looming threat of torture at the hands of the police and groups that the police cannot control, such as death squads (paramilitary groups that act outside of the formal auspices of the state) that enact social cleansing policies against young male deportees who are imputed to have gang identity.

Social cleansing and other forms of repression facing deportees in El Salvador are real, and deportees must take great efforts to hide their identity as deportees because the mere label "deportee" often raises suspicion among the Salvadoran authorities and many people in civil society. Some deportees who are older and truly fluent in Spanish and do not speak with a US-based Latino street language may be harder to detect. For others like Marcos, however, who speak with a thick New York accent and scarcely speak Spanish, detection is a fact of life.

A: Do people here recognize that you are from the US?
M: Fast. The way you dress, the way you walk, the way you talk.
A: How about when you speak Spanish?
M: Ah, that's faster![52]

Marcos's comment was a reminder that how one speaks Spanish is also a signifier of where one is "from" in the transnational model of society and economy. In fact, it was my Spanish with a Chicano accent that gave me up to a deportee named Carlos whom I met at a conference that I was attending in San Salvador. I was walking through the front door to the parking lot when, after a brief exchange of words in Spanish, the doorman asked me, "Hey, are you from Los?" [a shorthand Chicano term, adopted by Salvadorans, used to refer to Los Angeles]. I said that I was from the Inland Empire located just outside of Los Angeles. After a few days of light conversation, I asked him if he would grant me an interview. He agreed. I asked Carlos about his deportation and living conditions in El Salvador. Carlos went to the United States when he was nine and grew up near Vermont and Pico in the Korea town neighborhood of Los Angeles and attended Hollywood High School.

A: When did you get deported?
C: I was deported about four years ago. I spent most of my life in the states. After that, I was trying to fight the case to stay in the states. Even though they knew I was going to get killed [in El Salvador]. But thank God, I haven't. I mean, I am alive [looks at his hands in disbelief]. And I got a job.
A: Have you had any contact with the police?
C: Cops used to fuck with me every day. First they stop you, then after they stop you, they ask you to lift up your shirt. You could tell them I am not a gang member. They say shut the fuck up. I got beat down once.
A: This was the PNC?
C: Soldiers too! It was in the morning. They were looking for someone. They asked if I seen something. "Stop right here, we are going to search you." I told them that I did not see anything. The cops started hitting me. They were talking about they were going to take me to jail. "Because you should not be here. You probably killed someone in the states. We don't want to see you here."
A: Do you fear for your life here?
C: Hell yeah, every day, dog! I want to go back to the states. I got four years right here. I still have to go through six more [there is a ten-year bar on reentry for deportees]. I hope I don't get killed. I have to survive in El Salvador.[53]

The narrative shared by Carlos confirms the experience of many deportees upon arriving in El Salvador. They arrive in a country that they hardly know and are criminalized by the authorities and civil society after being deported by a country that sees them as perpetual suspects. Moreover, any contact with law enforcement, much as in the barrios of the United States, could lead to arbitrary arrest and violence. In the case of Carlos, he had the misfortune of being questioned and subsequently beat by the Grupo de Tarea Conjunto, a joint police and military patrol. These so-called temporary patrols first started in 1998 to temporarily assist the PNC in its police duties, but they have become more common since the implementation of the Mano Dura policies.

The young men who shared their stories with me were all legal permanent residents and held green cards while living in the United States. Although only one of them was a former gang member turned youth activist, they were all treated like gang members by the authorities. During my research several deportees told me that when the authorities were beating them, either in the streets or in prison, they often blamed deportees for all of the problems in El Salvador. Much like the nativists discussed in earlier chapters who scapegoat migrants in the United States, it was common for some of the PNC officers that I interviewed to blame deportees for the social ills in El Salvador.[54]

Most deportees, regardless of age or status as a former gang member or perceived gang member, are subject to the same type of criminalization and harassment by the Salvadoran authorities and disdain from many individuals in civil society. For instance, I met Roberto, a man in his early fifties, who had lived in the United States for thirty-eight years and left five children behind. He held steady jobs for several years at a time, worked in the merchant marine, in deliveries, and in a glass factory. Like all of the men I interviewed, Roberto was a legal permanent resident, a green card holder, who until the date of his first conviction in 2003 had never been convicted of a crime—but he was deported. He was different from most of the other deportees whom I interviewed because he had grown up in El Salvador and did not have a US-based Latino youth culture swagger. He also spoke fluent Spanish, unlike most other deportees with whom I came into contact, who often spoke Spanglish. Roberto arrived in 2003 before the implementation of the Mano Dura and witnessed how crime got worse in the aftermath of the so called anti-crime strategy.

R: Well, in reality the government has given the deportee negative propaganda. Because today they want to blame the social problems that the country has on other people. When the government can't make it with what it has, then it tries [to] figure out how someone could pay for what they did. When I got here in 2004 none of this was here, so then crime has increased, and the government could not be at the wrong place at the wrong time. So someone has to pay for the broken dishes, and who better than the deportee?[55]

Roberto succinctly noted that crime went up after the implementation of the Mano Dura policies. Indeed, not only crime but homicides went up after ARENA's war on gangs. Rather than attribute the increase in crime to deportees, he pointed to the poor socioeconomic conditions that currently exist in El Salvador. Moreover, he discussed how this dire socioeconomic situation leads to criminality, which is then attributed to deportees. This blame is attributed without identifying the root causes of this chain of events: neoliberalism, poverty, crime, displacement, migration, and deportation.

The narratives of the deportees interviewed for this chapter were confirmed in an interview with Mirna Perla a Supreme Court Justice in El Salvador. She narrated how deportees are generally treated by the police even when they are released from jail.

> Of course, I mean the police never provide protection. Even in jail if they [the police] say, Look, I want you to help me, they are threatening me, they are coming after me, they are extorting. Because in there they extort people; they tell them, if you don't give me $500 on that day, when your family comes, we are going to kill you, or rape you, or we are going to do this to you. So people agree right there. And the police are not capable of doing anything. They don't give these people any type of protection. On the contrary, they have them stigmatized, and every time there is a crime, they go and get them. Even though they have not done anything, they are trying stay out of trouble. When they get out of jail, they stay home just because they are scared to go outside of the house. But it is there where they are captured and persecuted. So if they go and ask for help, obviously it won't be provided.[56]

Judge Mirna Perla's words describe a dire situation facing deportees in which, as the Harvard Human Rights Clinic Report put it, deportees have "nowhere to hide."[57] Indeed, none of the deportees with whom I spoke could turn to the police for protection. In fact, as Mirna Perla elaborated, most must evade the police because the police may try to extort them for money. Moreover, even if deportees stay indoors and try to evade police because of fear of persecution, the police may enter their homes in the anti-gang sweeps and take them to jail.

The conditions described by deportees Javier, Marcos, Carlos, and Roberto and Judge Mirna Perla speak to a human rights crisis facing deportees in El Salvador. The crisis facing deportees is not limited to El Salvador, as similar conditions face deportees in other parts of Mesoamerica and in the Caribbean more broadly.[58] The bulk of the deportees, and other policy makers who I did not quote here, spoke to the conditions that deportees encounter as they are banished to live in El Salvador. The ironic thing about the war on gangs/terror in El Salvador is that it has resulted in a terrifying situation for deportees.

As terrifying as the conditions facing deportees may be, one cannot separate the transnationalization of the zero-tolerance police model in El Salvador and the policing of deportees from the geopolitical context of the war on terror and the homeland security state in the United States. After all, the increase in deportees arriving in El Salvador, the zero-tolerance police model, the military aid, the International Law Enforcement Academy, and the social anxiety that this new transnational system of policing produces are a direct result of the homeland security state's crackdown on migrants in the United States.

*   *   *

This chapter illuminated the transnational dimension of the homeland security state and the human rights consequences it has for deportees. Logically, this discussion suggests that any effort to secure justice for Latino families must take into account the current moment in which there is a transnationalization of zero-tolerance policing in the name of anti-terrorism with severe human rights consequences for deportees, regardless of the reason for their deportation. Immigration reformers and oppositional groups within the migrant rights movement have different reactions to the plight of deportees. Among the few organizations that have attempted to call attention to the human rights conditions facing deportees as a result of US migration and foreign policies is Homies Unidos in Los Angeles. Homies Unidos works closely with individuals fighting their deportation cases and with families separated by deportation. The organization led a campaign designed to put a moratorium on deportations and to denounce the Mano Dura. Organizers with Homies Unidos provide educational workshops about the plight of deportees with religious organizations, universities, and elected officials. Homies Unidos often works with migrants in detention to fight their deportation cases. They work with lawyers, detainees, and country conditions experts to prove to the court that a deportee is likely to face torture or death in Salvador. They base their efforts on the Convention Against Torture (CAT), an international human rights agreement ironically advanced by the United States in 1984 to help people fleeing torture and state violence to win asylum in the United States. According to the CAT, countries that have signed the agreement cannot deport individuals to another country where there is a more than likely chance that the person will face torture at the hands of the government or groups the government cannot control. Homies Undidos is rarely successful at winning CAT cases for Central American youth facing deportation because of changes in immigration case law and a variety of other factors that go beyond the scope of this chapter. Yet organizers with Homies Unidos clearly understand that there must be an effort to curtail the draconian police tactics in the United States and the zero-tolerance police model in El Salvador if there is ever going to be justice for deportees and their families in the United States.

As a short-term remedy to bring some relief to families facing possible separation because of deportation, Homies Unidos worked with the New York City–based organization Families for Freedom to support the Child Citizenship Protection Act, a bill introduced by Congressman Serrano from the Bronx in New York. The bill would have given immigration judges more discretion to cancel a deportation in cases in which US citizen children would be adversely affected by deportation. Had the Child Citizenship Protection Act become law, three of the men I interviewed for this chapter, all of whom had children who are US citizens, may have received some form of relief from an immigration judge. Unfortunately, the efforts of Homies Unidos and their allies fell upon politicians who lacked the political will to support the Child Citizenship Protection Act. This failure is partially because immigration reformers were focusing on comprehensive immigration reform (CIR) as the only viable solution. Yet, as we will see in the following chapter, CIR, as articulated by immigration reformers, would not help men or women with minor criminal offenses who—like all the men I interviewed for this chapter—would still be deported even if a CIR bill would have passed in Congress. Moreover, such a bill would leave the homeland security state and transnational system of migration control intact, despite the horrific human rights consequences for people on all sides of national borders. Even as the political conditions have changed with President Obama's election in 2008 and in 2012, immigration reformers, guided by the good immigrant– bad immigrant binary, were reluctant to fight for the rights of migrants with a "criminal record" and even less so to defend the human rights of deportees. In this next chapter we will see how these groups in Washington, D.C., and New York City struggled to win a CIR bill in Congress under the first term of the Obama administration.

Resisting "Passive Revolution": The Migrant Rights Movement in Washington, D.C., and New York City

I think the consensus is...the American people still want to see a solution [to undocumented immigration] in which we are tightening up our borders, or cracking down on employers who are using illegal workers in order to drive down wages.

—President Obama, June 25, 2009

The issues we're touching on here must be broached by liberals. The conservatives simply cannot do it without tainting the whole subject.

—John Tanton

Instead of mastering reality, they allowed themselves to be absorbed by it.

—Antonio Gramsci

In 2006, Latino rights activists began using the slogan *Hoy marchamos, mañana votamos* (Today we march, tomorrow we vote). The slogan reflects the coming to political consciousness of the new generation of Latinos participating in the mega-marches and in the political system more broadly. In the aftermath of the marches, many Latino advocacy organizations sought to capture the moment of mass mobilization and heightened politicization of Latino communities to build up their electoral power in support of a presidential candidate, Barack Obama, who promised to pass immigration reform and stop ICE raids in migrant communities.

Obama's promise energized Latino voters to come out for the historic 2008 election. Indeed, 67% of the ten million Latinos who voted in the election supported his candidacy.[1] After Obama was elected president, most sectors of the migrant rights movement were excited about the possibility of immigration reform. Compared to 2006 and 2007, when the movement was up against a Republican president and a Congress heavily influenced by the anti-migrant bloc and its allies, the moment seemed favorable for change. The 111th Congress began with a Democratic majority in both the House and Senate and the first African American president in the history of the United States. Many Latino migrant activists and their allies in the migrant movement thought the tables had turned as Obama appointed forty-eight Latinos to top-level positions with Senate confirmation. This numbered more than any previous administration and earned Obama the praise of many mainstream Latino organizations.[2]

Despite all the hope, immigration reform did not occur during President Obama's first term. Ironically, it was during this time, when Latinos were most integrated into the American political system, with more voters and elected and appointed officials than at any time previous in the history of the United States, that the country simultaneously witnessed a record number of deportations. This chapter is an effort to explain this apparent paradox.

I argue that the election of Obama created the conditions for a constellation of Washington, D.C.–based civil society organizations to pacify the migrant movement and channel the popular demands of migrant workers into a vision of reform that would in theory bring about some immediate relief in the form of temporary status for undocumented workers who qualify, while sacrificing the demands of the oppositional sector of the movement. By "pacify," I don't mean that the movement stood by idly and did nothing. In fact, in this study I focus on concrete days of action. But by pacification I am referring to how the demands, strategy, and tactics were tamed by forces other than an organic base of migrant workers and their organizations in an effort to bring about palatable reforms. This new constellation of immigration reformers financed by the major foundations and select fractions of global capital, and under the political leadership of groups close to the Democratic Party, fought for a limited set of reforms known as comprehensive immigration reform (CIR). While this vision of reform included real short-term benefits for a select group of undocumented migrants (such as a work permit and, in some cases, a pathway to citizenship), it sacrificed any radical challenge to the authoritarian nature of the homeland security state, the structural causes of migration, or the fundamentally racist policing, detention, and deportation of millions of Latinos and other migrants from other parts of the third world. Moreover, this vision of reform legitimated the emergence of a more efficient and robust homeland security state that was being built by the Obama administration and resulted in the deportation of over 1.5 million people under his first term alone. His office made modest reforms that would benefit a minority of noncitizens at the expense of millions of others.

This assessment is not to say that Latino migrant activists and their allies did not make any gains during Obama's first term. Immigration reformers were able to organize large mobilizations in support of their vision of CIR, and oppositional youth were able to pressure the president to use executive power to pass Deferred Action for Childhood Arrivals. Indeed, Gramsci noted that "the fact of hegemony presupposes that account be taken of the interests and the tendencies of the groups over which hegemony is to be exercised."[3] Thus the expansion of the homeland security state was accompanied by modest reforms and the reinforcement of the good immigrant–bad immigrant binary. A select group of migrants benefited from the reforms while the vast majority was targeted for a mass program of state-sponsored detention and deportation.

The period covered in this chapter—marked by Obama's election and first term—can be characterized by what Gramsci described as passive revolution. Gramsci used "passive revolution" to describe a political transition that appears to be a great transformation and resonates with the aspirations of the popular classes but ultimately only restores the hegemony of the ruling classes and the institutions of governance—without fundamentally changing society. His ideas on passive revolution are related to what he saw as a dual process of revolution-restoration. State leaders promise reforms and then incorporate moderate forces into the dominant ruling bloc that silence potentially counterhegemonic forces. Gramsci wrote, for instance, "The absorption of the enemies' elites means their decapitation and annihilation often for a very long time."[4] Stuart Hall, interpreting Gramsci wrote, "Passive revolution, simply put, designates all those strategies designed to put through reforms in order to prevent revolution."[5] In other words, the dominant classes seek to co-opt sectors of social movements by making moderate reforms without fundamentally transforming the structures of society. Thus the dominant class brings those movements into a game of perpetual compromise.

To illustrate how the migrant rights movement was pacified by the Obama administration and its civil society allies, I draw upon interviews with activists, organizers, and political operatives and my own observations in Washington, D.C., and New York City between January 2008 and July 2011. During this period, I interviewed several dozen activists at migrant rights actions, ranging from a civil disobedience action led by CASA de Maryland in January 2009 to the two largest migrant mobilizations held in the Northeast during 2010: March for America, a mass mobilization organized by Reform Immigration for America (RIFA) on March 21 in Washington, D.C and the May 1st mobilization in New York City. Most of the activists whom I interviewed were working-class Latinos: construction workers, restaurant workers, street vendors, day laborers, housewives, domestic workers, and students. They were men and women, migrants and nonmigrants, from Latin American countries such as Mexico, Peru, Colombia, Ecuador, Nicaragua, El Salvador, and the Dominican Republic. In addition to interviewing migrants and their supporters on the ground during the heat of a mobilization,[6] I also interviewed grassroots organizers, executive directors of nonprofit organizations, and political operatives from think tanks and advocacy organizations in Washington, D.C., and New York City, including members of RIFA's management team. In Washington, D.C., I interviewed top leaders from the Service Employees International Union (SEIU) and from national Latino and immigration policy organizations, including the National Council of La Raza, the Center for American Progress, and the National Immigration Forum. I draw on these interviews to provide an analysis of the period between the mega-marches and the end of Obama's first term. In New York, I interviewed leaders from the May 1 Coalition, the New York Immigrant Rights Coalition, Make the Road New York, SEIU Local 1199, the Teamsters Local 808, Families for Freedom, Bayan International, the New Sanctuary Movement, Jornaleros Unidos de Woodside, and New Immigrant Community Empowerment.

The Mega-Marches, the Global Economic Crisis, and RIFA

Passive revolution is a way of dealing with a crisis of hegemony. Indeed, Gramsci describes it as a "brilliant solution" to a crisis or as "revolution without a revolution."[7] Gramsci maintained that when a crisis emerged that could potentially threaten the hegemony of the dominant classes, the state would implement a strategy for debilitating potentially transformative social movements. The crisis of hegemony could come about for many reasons, including "because the ruling class has failed in some major political undertaking for which it has requested, or forcibly extracted, the consent of the broad masses (war, for example)."[8] In response to such a crisis, Gramsci maintained that the dominant class may "make sacrifices, and expose itself to an uncertain future by demagogic promises; but it retains power, reinforces it for the time being, and uses it to crush its adversary."[9]

Obama was elected in the context of the global economic crisis and a crisis of the broad constellation of forces that constitute the conservative right in the United States. The Bush administration and the neoconservative movement faced a public that had become opposed to the war in Iraq and Afghanistan. This period was also the time of the global economic crisis, or what is known in the popular media as the Great Recession of 2008. Moreover, Obama was elected two years after the 2006 mega-marches, which marked the rapid ascent of the migrant rights movement into a powerful and large-scale social force that momentarily was able to challenge the hegemony of the anti-migrant bloc. The election of the first African American president at such a moment created the appearance of a great transformation in American politics—to the point that it reestablished the legitimacy of the American political system in the United States and in many areas around the world. Most important, this period marked the Latino migrant movement's transition from a mostly grassroots and activist-led social movement to a professionalized movement led by a class of professional nonprofit activists and political operatives. This latter group relies on electoral politics and an "insider game" based on connections with powerful figures in the administration.

As noted by Nativo Lopez, the former director of Hermandad Mexicana and leader in the Southern California Latino migrant movement, in an interview conducted in 2008, the slogan *Hoy marchamos, mañana votamos* (Today we march, tomorrow we vote) was not a coincidence but rather part of a strategy led by labor, the Catholic Church, think tanks, and liberal foundations based in Washington, D.C. In retrospect, Lopez was correct.[10] Although this constellation of forces maintained an official nonpartisan posture, for all intents and purposes, they prepared Latino communities to become a base of voters for the Democratic Party. This coalition of voters is most clearly illustrated through the campaign called Mi Familia Vota (My family votes) and the coalition known as Ya Es Hora (The time is now).

This campaign was organized by the SEIU along with Univisión, the National Association of Latino Elected and Appointed Officials, and the National Council of La Raza. Eliseo Medina, secretary-treasurer of the SEIU noted, "The goal was . . . to have a national campaign of civic education and say to Latinos that your vote matters!" Eliseo continued, "We went out on a national citizenship campaign and we actually had a goal of one million new citizenship applications and we actually wound up with 1.2 million new citizenship applications from all over the country."[11] While the campaign was officially nonpartisan, this newfound Latino electoral power was in place for the run-up to the historic 2008 presidential election. This was a time when most Latinos associated Republicans with anti-migrant policies.[12]

After the primary election, many Latino voters were particularly drawn to Illinois senator Barack Obama, who cautiously expressed a public solidarity with migrants. Speaking before the League of United Latin American Citizens in July 2008, candidate Obama promised a more just and humane approach to immigration:

> The system is not working when a young person at the top of her class, a young person with so much to offer this country, cannot attend a public college or university. . . . The system isn't working when . . . communities

are terrorized by ICE immigration raids.... When all of that is happening, the system just isn't working, and we need to change it![13]

With promises to end the raids, to give undocumented students an opportunity to stay in the United States, and to pass immigration reform, most Latinos identified with Obama. In fact, exit polls from the polling group Latino Decisions indicated that 68% of Latinos voted for Obama to become president in 2008.[14]

Once Obama was elected, RIFA was designed to channel local migrant rights groups across the country into a centralized campaign structure to push through a CIR during Obama's first term. The campaign was run top-down, with political direction coming from Washington, D.C., leading progressive think tanks and policy organizations. RIFA was closely associated with the state–civil society nexus, especially with the president's civil society allies, and select fractions of global capital in the form of private foundations and direct corporate sponsorship of many of its member organizations. From Washington, D.C., RIFA soon established its ideological and organizational leadership over Latino migrant activists across the country. Some oppositional groups in the migrant rights movement tried to resist this effort at passive revolution from within the RIFA structure, and many more did so from outside it. However, these groups were eventually marginalized from the overall political direction of the coalition and the policy discussion around reform during Obama's first term, especially between 2008 and 2010, when CIR was potentially on the congressional agenda.

RIFA and the Pacification of the Migrant Rights Movement

Launched in June 2009 with the specific goal of passing CIR during the 111th Congress, RIFA arguably played a bigger role in the fight for CIR during the first two years of the Obama administration than did any other coalition or campaign.

Rationale and Structure

The rationale for creating RIFA came out of the experience of national migrant advocacy organizations' fight for immigration reform during 2006 and 2007. RIFA chair and executive director of the National Immigration Forum, Ali Noorani, explained that the coalition was created because the movement "needed an integrated strategy that goes field, communications, and then legislation—that's why it was created, to build that kind of infrastructure and that type of coordination." RIFA drew on lessons from previous national coalitions, such as the Somos America coalition, which was the main coalition during the mega-marches and pushed for the Kennedy-McCain bill in 2006 and a similar bill in 2007. In such a coalition, membership is based on shared policy preferences, not necessarily shared resources, responsibility, and accountability to the rest of the coalition. Noorani related, "RIFA was different because we had to raise the resources to hire organizers in key districts or hire organizations in key districts across the country. This was a campaign, not a policy coalition."[15] Indeed, RIFA was structured from the top-down, with a management team providing it direction.

The RIFA management team brought together different stakeholders in the immigration debate—from business, clergy, labor, national civil rights organizations, policy groups, and local migrant rights groups across the country—to help coordinate a national strategy. Among those from the business sector was the Agricultural Coalition for Immigration Reform. National migrant rights and civil rights groups included Americas Voice, the National Immigration Forum, and the National Council of La Raza. Local migrant rights organizations on the management team included *Pineros y Campesinos Unidos del Noroeste* (Pine Workers and Farmworkers of the Northwest), CASA de Maryland from the metro Washington, D.C., area, Make the Road New York, CAUSA from Oregon, and the Coalition for Humane Immigrant Rights of Los Angeles, among other groups. In addition, hundreds of local migrant rights groups across the country were members, helping coordinate RIFA's local activities in distinct regions. Labor also played a major role in RIFA, with unions such as the United Food and Commercial Workers, the AFL-CIO, the SEIU, and the United Farm Workers of America also on the management team. A coalition of clergy that included groups such as the Leadership Conference for Civil Rights also provided support within the management team. In addition to the base organizations, there were think tanks and policy groups, such as the Center for American Progress and the Center for Community Change, that provided political direction, communications strategy, and legislative expertise to the coalition.

RIFA's Strategy and the State–Civil Society Nexus

RIFA sought to build a coalition that could amass the political power necessary to win enough votes for CIR in the 111th Congress. Ali Noorani stated, "At the outset of the campaign we asked people to focus on 279.... To win anything, you need 218 [votes] in the House, 60 in the Senate, and then you are missing the president, that is 279. So when we talked about it that way, people realized that they could deliver Xavier Becerra [D-CA], but that we still need 279."[16] In other words, RIFA sought to build the political infrastructure that could move not only liberal members of Congress but also congressional voters in swing districts across the country to support CIR. This campaign strategy stressed mobilization, legislation, and communications.[17] The idea behind these three components was that one sector of the immigration rights movement, the base organizations throughout the United States (what RIFA calls "the field"), would mobilize the masses of migrants and their allies to create pressure on Congress to adopt legislation. The communications part of the strategy, according to RIFA leadership, was designed to create a sense of inevitability around immigration reform.[18] RIFA's legislative strategy was straightforward: garner the votes necessary to pass a bill. But RIFA publicly questioned the enforcement-heavy components of the CIR package proposed by congressional Democrats.

While all groups played a role in guiding the political direction of RIFA, its political strategy was shaped primarily by the Center for American Progress (CAP), the Center for Community Change, and the National Council of La Raza. These Washington, D.C.–based institutions, which had close ties with the administration, provided direct linkages to the state–civil society nexus, between the migrant rights movement and the president. For instance, Janet Murguía, who is president and CEO of the National Council of La Raza (2005 to present), joined the president's cabinet, and John Podesta, the chair of CAP, ran Obama's transition team. CAP was especially influential within RIFA. A *Time* magazine article described CAP as a think tank on steroids, noting that Podesta was the former chief of staff of the Clinton administration and that the organization had an annual budget of over $25 million.[19] Angela Maria Kelley, head of immigration policy for CAP, stated, "We are so associated with the Obama administration because John [Podesta] ran the transition team for Obama [and so] he helped select the cabinet that is there now. CAP has a lot of staffers at the White House. I think like fifty people left to go and work in the White House with the administration after he [Obama] was elected."[20] Indeed, CAP was to the Obama administration what the Heritage Foundation was to the Reagan administration: a factory of ideas that provided the intellectual resources to move the president's agenda forward.[21] With groups like CAP helping to design RIFA's legislative and communications strategy, the management team was firmly planted in the state–civil society nexus that emerged after Obama's election.

Much of RIFA's strategy depended on "insider" connections with the administration and the Democratic Party. Indeed, RIFA sought to reproduce a certain discourse on immigration reform that had already been adopted by the Democratic Party in 2007, after CIR did not pass during the 109th Congress. At that time, the Democrats concluded that the only way to pass immigration reform was to talk more like Republicans and reproduce the same law-and-order arguments.[22] This shift in the Democratic Party's strategy was a result of a study funded by CAP that concluded that any effort to win immigration reform should appeal to the sensibilities of the public that was undecided on immigration issues. This strategy translated into developing a discourse on immigration policy that appealed to the common sense of middle-class white Americans—what many Washington, D.C., political operatives and communications specialists call "the middle." The pollsters and linguists who conducted the study advised immigration advocates to start using buzzwords like "illegal alien" instead of "undocumented" and to insist that it is "unacceptable for there to be twelve million undocumented people in the United States" and that the undocumented must "get right with the law, pay taxes, and learn English—or face deportation." Angela Maria Kelley explained,

> We did polling at CAP. One of the strategic engagements was to convene several pollsters to look at the issue of CIR and to look at the issue of the undocumented and to find language that you can use that speaks to policy that we support and that wins over the middle.... The messaging is if you talk about requiring undocumented immigrants to register, to pay taxes, learn English, and go through background checks, then you get very, very high support, in the mid to high 80s even, in bright red districts. It is tried and true. It does not matter when you use this language, who says it—if you use those words, the public buys it, they support that, and they want people to be part of that program. I think that most undocumented immigrants would be OK with it.[23]

Although this messaging strategy resonated with pollsters and Washington, D.C., political operatives, it did not resonate with Latino migrant activists across the country. On the contrary, it created skepticism and undercut unity between oppositional forces and immigration reformers within the overall movement.

RIFA's overall political strategy was likewise problematic. It rendered mass mobilization in the forms of marches and large protest rallies subordinate to the legislative lobbying, and it sought to make mobilization efforts fit into a tightly managed messaging scheme that reinforced the good immigrant–bad immigrant binary. Rather than allow the migrants most affected and veterans of the movement to develop their own strategy organically, as occurred during the planning meetings for the mega-marches in 2006, RIFA was waiting for the president and Congress to get ready to take on immigration reform. But this strategy was problematic because it rested on the assumption that the president would act on his own without an autonomous social movement pushing him to act. If the migrant rights movement would have been led by an independent and autonomous movement, it could have pressured the president to act on immigration reform sooner and under different terms. But instead, Gustavo Andrade of CASA de Maryland noted, "people [in the coalition] were operating under the position that the administration was on their side, which is fairly obvious to anybody that they were not. Rahm Emanuel and the administration were actively blocking immigration reform from ever seeing the light of day."[24] Other leaders within RIFA at the National Council of La Raza and SEIU argued that they could not get the president to act because he had health care and the economy on his legislative agenda. Yet, as one of the few movements in the United States with a large, passionate base, the migrant rights movement could have pushed harder and sooner on the president without worrying about what was on his agenda. This is why social movements all over the world are most often ardent defenders of their autonomy from state leaders and political parties.

Resistance from within RIFA and Civil Disobedience

RIFA was a centralized but never a homogeneous coalition. By August 2009, it became apparent even to members of RIFA's management team that the inside-the-Beltway strategy of waiting for the Democrats and the president was not going to work. Some groups within RIFA were pressuring the management team to push for a major mobilization that would use the passion of the base of migrant workers to create a mass mobilization to compel the president and Congress to act. Most on the management team resisted this idea, until one of the larger organizations within the coalition broke with the consensus. This break put tremendous pressure on RIFA's leadership. Ali Noorani noted, "We had to go through a process of really making sure that the coalition was comfortable challenging the president, because not everyone was there necessarily. We had assumed that we could have lost the coalition."[25] CASA de Maryland gambled on this chance to jump-start the movement in January 2010.

One of the first organizations within the RIFA management team to break with the consensus on strategy, CASA de Maryland, spearheaded an action on January 26, 2010, just one day before President Obama was to deliver the State of the Union address. By denouncing the record number of deportations under the Obama administration, the action aimed to escalate the demand for immigration reform and pressure Obama to commit to a timeline on immigration reform during the speech. Forces within the broader movement could then, the organizers hoped, mobilize around this timeline.

At the action, roughly two hundred activists gathered in front of the headquarters of DHS to demand that Obama make good on his promise of immigration reform. Twenty-three protesters then attempted a civil disobedience action that broke with RIFA's messaging strategy. The group of mostly Latino migrant activists that I interviewed at the action explained that they were disappointed with President Obama and the Democrats for whom they voted in 2008. For instance, Elsa, a waitress who had left law school in El Salvador to make money to send back to her family there, gave the following explanation for her participation in the protest: "*Estoy aquí por muchas razones. La primera es que necesitamos que toda nuestra gente sea legalizada! Todos los inmigrantes que estamos en este país para poder tener un estatus legal y poder ayudar a tener, a poder tener decisiones para contribuir tanto en las leyes de este país como para ayudar nuestra gente de Latinoamérica*" (I am here for many reasons. First, we need all our people to get legalized! All of us immigrants that are in this country so we could get our legal status and be able to help to have the power to make decision to contribute to both the laws in this country and also to help our people in Latin America).[26] Elsa's position that she wanted legalization to be able to help her people in Latinoamérica is a common one among many migrants, yet it was not represented in RIFA's communication strategy, which sought to portray migrants as Americans in waiting who can't wait to assimilate into the American mainstream. Yet this goal is not one of Elsa's demands. Indeed, as noted by Fernandez and Olsen, a significant number of Latino migrants maintain that they are demonstrating not just for liberal citizenship within the United States but also for legalization as something that will allow them to exert a transnational citizenship through which they can be political and social actors in the United States and for their families in Latin America.[27]

On a similar, albeit more critical, note, Antonio, an Afro-Colombian, activist gave the following explanation for his participation in the action:

> *Estoy aquí porque ya estamos cansados. Queremos que el gobierno de Obama cumpla sus promesas de campaña. Necesitamos una reforma migratoria ahora! Ahora! Somos doce millones o más que estamos trabajando, aportando la economía de este país. Por eso le estamos diciendo hoy, le estamos diciendo al gobierno nacional que cumpla su promesa de campaña y que estamos aquí en la lucha. Siempre y fuerte.* (I am here because we are tired. We want Obama's government to fulfill their campaign promises. We need immigration reform now! Now! We are twelve million or more who are working, helping the economy of this country. That is why we are telling him today, we are telling the national government to fulfill their campaign promise and we are here in the struggle. Always and strong.)[28]

Antonio's passionate demand for reform *ahora* (now) and emphasis on the eleven to twelve million undocumented workers who contribute to the economy reflects the position of many migrants that they have earned their right to be in the United States based on their labor. This common-sense position of many migrants was not reflected in RIFA's talking points around "paying a fine, registering with the government, and speaking English."[29] The growing frustration that Antonio expressed was reflected in the words of María, a Mexican migrant and pastor at a Lutheran church in the Washington, D.C., area, who gives the following argument for her participation:

> *Estoy envuelta en esto porque estoy dándole voz a mi comunidad latina y a la comunidad inmigrante en general que está sufriendo deportaciones a pesar de que es gente que paga impuestos y que ha trabajado. Estoy aquí porque tengo el compromiso de ayudar a la comunidad a que tenga una reforma migratoria y en ese sentido puede estar trabajando con documentos, pueda visitar a su familia, porque eso es lo más cruel que ellos no puedan visitar a sus familias.* (I am involved in this because I am giving my Latino community a voice and a voice to the immigrant community in general that is suffering deportations despite the fact that they pay taxes and have worked. I am here today because I have an obligation to help the community to be able to get immigration reform and in this sense be able to work with legal documents, be able to visit their families, because that is the cruelest thing, not being able to see your family.)[30]

María's position reflects a righteous indignation felt by many migrants who feel they have earned the right to be here through the sweat of their labor and payment of taxes. Such migrants dislike being separated from their families by unfair and unjust US immigration laws. This stance does not conform with the image of the passive assimilationist Latino put forth by immigration reformers.

This action in Washington, D.C., was held in conjunction with several actions throughout the country in which activists sought to escalate the pressure on the Obama administration by bringing attention to the plight of migrants and highlighting the need for CIR. In Phoenix, Arizona, for example, people demonstrated against the actions of Sheriff Joe Arpaio, the flamboyant head of the Maricopa County Sheriff's Department who had ties to neo-Nazi groups and humiliated migrants by putting them in pink jumpsuits and diapers in makeshift Arizona tent city jails. In Florida, a group of students began a march to Washington, D.C., in solidarity with undocumented students. Nonetheless, the Washington, D.C., action was particularly important, because it was organized in the nation's capital and spearheaded by Washington, D.C., rights groups with a large base of Latino migrant workers. CASA de Maryland sought to use the January direct action at the DHS office as a way to escalate the struggle and build the momentum to pressure other members of RIFA and the administration to act. Accordingly, they used the action to call for a major mobilization to be held on March 21, 2010. Gustavo Torres, the director of CASA de Maryland, ended the protest with the following announcement: "*Queremos anunciarles a ustedes que estamos preparando una marcha extraordinaria para el mes de marzo. Nos van a acompañar de todo el pais. Desde Florida hasta el estado de Washington*" (We want to announce to all of you that we are preparing an extraordinary march in the month of March. People will join us from all over the country, from Florida to the state of Washington).[31] CASA de Maryland and the rest of RIFA spent the next month and a half preparing the March for America mobilization to be held on March 21, 2011. This march was supposed to be the catalyst for passing CIR in the 111th Congress.

The March for America Mobilization

The March for America was one of the largest single migrant rights mobilizations held after the 2006 mega-marches and perhaps the largest during the first two years of the Obama administration. It was attended by more than 250,000 participants—including workers, students, migrants, and those of the second generation—who had come to Washington, D.C., from all over the country. The night before the protest, I was impressed with the number of buses in the city; a labor and migrant rights organizer who helped plan the action told me that more than three hundred buses of protesters had arrived in the city. The next morning, members of organizations poured in on buses from Chicago, Kansas City, New York City, and elsewhere. Javier Valdez of Make the Road New York, which took forty-three buses, noted, "It was really inspiring to be part of such a large mobilization. On the way down to DC, we did five conference calls [with members of Congress]."[32] Altogether, other New York City–based groups, including New York Immigrant Community Empowerment (NICE), Families for Freedom, Desis Rising Up and Moving (DRUM), Jornaleros Unidos de Woodside, and the May 1 Coalition, took hundreds of migrants activists to the action.

On the day of the march, it was apparent that the protest was going to be enormous. Not since the first mega-marcha, held on March 25, 2006, in Los Angeles, had I gotten the feeling that I was about to participate in a colossal protest. From the bus driving down Fourteenth Street, from Columbia Heights to the Capital, I could see thousands of Latino protesters dressed in white and heading to the National Mall. It was the first time that I had been to a demonstration at which there were apparently more Central American (Salvadoran, Honduran, and Guatemalan) families than Mexicans. This percentage was obviously not an accident; the majority of those in attendance were from the massive Central American community that resides in the metro Washington, D.C., area. Gustavo Andrade from CASA de Maryland explained how the massive turnout came about: "We mobilized 268 buses. We estimate that at least 75,000 people came through the efforts of a small team of very dedicated people and local leaders from Maryland."[33]

Participants articulated powerful explanations for why they were demonstrating. For instance, Alonso, a construction worker originally from Celaya,

Guanajuato (Mexico), traveled thirty hours on a bus from Garden City, Kansas, to the Washington D.C., action. Alonso explained that he and the group he traveled with came for the following reasons: *"Nosotros estamos aquí porque queremos decirle a Obama que aquí estamos y no nos vamos a ir hasta que nos dé una reforma migratoria porque él prometió y nos tiene que cumplir"* (We are here because we want to tell Obama that we are here and we are not going anywhere until we have immigration reform, because he promised and he must keep his promise and that we are not going to leave until he gives us immigration reform, because he promised us and he has to comply).[34] Alonso's words conveyed a sense of dignity. He spoke as a migrant worker demanding rights promised to him by the president. He was not declaring guilt or a willingness to "get right with the law" and forgo his culture and language.

Alyssa, a middle-aged migrant with a Chicago-based organization, laid out her reasons for attending: *"Soy de Perú y estoy aquí para exigir una reforma, una reforma migratoria, porque ya es tiempo de salir de las sombras y exigir los derechos que tenemos en este país como cualquier otro ciudadano, porque trabajamos, aportamos y hacemos más grande a este país"* (I am from Peru and I am here to demand reform, immigration reform, because it is time to come out of the dark and fight for our rights that we have in this country like any other citizen, because we work, we pay taxes, and we make up a big part of this country).[35] Her demands were based on a sense of equality (*como cualquier otro ciudadano*). When I asked her if she thought the protest would provide results, she said, *"Pues, yo no estoy segura de verdad porque se ha prometido tanto, hace tantos años y no se ha cumplido. Pero lo único que yo sé es que si ahora no se cumple, vamos a regresar cuantas veces sea necesario hasta que tengamos una legalización"* (Well, I am not really sure, because so much has been promised, so many years and nothing has been done. But the only thing that I do know is that it is time for these promises to be fulfilled; we are going to return as many times necessary until we have legalization).[36] Alyssa expressed dignity and a will to keep fighting even if the president failed to make good on his promise. This sense of determination and the need to wage a long-term struggle was also conveyed by an indigenous organizer named Sylvia Herrera, who was from Puente, an organization at the epicenter of the migrant rights movement in Phoenix, Arizona. She put it:

> With or without immigration reform, what we need to focus on is the criminalization of our communities.... We do not want it to be just any reform, because what is happening now... this country is adopting laws that are criminalizing workers, that are criminalizing children. In Arizona, laws are being passed basically denying services to US children that were born in this country but because their parents do not have papers, the state has passed laws that are denying social service, health

services to these children and also they're at the point of adopting a law that would make it mandatory for schools to report parents when they're enrolling their children. The right to education is being denied, and if this happens in Arizona, it is going to happen in other states, and this is what we need to focus on. I know that reform is important, but with or without it we cannot continue to have deportations, we cannot continue to have separations of families.[37]

Sylvia's powerful words remind us that one must struggle to find justice that goes beyond fighting for legal status or a piece of legislation. Moreover, she recognized that the migrant rights movement must struggle even for those born in the United States but who are racialized and excluded from society.

The authoritative words of Alonso, Alyssa, and Sylvia resonated with those of others whom I interviewed on the ground throughout the day. They conveyed the sense of collective power and solidarity between Latino migrant workers and the second generation, both of whom expressed a sense of righteous indignation over immigration policies that separate families and deny them the right to live and work in the United States. But the voices of people on the ground contrasted drastically with the voices of those on the stage.

March 21 on the Stage

It seemed as if there were two separate actions going on: the mass turnout as expressed in the hundreds of thousands who protested and the rally on stage hosted by RIFA. The stage area was protected by a sea of labor organizers. Speakers included such Washington, D.C., elites as then-president of the SEIU, Andy Stern; Senator Charles Schumer of New York; Senator Bob Menendez of New Jersey; and Obama administration cabinet member Cecilia Muñoz, among others. A videotaped address by President Obama was screened on the Jumbotrons that surrounded the red-white-and-blue-covered stage, which, according to one organizer with the SEIU, cost thousands of dollars to set up.[38] It looked like a stage at a typical concert or mainstream political convention.

The event was carefully choreographed from above to convey the "right" message. Labor organizations that were staffing the stage area passed out American flags and asked protesters holding flags from various Latin American countries to put them away. The ceremony was opened by a group of all-white students from the Midwest holding American flags and singing the national anthem. While it is perfectly legitimate and necessary for there to be broad working-class solidarity across ethnic and racial groups around questions of migrant rights, it is important to note how careful the political messaging was managed at this action. Moreover, it was managed in such a way as to suggest that the very people who made up the bulk of the protesters—including Elsa, the Salvadoran waitress living in D.C., and Alonso, the Mexican construction worker who traveled from Kansas—had little to say.

Latino migrants were not the only ones disappointed with the action. Janis Rosheuvel of Families for Freedom, a New York City–based organization that works with a large base of migrants from all over the African diaspora, said, "Even on the bus coming back home, I remember a lot of our members being like, where were the people that were affected by these issues on the stage? Where are the black folks on stage? The Afro-Caribbean people, the African people, where are they? There was disappointment from folks. We went, but it didn't seem like they were talking about stuff that are going to affect us."[39] While Rosheuvel was correct to point out that the base of Families for Freedom did not feel represented, it could also be said that many of the Latino migrant workers who were there did not feel represented with the political messaging at the mobilization—albeit for different reasons.

Despite the disjunction between what the base of migrant workers demanded and what RIFA's careful communications strategy sought to convey, the March 21 mobilization was still an important milestone in the migrant rights movement, thanks in large part to the hundreds of thousands of Central American migrants from the Washington, D.C., metro region and their allies who came to the protest from throughout the country. It conveyed that the base of Latino migrant workers was still demanding legalization. In fact, the March 21 mobilization was the largest for immigration reform in Washington, D.C., since April 10, 2006.[40] Jaime Contreras, a Salvadoran migrant and district chair for SEIU Local 32BJ for the capital area, stated that the March 21 mobilization "made the community within the D.C. region and from other states that they came from realize that this movement is not finished: we still have major problems with immigration reform—it helped wake up people again."[41] Jaime made these remarks because after 2006 major mobilizations in support of immigration reform in Washington, D.C., had become a thing of the past. As indicated by the words of Contreras, the March 21 RIFA mobilization illustrated that the migrant rights movement could still flex its muscle, albeit for a vision of reform that many migrants at the protest would probably find problematic.

The Democrats and the CIR Bill That Never Was

By the beginning of 2010, even some of the forces most integrated into the state–civil society nexus within RIFA realized that only a mobilization could help persuade Congress to act on immigration reform. Angela Maria Kelley explained, "We could not get an inside game going; we did not have enough juice.... We needed outside pressure, just like the marches [in 2006], and we needed to show that we had that type of power."[42]

The March for America was RIFA's attempt to pressure the president and leaders in the Senate to commit to CIR but to no avail. The most they were able to get was a *Washington Post* op-ed piece just a few days before the March 21 protest jointly authored by Senators Charles Schumer and Lindsey Graham. Having agreed on a set of principles that would guide an immigration reform bill, the Democratic senator from New York and the Republican senator from South Carolina made their principles public in an article titled "The Right Way to Mend Immigration."[43] The Schumer-Graham principles essentially reinforced the status quo by calling for an enforcement-first approach to immigration reform that would tighten US control over migrant labor. This process would happen through a biometric national ID card and an employment verification system, with an "earned" path to citizenship. RIFA had for all intents and purposes endorsed the Schumer proposal before it was even made public. According to Clarrisa Martinez of NCLA, her organization and RIFA were "ready to support something along the lines of that construct" [the Schumer proposal]. From her perspective and that of most immigration reformers "on the merits of policy the debate has been won."[44]

The Schumer Proposal

It was not until Thursday, April 29, just over one month after the March 21 mobilization, that Senator Schumer and his Democratic Party allies Senator Menendez and Senate Majority Leader Harry Reid released a twenty-six-page document outlining their proposal for immigration reform, which they dubbed REPAIR (Real Enforcement with Practical Answers for Immigration Reform).[45] Although not an actual bill, the proposal provided details on the type of immigration reform bill that the Democratic Party leadership and most groups within RIFA were willing to embrace. The proposal confirmed the fears of those who thought it would be an enforcement-first approach to immigration reform. The first paragraph of the proposal laid out eight benchmarks that would be required for a legalization program to be considered:

> These benchmarks must be met before action can be taken to adjust the status of people already in the United States illegally and should include the following: (1) increased number of Border Patrol officers; (2) increased number of US Immigration and Customs Enforcement

(ICE) agents to combat smuggling operations; (3) increased number of ICE worksite enforcement inspectors and increased inspection
resources; (4) increased number of ICE document fraud detection
officers and improved detection capability; (5) increased number
of personnel to conduct inspections for drugs, contraband, and illegal immigrants at America's ports of entry; (6) improved technology,
infrastructure, and resources to assist the Border Patrol and ICE in their
missions; (7) increased resources for prosecution of drug smugglers,
human traffickers, and unauthorized border crossers; and (8) increased
immigration court resources to expedite the removal of unlawfully
present individuals.[46]

The proposal lends unequivocal support for further militarizing the US–Mexico
border and interior enforcement, with a punitive path for people to adjust their
immigration status. In fact, most of the twenty-six-page document focuses on
enforcement-related items and control over labor. It is not until page twenty-
three, section ten, that a path toward legalization is outlined. This section
bears the subhead "MANDATORY REGISTRATION, ACCEPTANCE OF
RESPONSIBILITY, AND ADMINISTRATION OF PUNISHMENT FOR
UNAUTHORIZED ALIENS PRESENTLY IN THE UNITED STATES." As
this language suggests, the fundamental assumption built into the document is
that those in this country without documents are criminals who must be pun-
ished for their transgression.

The section further outlines the Democrats' vision for adjustment of status.
The proposal calls for granting "lawful prospective immigrant" (LPI) status to
those undocumented workers who pass a rigorous screening process and provide biographic and biometric data:

> After eight years, individuals who have been granted LPI status will be
> permitted to apply for adjustment of status to lawful permanent resi-
> dence (LPR), provided that they can demonstrate that they meet cri-
> teria related to: (1) basic citizenship skills; (2) English language skills;
> (3) continuous residence in the US; (4) updated terrorism, criminal
> history, and other checks; (5) payment of all federal income taxes, fees,
> and civil penalties; and (6) registration for Selective Service.[47]

In short, the Schumer, or REPAIR, proposal offers the same old solutions proposed by the Republican-controlled House and Senate in 2006. During that
period, the country's political leaders suggested strengthening the homeland
security state through increased militarization of enforcement in exchange for a

punitive form of legalization. The Schumer proposal contained many of the components of the enforcement-through-attrition strategy proposed by the nativist Right, and actually added elements that not even the nativists had thought up— biometric IDs and an expanded E-Verify program.

RIFA held the position that the Schumer CIR proposal was the best that the migrant rights movement could possibly attain in 2010. For instance, in a RIFA press release strategically distributed on April 29, 2010, just after the Democrats' CIR proposal was made public, RIFA chair Ali Noorani made the following statement: "The invitation by Senate Democratic leaders to Republicans to come together to negotiate, starting with the framework released today, is a step toward the federal government and Congressional leaders stepping up their efforts to fulfill their responsibility to fix the broken immigration system."[48] When I interviewed Noorani about what could have been done differently to win justice for migrants in 2010, he limited his point to the tactical means, not the end goal, of CIR:

> At that moment we were at the peak of our power as a campaign, if you will. The mistake we made is that we should have told Schumer, Reid, etc., you have to drop a Democratic Party bill [without the support of Republicans].... Then because what would have happened is that would have led to us rallying around a bill and pressuring Republicans on that bill... that was our mistake [not dropping a Democratic Party only bill], but that was not a function of the rally, that was a function of the legislative strategy. Now I don't think we could do that again moving forward, because Congress is never going to be like that again.

Rather than question the terms of the Schumer proposal, or of any CIR package, Noorani and others on the RIFA management team simply questioned the timing and tactics behind their legislative strategy. RIFA was unwilling to push for a genuine, humane, and just immigration reform package that reflected the desires of the millions of workers for dignity and full legalization. Rather, groups like the National Council of La Raza, the National Immigration Reform, the Center for American Progress, and other RIFA member organizations never questioned the nature of the CIR; in fact, they kept the movement from demanding anything that would deviate from an ominous CIR bill. Angela Maria Kelley remarked: "I don't think there is some new big, creative idea on how to fix the immigration system. It's pretty basic. You have to control people coming in, they have to come in with visas, not smugglers; you have to deal with the people who are already here. Enforcement is best done at the point of hire, so a verification system is needed, smart technology at the border."[49] As the words of Angela Maria Kelly suggest, the leadership of RIFA was willing to agree to a bill that would result in the deepening of the homeland security state and a twenty-first-century labor-control system in exchange for legalization.

While RIFA and its allies found CIR to be a fair compromise, for the oppositional sector of the migrant rights movement, the Schumer proposal was a line in the sand that they were not willing to cross.

CIR and Fragmenting the Migrant Rights Movement in New York City

At the time of the March 21 protest, it seemed as if RIFA and the Democratic Party had pacified most of the leadership of the migrant rights movement. Nonetheless, there was a burgeoning but fragmented oppositional sector of the migrant rights movement that sought to resist the process of passive revolution. Oppositional elements of the migrant rights movement rejected RIFA's structure, strategy, and vision long before the March for America. One of the main groups opposing the Schumer proposal in New York City was the May 1st Coalition for Immigrant and Workers Rights.

Established during the 2006 mega-marches in New York City, when half a million migrants and their allies hit the streets to denounce HR 4437 and to demand legalization, the May 1st Coalition is informed by genealogies of struggle that are unique to New York City. Among its key members one can find organizers and leaders from the Nuyorican movement of the 1960s and 1970s, recent New York Mexican migrant struggles, the city's Dominican community, and Central and South American migrants. In addition, and unlike its counterpart in Los Angeles (see chapter 2), the New York May 1st Coalition includes many non-Latino migrant organizations, including Pakistani and Filipino groups, African American and African organizations, and rank-and-file labor leaders. The May 1st Coalition thus represents a heterogeneous and multinational Left tradition that is specific to New York City. Like its counterpart in Los Angeles, it is a coalition that is autonomous from the Democratic Party and the political machinery of US labor.

This political autonomy has allowed it to articulate a position that was unequivocally opposed to the Schumer proposal and that called for an immediate moratorium on all enforcement policies and practices (raids, deportations, and border militarization) and for the full and immediate legalization of all undocumented workers. Indeed, Melanie Dulfo, a Filipina migrant organizer with Bayan USA, which works with May 1st Coalition, articulated, "No matter how much we do advocacy through parliamentary struggle and expect our representatives to hear our voices and represent us...we can never, never, never replace the primary struggles, which are out on the streets...which is always from the people—from what we want...what is in mind with what our principles are...that includes legalization for all....That's not something they're ever going to carry for us."[50] Melanie's position was echoed by other Latino migrant activists who supported the May 1 mobilization at Union Square in 2010.

Teresa Gutiérrez, co-coordinator of the May 1st Coalition, recalled how on Labor Day 2009, she approached Senator Schumer at a parade:

> He was walking the line, shaking hands. He is very tall. He seems seven feet, I'm sure he wasn't, but I'm five one. He was working the line and everyone was shaking his hand. I had to take the occasion of telling him how opposed we were to the Schumer plan and that immigrants have earned legalization and that 100% of the undocumented should get legalization. He got almost violent, he was raging, spit was coming out of his mouth, he got so angry, and he told me that immigrant organizations were for his plan. I said no, not all of the immigrant organizations support his plan. He was very aggressive in saying what the Democrats always say, that this is the best we could get.[51]

Teresa was willing to confront Senator Schumer and articulate why she and her allies were critical of his bill. The senator likely became irate partially because he is not accustomed to activists challenging him. In fact, it was much harder for the unions and the established immigration nonprofits to challenge the senator openly because many of these groups were on board with RIFA's message. For instance, when I asked the vice president of SEIU Local 1199, Rhadames Rivera, about his position on the Schumer proposal, he responded, *"Para mí, no hay propuesta mala, lo que hay son propuestas incompletas"* (For me there are not bad proposals, but there are incomplete proposals).[52] Rivera, like others associated with RIFA in New York City, was too close to the Democrats to criticize the Schumer proposal openly. Teresa Gutiérrez related, "They might not have called for the Schumer proposal overtly, but they did not denounce it, and the May 1 Coalition did."[53] Given this difference over the willingness to push Schumer on the details of his proposal, it was almost inevitable that the long-standing tensions between these two coalitions would lead to further differences.

These political differences between the May 1st Coalition and RIFA affiliate organizations in New York City led to further divisions in the migrant rights movement and ultimately to two separate actions for May 1, 2010. The march and rally organized by the May 1st Coalition was, at its height, attended by roughly 25,000 people. The action started at Union Square and ended at Foley Square in downtown Manhattan later that evening. Unlike at the carefully choreographed

RIFA rally in Washington, D.C., on March 21, migrant workers had the largest presence on stage and their voices were heard loud and clear. The program featured a broad array of speakers from the grassroots Left in New York City, including Dominican organizations and hip-hop groups from the South Bronx and Washington Heights; Ecuadorian and Filipino organizations from Queens; Honduran activists; progressive religious leaders; and street vendors; day laborers; youth active in the fight for the Dream Act; rebellious labor organizers from the Teamsters Local 808, SEIU Local 32BJ, and the Longshoremen Union;[54] and students and educators. Not a single politician or political operative from the Democratic Party spoke at the rally. But perhaps most important, migrants spoke out against the Schumer proposal. I recall a letter written by an undocumented indigenous Mexican women from the Bronx-based street vendor organization Vamos Unidos that explicitly denounced the bill. The letter, which she wrote from her hospital bed, said, "*No queremos los papeles si estan manchados de sangre!*" (We do not want papers if they are stained in blood!) The woman's letter and the words of many of the popular migrant organizations on the stage articulated a series of positions that came directly from the migrant working class and not a carefully choreographed political messaging plan designed to win over the middle or to reinforce the good immigrant–bad immigrant binary.

There was a great synergy between what people said on stage and what the masses of migrant workers on the ground were saying. Many of the participants in the May 1 Union Square rally noted that they were angry over SB 1070 in Arizona. For instance, Juan, an Ecuadorian migrant waiter in his early twenties who had never participated in a protest while in the United States, gave the following analysis of the Arizona law:

> *Eso es la cosa más ridícula...se trata de puro racismo. Racismo, que nos quieran echar de acá. Porque los que están cazando son latinoamericanos? Porque no migrantes europeos, italianos, de otros países? Ellos no están siendo cazados, los que están siendo cazados son nosotros. Eso es racismo....Esta es la primera vez que salgo por la ley de Arizona porque es una cosa que está muy mal. Ahí no están respetando los derechos humanos y este país se caracteriza por derechos, valores, libertad de expresión, y todo?* (That is the most ridiculous thing. It's about pure racism. Racism is the reason they want to get out of here. Why are they hunting Latin Americans? Why not European immigrants, Italians, and from other countries? They are not being hunted; we are the ones that are being hunted! That is racism. This is the first time that I come out to protest, because of the Arizona law, because it is something really wrong. They are not respecting human rights there, and this country is supposed to be characterized by rights, values, free expression and all?)[55]

Juan was not afraid to denounce policies that he saw as racist and that resulted in what he explicitly described as the hunting of Latinos. Such an argument gets to a critical point that rarely is discussed in the press releases of immigration reformers: the differential racial treatment that Latinos receive compared to European-origin groups. Moreover, this humble Ecuadorian waiter had the good sense to make a claim against such racist treatment based on his human rights and to call into question the democratic credentials of the government of the United States for its treatment of Latinos.

Clearly, Arizona's SB 1070 was not the only factor leading people to protest. Others noted that they were there to fight for their family. For instance, a twenty-two-year-old US-born Salvadoran woman from Manhattan named Zoila gave the following explanation for her participation:

> I'm here fighting for my father because right now...they're trying to send him back to his country. He's been here twenty-five years now. When he filed last year to get his papers, they took him in right then and there so now we're trying to fight for him to stay because if not, then I'm going to be the one taking care of the family.[56]

Zoila was at this rally to demand justice, in this case an end to the suffering for her family. While I never learned the details about Zoila's father's case, it is important to note that the CIR bill that was being proposed by Senator Schumer and that is now being proposed by the president would not put an end to the draconian practice of detaining migrants who are trying to fix their status when they visit immigration authorities. Thus, Zoila, at just twenty-two years of age, would still likely face the possibility of having to raise her family in the absence of her father.

The migrant workers and their family members whom I interviewed at the May 1 rally felt the pain of deportation, and they expressed a righteous indignation over racial profiling and draconian police practices like Arizona's SB 1070. Despite the variety of positions and social locations of the speakers, they all called for a just and humane immigration reform that went beyond what was outlined in the Schumer proposal. A US-born Filipina woman named Sabia gave the following explanation for her opposition to the Schumer proposal.

> I know that one of his main points is trying to make a national identification system or some sort of biometric and trying to get your fingerprint, some type of retinal scan. But that is not right, because you don't have to live in such a society where we are policed like that and where they must know our identity. We are human, we should be able live freely without being harassed by people just to know if we have documents.

> Just because I have a passport does not mean, should not mean that
> I have more rights than the person that also works here twelve hours a
> day and is undocumented.[57]

The points made by Sabia reflect a broader critique laid out by many migrants. She rejected the Schumer proposal because it would subject migrant workers to a draconian social control system based on the inalienable human rights of migrant workers. The positions voiced by migrant workers and their children at the Union Square rally should be distinguished from what took place at the Foley Square rally.

That same morning, forces associated with RIFA also held a demonstration in Foley Square. Attended by roughly 3,000 people, the rally primarily featured organizations and leaders closely linked to the Democratic Party leadership and the major labor unions in the New York City area. Speakers included Arlene Holt Baker, executive vice president of the AFL-CIO, leaders from nearly every major union (AFSCME, LIUNA, SEIU 32BJ, and SEIU Local 1199, among others), and a host of elected officials, including Congressman Charles Rangel, Congresswoman Nydia Velázquez, and City Council Speaker Christine Quinn. The speakers at the RIFA action did not question Schumer's CIR proposal and the Democratic Party leadership. Although the action's messaging was one that denounced Arizona's SB 1070 and called on Congress and the president to support so-called CIR, the rally's organizers did not recognize that the Democratic Party's immigration proposal would essentially result in the same type of racial profiling as the Arizona law being institutionalized at the national level. Rhadames Rivera, vice president of SEIU Local 1199, one of the most powerful unions in New York City and one of the main organizers of the Foley Square action, stated, "*No podemos pensar que vamos a lograr una amnistía general. Eso no va pasar!*" (We could not think that we are going to reach a general amnesty! That is not going to happen!)[58] Rivera was essentially capitulating to the Schumer proposal and to the anti-migrant bloc. Rivera was not alone in this thinking; most RIFA-affiliated groups that organized the Foley Square action were demanding CIR without questioning the content of the Schumer proposal.

Other groups attending the Foley Square rally, such as the New York Immigrant Coalition and Make the Road New York, held a position similar to Rivera's. For instance, Javier Valdez of Make the Road New York agreed that an immigration reform package would have to exclude some migrants and include more enforcement: "If legislation is going to be the venue on immigration, then we have to understand that there are going to be some things that we negotiate...there is going to be good things and bad things....I think he [Schumer] was honestly doing the work; he was going to a lot of meetings and trying to persuade conservative Democrats and marginal Republicans to get on board. It just shows that he knows how to do legislation."[59] Valdez explained the separate May Day rallies as just a matter of territorialism between the two coalitions. Although groups in New York City are certainly territorial, since 2006 the real difference between the groups has been political: the question of who is the real and legitimate force in the migrant rights movement reflects the different positions that these groups hold on immigration reform. Just as there was in Los Angeles in 2006, there is an oppositional current that demands the full legalization of all twelve million undocumented people in the United States, and there is a current of immigration reformers who stand behind CIR and who are willing to compromise on who should qualify for such a legalization package.

RIFA's strategy failed at its principal goal of winning CIR during the 111th Congress. This failure occurred for a variety of reasons that were out of its control, such as the development of an ultra-Right social movement funded by conservative foundations in the United States that pushed the national debate on immigration—and just about everything else—to the right. However, the principal reason why RIFA's strategy failed was internal: its management team assumed that the president and the Democratic Party would prioritize immigration to win over the Latino vote before the 2010 midterm election, as conventional political science would predict. Rather than prioritizing immigration, the president and his party spent most of their political capital fighting legislative battles over health care and energy. Moreover, as Clarissa Martínez De Castro of the National Council of La Raza related, "In many ways the biggest friend to Democrats when it comes to the Latino electorate, for example, are Republicans. And in many ways some Democrats expect that as long as Republicans continue to be as bad as they are being, then Democrats do not have to work very hard."[60] In the meantime, the Obama administration sought to placate Latinos with high-level appointments, minor changes to immigration policy, and the promise of immigration reform.

Some of the organizations within the RIFA management team eventually realized that they had been too restrained with the president and that they should have intensified the pressure much sooner. This realization, however, came too late, as the summer recess began and Congress geared up for the 2010 midterm elections. CIR did not pass during the 111th Congress; in fact, a CIR bill was never even formally introduced on the Senate floor. Not only did RIFA's strategy fail but also the question over what type of immigration reform should be demanded further divided the migrant rights movement. Most organizations within RIFA were willing to consent to a CIR legislative package that contained many of the enforcement measures proposed by the nativist faction of the anti-migrant bloc, such as the further militarization of the border and programs such as Secure Communities and E-Verify, among other draconian policies in exchange for legalization. The compromise on CIR had the effect of fragmenting the migrant rights movement and alienating many in the leadership from the base of migrant workers. Juan Carlos Ruiz, a Mexican priest and migrant activist, noted, "At this point there is no intention of working together. I think that organizing on the ground has become so politicized that we have allowed our own interests to come before organizing the community people who are in front of organizations."[61] Further reflecting on the state of affairs of the migrant rights movement in 2010 and 2012, Ruiz noted, "We have become so corrupted by the politics by the state that instead of being the voice and demands of our people.... we are in debt with the state, with those institutions. And as results we have two marches" and a divided movement.

Little Carrots and Big Sticks: Obama's Immigration Policies

Despite divisions among Latino migrant activists, hope turned into despair for many Latino migrant families during Obama's first term in office. The Democratic Party leadership failed to push for an immigration reform bill, and the administration sought to implement a program of passive revolution. Indeed, it pacified the movement with a series of reforms that could be classified as carrots and sticks. The carrots were minor reforms to its enforcement system coupled with the promise of a CIR bill, and the sticks were policy changes that resulted in a more robust and efficient homeland security state apparatus responsible for the deportation of more than 1.5 million people.

Carrots

The Obama administration used its executive power over DHS to make several changes to the migration control system. While some of these changes appear to make the system more efficient and humane to some, the reality is that the changes to the migration control apparatus reflect the broader strategy of passive revolution that has played out against Latino migrant activists and their allies. It is also alienating the leadership of the movement from the base of migrant workers who face the brunt of state violence.

The administration has certainly made some adjustments that make the migration control system appear more fair and humane to the casual observer. For instance, the Obama administration moved away from aggressive work-site raids. Moreover, under the Obama administration, assistant secretary of ICE John Morton issued a memo in which ICE would ostensibly deport those migrants whom it has dubbed a "high priority" or a threat to public safety or national security. According to the memo, the DHS will exercise what it calls prosecutorial discretion, which gives ICE agents more power to decide how to proceed in what they consider to be low-priority cases. Assistant Secretary Morton also announced that ICE would attempt to create a more "civil detention system" which supposedly releases asylum seekers on bail who pass a credible fear interview, provide an online prisoner locator system, and look for alternatives to detention, among other reforms.[62] Moreover, the Department of Justice under Erik Holder brought charges against the Maricopa County Sherriff, Maricopa County, and Sherrif Joe Arpaio for violating the civil rights of Latino groups. The administration also made adjustments to the provisional waiver program, which forgives unlawful presence for those who have no criminal history or administrative violations. And in the face of intensified activism from Obama's strongest critics—undocumented youth and their allies—he announced the implementation of Deferred Action for Childhood Arrivals. Finally, Obama gave his symbolic support for a series of CIR bills that never made it past both the House and Senate.

Yet these minor reforms to the migration control system and symbolic gestures were accompanied by efforts to create a more robust and homeland security state. Indeed, Obama continued the Bush administration's spending on enforcement, which has climbed steadily from almost $7.5 billion in 2002 to $17 billion in 2010.[63] Moreover, President Obama expanded the capacity of homeland security by stepping up what is euphemistically called interior enforcement and border enforcement. This enforcement has occurred primarily through two programs that represent a new generation of technology-based social control policies: E-Verify and Secure Communities.

E-Verify

The Obama Administration may have abandoned the use of work site raids, but it replaced them with electronic raids through E-Verify. E-Verify is the online worker identification verification system of the federal government. The program works by comparing information from employee work documents to government records to check the legal status of workers.[64] The program, which has been around as a pilot program since the Illegal Immigration Reform and Immigrant Responsibility Act of 1996, became E-Verify in 2007 under the Bush administration. The Bush administration, however, did not make the program mandatory for all federal contractors until after 2007, when CIR did not fall through. In 2009 the Obama administration continued the practice of requiring E-Verify for all federal contractors.[65] In light of this policy reform, the number of employers participating in the program more than doubled, according to the Migration Policy Institute. In fiscal year 2009 there were 157,000 employers enrolled in the program, and the government processed more than eight million queries. The program increased to thirteen million in FY 2010 and seventeen million queries in 2011. As a consequence undocumented workers are being fired when employers can not match their information through the E-Verify database.[66]

287(g) and Secure Communities

As part of the administration's efforts to expand the capacity of the homeland security state, it has begun to replace the 287(g) program, which allows ICE to partner with local law enforcement agencies and effectively gives local police the powers of federal immigration agents. Despite its popularity and growth in the aftermath of the mega-marches, the 287(g) program fell under much scrutiny from the Department of Justice and Latino migrant activists and their allies who viewed it as a program that uses racial profiling. In light of this critique and other contentious points around the program, DHS began plans to replace 287(g) with another program called Secure Communities. The DHS claims that Secure Communities does not use racial profiling to identify undocumented people because all people arrested, regardless of race or nationality, are subject to screening. Still, the vast majority of those deported through the program are Latinos, many of whom are taken into custody because of racial profiling on the streets by regular police officers.

Secure Communities runs the fingerprints of suspects arrested by local authorities through two federal databases, one belonging to DHS (IDENT checks immigration history) and another belonging to the FBI (IAFIS checks criminal history).[67] These two compatible databases are used to determine whether a person is in the United States without documents. These searches will most often result in an immigration detainer being issued for people who are undocumented or are deemed deportable by federal authorities. A detainer allows local law enforcement to hold a person for seventy-two hours or until immigration authorities can arrive to detain the individual and begin immigration proceedings. Moreover, the program was originally implemented through a Memorandum of Understanding like the ones used to implement the 287(g) program in which states could opt out of the program. However, after Latino migrant activists and their allies in Chicago and New York City began campaigns to opt out of the program, the DHS revised the program and made it mandatory across the United States and its territories.

The Obama administration aggressively expanded the program. For instance, Figure 5.1 illustrates how the program went from being implemented in only 77 jurisdictions in July 2009 to 3,074 in July 2012. The expansion of the program is partially responsible for the increase in deportations under the Obama administration. For instance, in 2009 the program accounted for 4% of all removals, whereas in 2011 it accounted for 20% of removals.[68] DHS plans to expand the program to all 3,181 jurisdictions in the United States and its territories by March 2013.[69] The Migration Policy Institute indicated, "The total number of fingerprints submitted through the program increased from 828,119 in FY 2009, to nearly 3.4 million in FY 2010, to approximately 6.4 million

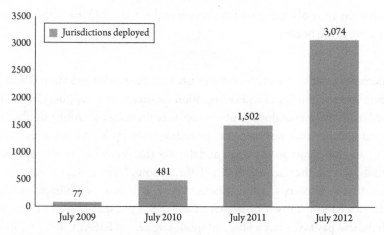

Figure 5.1 Expansion of Secure Communities

Source: Immigration Policy Center, A Decade of Rising Enforcement (American Immigration Countil, Janurary 2013). http://www.immigrationpolicy.org/sites/default/files/docs/enforcementstatsfactsheet.pdf

in FY 2011."[70] This massive interior enforcement apparatus of the homeland security state cannot be separated from the unprecedented buildup of border enforcement.

Border Enforcement

As part of its move toward using so-called smart technologies to enforce migration control efforts, the Obama administration has also continued to expand border enforcement using the latest state-of-the-art technology and surveillance equipment. In 2010 the Obama administration deployed 1,500 National Guard troops to the border, together with about three hundred new Customs and Border Protection agents, through a program called Operation Phalanx. The program, which was supposed to be discontinued in 2011, was still in place as of December 2013, according to the Migration Policy Institute.[71] The continued presence of these troops, who provide logistic, surveillance, and technological support, among other types of "support," is part of a broader border enforcement strategy for 2012–16 implemented under the Obama administration. Under this program US Customs and Border Protection seeks to develop mobile rapid response teams of up to five hundred agents at a time to respond to "terrorism" and other emergencies. While the Obama administration has kept funding and personnel levels steady compared to the several years of sustained and significant growth since Operation Gatekeeper in 1994, it has completed 651 miles of the 700-mile border fence approved by Congress in the Secure Fence Act of 2005.[72] This marks a milestone in the rapid expansion of border enforcement,

which at the time of Operation Gatekeeper in the mid-1990s had fourteen miles
of fencing at the border.

*   *   *

As noted by political theorists and activists Luis Fernandez and Greg Olson, the
"debate" between nativists and immigration reformers who support CIR is often
at odds with the way undocumented people see themselves.[73] Along similar lines,
I found a disjuncture between the messaging used by RIFA's communications
strategists and campaign managers and the way that many Latino activists on the
ground perceive themselves, even at RIFA actions.[74] For instance, not a single
migrant from Mexico, Central America, the Caribbean, or Philippines whom
I interviewed saw himself or herself as an "illegal person" who must "get right
with the law, pay taxes, pay a fine, and speak English," as RIFA's talking points and
communications strategy seek to convey.[75] Nor did any of the individuals whom
I approached at the protests at RIFA's own actions or at the actions of the May 1st
Coalition say that they were there demonstrating for CIR. Almost all of the people
whom I interviewed at these protests and actions, migrant and nonmigrant alike,
offered a different message: they all unequivocally were calling for legalization in
the face of what many of them described as racist policies that target Latinos.

But these popular demands were never met by the 111th Congress, nor
are they likely ever to be met without a massive autonomous grassroots social
movement with sufficient power to make the demands of migrants a reality. The
beauty and power of the 2006 mega-marches was that migrant workers had organizations and venues that were capable of articulating those demands, if momentarily, in the face of the homeland security state that viewed them as passive
objects. By 2008, however, a new leading ideological force among Latino migrant
activists and their allies had emerged. Moreover, these immigration reformers
demonstrated a willingness to concede to a CIR bill that contained most of the
enforcement-through-attrition measures proposed by the anti-migrant bloc in
exchange for legalization. Clearly, this concession is not simply a matter of being
satisfied with the CIR framework; there are well-intentioned activists with a
long trajectory of fighting for workers and migrant rights who temporarily and
strategically adopted such a discourse as part of a campaign strategy to win a
path toward legalization. Nonetheless, the fact they were willing to adopt such a
discourse and set of policy proposals at a time when the Democratic Party controlled the presidency and Congress is a reflection of the ideological leadership
over the immigration debate established by the anti-migrant bloc. They pushed
the public discourse so far to the right that even when they were no longer the
majority in the legislative apparatus of the state, the immigration reformers and
the Democrats continued to use the same discourse. Indeed, the nativist Right
spent the last thirty years preparing the moral and intellectual groundwork to

reduce the immigration debate to a binary that forced activists to agree to police the "bad immigrant" to save the "good immigrant."

The president, the Democratic Party, and RIFA structured their position on immigration reform in such a way that they played directly into this binary opposition. The logical consequence of adopting the good immigrant–bad immigrant binary is agreement that the undocumented are criminals, and thus the natural and ostensibly race-neutral solution must be to punish and deport the undocumented for their reputed transgression—not to challenge the underlining structural reason people migrate. Thus, rather than providing an opportunity to fight for the most popular demands that came from the base of migrant workers, the election of Obama had a pacifying effect.

Rather than being a "revolution" or great transformation, the election of President Obama, in classic Gramscian fashion, resulted in the strengthening of the very structures that Latino migrant activists and the migrant rights movement were fighting. Obama the candidate and later president pacified immigration reformers by making promises to push through a CIR bill and to curtail state violence against Latino communities. Immigration reformers and their allies across the county sacrificed radical challenges to lethal migration control policies for the sake of short-term gains and access to powerful administration figures.

This sacrifice resulted in a rather ironic outcome as immigration reformers got behind the president and his party's ominous immigration reform proposal while he and his administration did more to expand the repressive capacities of the homeland security than any of his Republican predecessors. As a veteran Chicano migrant rights activist and lawyer put, "It's like a Republican plan but it's executed by the Democrats, *güey!*"[76]

Beyond "Immigration Reform": The Latin Americanization of Latino Politics, Authoritarian Statism, and Democracy from Below

> It is impossible to disentangle the migration and labor question today without a deep understanding of the nature of contemporary capitalism, namely, neoliberal globalization.
>
> —Raúl Delgado Wise

This book was born out of both inspiration and frustration with the gains made by Latino migrant activists and the migrant rights movement in the face of the homeland security state during the conjuncture of 2001–12. I use the concept of the homeland security state to refer to the post-9/11 migration and social control regime that emerged under the discourse of the war on terror but that is also part of a thirty-year long symbiosis between the prison-industrial complex and the war on drugs with immigration control efforts of the 1980s and 1990s.

After more than a decade of struggle the movement has not been able to win justice for people like Bernardo, the father and veteran deported to Mexico because of a minor criminal offense, the several Salvadoran men interviewed for chapter 4, or the millions of others who have been deported in the aftermath of the post-9/11 homeland security state. Clearly, this is not due to a lack of effort. Even before 9/11, there have been major mobilization efforts to fight for migrant rights: actions against Proposition 187 in California; protests against similar bills in places like Arizona; and numerous actions against the border wall in the southwest in the 1990s. Following the post-9/11 crackdown, there have been countless actions, including the 2006 mega-marches, which put three to five million people on the streets nationwide; the Ya Es Hora and the Ve y Vota campaigns in 2007, which produced over one million new Latino citizens and voters; the 2010 rally at the National Mall, which brought 250,000 mostly Central American migrants and their allies to demand immigration reform under the Obama administration; sit-ins, hunger strikes, teach-ins, and other actions against racist ordinances and state proposals; the struggle for driver's licenses; and the student-led struggle for the Dream Act across the country.

I asked a simple question at the outset of this book: how is it that after this entire struggle, Latino migrant activists have not been able to win sustainable and transformative social justice victories for migrants and their families beyond the conventional policy solutions embedded in most CIR proposals from 2001 to 2012? I argued that the reason Latino migrant activists and their allies were in such a position was that, starting in the 1980s, a dynamic and contradictory constellation of forces that I call the anti-migrant bloc built the political and intellectual infrastructure to establish its hegemony over the immigration debate. This bloc used its ideological leadership, which I call anti-migrant hegemony, to call for the expansion of the state's police powers at the local, federal, and transnational levels of governance. The post-9/11 security context created the conditions for an anti-migrant bloc born out of an alliance between the nativist Right, state actors, and strategic fractions of capital that benefit from undocumented migrants as a flexible labor force that is detainable and deportable. Together, these contradictory forces have set the ideological boundaries of the immigration debate in such a way that many immigration reformers consent to, and in some cases defend, many of the components of the homeland security state and the enforcement-through-attrition strategy devised by the nativist Right in exchange for legalization. As a result of this ideological leadership, the anti-migrant bloc has been able to divide and disorganize Latino migrant activists and their allies. Indeed, until the day of this writing, migrant activists are divided over their vision of reform and strategy on how to best proceed.

As I have shown in the last five chapters, the key to the anti-migrant bloc's success has been the criminalization of Latinos at nearly every level of the state–civil society nexus, from local county boards to Congress to US foreign policy institutions and in civil society. The anti-migrant bloc won the ideological battle on immigration reform long before Barack Obama became president of the United States and long before Latino organizations and their allies built the political machine that brought about the results of the 2012 election and renewed efforts to pass immigration reform in Congress.

The 2012 Election and Beyond

Like all major elections, the 2012 presidential election proved to be an important gauge of political attitudes and trends more broadly. A record 11.5 million Latinos turned out to vote in this election, according to the Pew Hispanic Center.[1]

Although Latinos are yet to realize their full electoral power, further analysis of the 2012 election indicates that Latinos are gaining electoral influence and that support for the anti-migrant bloc—at least in its previous configuration—is waning.

In the 2012 presidential election Republican candidate Mitt Romney promised to promote the enforcement-through-attrition strategy pushed by the nativist Right. He hired Kris Kobach, mentee of the late Samuel Huntington and author of Arizona's SB 1070, as his immigration adviser. Republicans felt that they could galvanize the racial resentment of their base against a group that they portrayed as noncitizens who do not and cannot vote. Yet this strategy proved to be a total failure. Latino organizations through the Ya Es Hora (The Time Is Now) campaign and the efforts of grassroots organizations made good on their promise when they said *Hoy marchamos, mañana votamos* (Today we march, tomorrow we vote).

Some of the leading Latino political scientists, including Gary Segura and Matt Barreto, have called the election a "watershed" moment.[2] Nearly 72% of Latinos voted for President Obama. According to the polling group Latino Decisions, Latinos were "nationally decisive" in a US presidential election for the first time in history. According to Decisions, "Latinos' net contribution to Obama [was] a 5.4% margin" when the national popular vote margin for Obama was +2.3%. The polling group concluded that, if Latinos had split their votes evenly for both parties, Obama may have lost. From this perspective, Romney could have won with 35% of the Latino vote.[3] Moreover, the Latino vote played a decisive role in the battleground states of Arizona, Colorado, Nevada, Florida, and Virginia.

Indeed, a major reason why Latinos voted for Obama and the Democratic Party more broadly is that they associated the Republican candidates with more aggressive anti-migrant and, hence, anti-Latino policies. Latino Decisions noted that 56% of Latino voters believed that Romney did not care about Latinos, whereas only 23% of Latinos felt that Obama does not care about Latino issues.[4] In fact, 66% of Latino voters thought Obama cares about Latino issues, compared with only 14% who thought that Romney did.[5] Moreover, 58% of Latino voters felt more enthusiastic about voting for Obama after he announced his Deferred Action for Childhood Arrivals (DACA) policy, which allowed undocumented youth between the ages of fifteen and thirty, with no felonies or fewer than two misdemeanors temporary legal status for two years. Compare this figure to 57% of Latinos who felt less enthusiastic about Romney's immigration policies.[6]

These political attitudes must be seen as a response to the racist vitriol of the anti-migrant bloc over the last decades, which led to the increased politicization of Latino communities. According to the Pew Hispanic Research Center, from 2008 to 2012 the number of eligible Latino voters grew from 19.5 million to 23.3 million.[7] Moreover, the Center for American Progress expects that by the 2016 election there will be over four million new eligible Latino voters, an increase of 17% over the current number of eligible voters.[8] In addition, the Pew

Hispanic Center reports that, as of 2012, "some 800,000 Latinos turn 18 each year; by 2030, this number could grow to 1 million per year, adding a potential electorate of more than 16 million new Latino voters to the rolls by 2030."[9] This increase in potential voters could double the Latino electorate by 2030 and turn Arizona and Texas into blue states where Democrats will be positioned to win the Electoral College and dramatically shift the outcome of presidential elections for generations to come.

In the aftermath of the 2012 election some of the most rabid anti-migrant forces most closely associated with the nativist Right, including Representative Brian Bilbray of San Diego's 50th Congressional District, who chaired the notorious House Immigration Reform Caucus, are now out of office thanks in part to the Latino vote.[10] In fact, several conservatives who supported the slew of anti-migrant legislation introduced in Congress since 2001 have been voted out of office. In Riverside County, California, conservative Republican Mary Bonno Mack, who held a firm grip over her congressional seat, was defeated by political newcomer Democrat Raul Ruiz, an emergency room doctor with humble Mexican roots.[11] This change happened, in part, because of the changing demographics in places like Riverside County and more competitive districts that were redrawn based on the 2006 Census. In light of these demographic changes and restructuring of the political system, it is unlikely that the hard-core nativist Right will continue to maintain the same type of ideological leadership over policy and the public discourse on migration control, especially in places with rapidly changing demographics.

This confluence of forces set the context for the 2012 presidential race and will create a new set of conditions for Latino migrant activists and the broader migrant rights movement vis-à-vis the homeland security state in the years to come. Stanford political scientist Gary Segura succinctly made this point:

> The results of the 2012 election have awakened the Republican Party to their impending demographic disaster. Substantial growth in the size and power of the Latino vote—and an overwhelming tilt in that vote against their nominee—paints a bleak future for Republican electability. Coupled with startling Democratic vote share among Asian Americans (73%), and an ever more resolute and motivated African American vote, demography may be destiny for the GOP.[12]

Segura is pointing to an emerging coalition of color that is strongly identified with immigrants and that is skeptical if not adverse to the GOP's broad agenda on a variety of issues.

Political scientists such as Segura are not alone in their optimism about changing political and demographic trends. Noting that by 2040 the majority of Americans will be people of color, sociologist Joe Feagin stated, "We will in all likelihood have fewer winning white candidates opposing antidiscrimination laws and pressing for laws further restricting Latin American and Asian immigration as well as more candidates of color."[13] Segura and Feagin are correct to point to an inevitable shift in politics due to the changing demographics and emerging voices in our society, but demography is not always destiny, and if history has taught us anything, having large majorities of people of color does not guarantee access to social justice, much less a democratic polity.

Reconfiguring the Anti-Migrant Bloc: The Latin Americanization of Latino Politics in the United States

Although recent demographic trends and the influence of the Latino vote may make it seem like the immigration debate has changed for the better, there are no guarantees that these changes will lead to sustainable and transformative social justice victories for Latino communities. Nor do these changes mean that the anti-migrant bloc has been defeated.[14] Rather, the anti-migrant bloc and its hegemonic leadership over the immigration debate is being reconfigured.

In response to the demographic changes and evolving political attitudes in Latino communities, I see a reconfiguration of the anti-migrant bloc and of politics in the United States in general. I conceptualize this phenomenon as the Latin Americanization of Latino politics in the United States to refer to how a mostly Euro-descendant and affluent Latino elite is attempting to represent the interests of nearly 50.5 million Latinos, the vast majority of whom are working class and many of whom are descendants of the African and indigenous communities of Latin America, and in some cases of the United States.[15] I developed this concept as a corollary to Eduardo Bonilla Silva's argument on the Latin Americanization of race in the United States. He uses this sociological concept to discuss how race relations in the United States are changing in such a way that some Latinos are able to pass as honorary whites, while large sectors of dark-skinned Latinos continue to bear the brunt of racism.

Building upon the ideas of Bonilla Silva, I foresee a new generation of mainstream Latino politicians, alongside political operatives and media personalities, emerging and taking on the role of representing the vast majority of working-class Latinos before the United States political system without challenging the structural causes of migration and the racial politics that make state violence against migrants and people of color all too common. Much like Latin American elites who use nationalism to make broad appeals to national unity in racially and linguistically diverse societies that are also divided over class, the Latino political elite often appeal to a sense of *Latinidad* that conceals the racial, class, sexual, and linguistic discontinuities in Latino communities to become brokers between Latinos and the homeland security state.

Among Republicans we have a new generation of politicians such as Senators Ted Cruz and Marco Rubio who are quickly emerging as a new class of conservative Latino politicians across the United States. These two particular cases are emerging as the Latino face of the anti-migrant bloc in what is a transparent attempt to recast the image of Republicans as being inclusive and to lend credence to the claim that anti-migrant policies are colorblind. In fact, just seven months after the 2012 election, Republicans in the House of Representatives have sponsored a bill to defund the DACA program and to increase funding for the DHS's detention and deportation programs. The main spokesman in the Senate against the immigration reform in the 113th Congress was Senator Ted Cruz, who proposed poison amendments to remove any pathway toward citizenship in the 2013 Senate immigration bill. Cruz, a Tea Party Republican who is to the "right" of even Senator Rubio, has appeared on *The Rush Limbaugh Show* and other conservative talk radio programs to boost opposition to the immigration bill. Rubio has also called for expanding the "border fence" and threatened to revoke his support from the very bill that he helped draft if certain border triggers are not met. Politicians like Cruz and Rubio are not going away; in fact, conservative Latinos like them are being groomed across the country. They will become the new face of the anti-migrant bloc for years to come.

Republican Senators such as Ted Cruz and Marco Rubio are extreme examples of this phenomenon. But it would be a theoretical and conceptual mistake fraught with serious political consequences to limit an analysis of the Latin Americanization of Latino politics to Republicans and conservatives. As political theorist Kathleen R. Arnold writes, when it comes to immigration politics "the separation between Right and Left is a matter of degrees, rather than leading to debate or exposing the complexities of immigration . . . Both Democrats and Republicans have backed the border fence, the guest workers program, and tighter immigration control."[16] In fact, she notes that even the much-celebrated Hispanic Democratic governor of New Mexico Bill Richardson "declared the border area a 'state of emergency' and deployed his state's National Guard before President Bush did in May 2006."[17] In a similar fashion throughout this book, I have shown how the anti-migrant bloc has gained ideological leadership over groups that have traditionally been viewed as progressive and aligned with migrants. The Latin Americanization of Latino politics in the United States is a bipartisan and bilingual racial and class project.

The Latin Americanization of Latino politics in the United States has its manifestations from above and from below. From above, it is made possible by the affluence and corporate connections of the mostly Euro-descendant Latino political elites who do the work of representing the masses of Latino workers before a system that they ultimately seek to preserve. As in Latin America, there is also a politics from below. This form of politics come via the proliferation of labor organizing among warehouse workers, street vendors, car wash workers, guest workers, and other marginalized workers. It also comes in the form of new social movements comprised of students, marginalized youth, women, sexual minorities, and indigenous people, Afro-Latinos—all of whom have emerged to make rights claims from the margins of society. Perhaps nowhere else are the differences between these two class projects more visible than in the struggle for immigration reform.

The Gang of Eight Bill (S. 744): Forging a Twenty-First-Century System of Labor-Migration Control

On June 27, 2013, the United States Senate passed the Border Security, Economic Opportunity, and Immigration Modernization Act (S. 744). The bill, which was originally drafted by the Gang of Eight, named after the eight senators who have come together to work out an immigration bill, passed with a vote of 68 to 32. Most liberal media pundits and immigration reformers celebrated the bill as a major step forward for bringing the eleven million undocumented people in the United States out of the shadows and toward fixing our broken immigration system.

The most celebrated aspect of the bill is that it will grant undocumented people who qualify and overcome certain hurdles Registered Provisional Immigrant (RPI) status for ten years with an eventual path toward a green card that ostensibly makes those who qualify eligible for citizenship after waiting another three years, if certain security triggers are met. The bill also puts about two million undocumented migrants, primarily Dreamers and agricultural workers, on an expedited five-year path toward receiving a green card, which, in turn, would make them eligible to apply for citizenship. If S. 744 becomes law, it will surely provide much-needed temporary relief to undocumented migrants that qualify by allowing them to travel, obtain a driver's license, and to have some type of temporary legal status. The bill would make some important changes to detention and immigration court practices. For instance it would limit the use of solitary confinement, it would provide court-appointed counsel to unaccompanied children and people with mental illness, and would allow judges a bit more discretion in certain immigration cases, among other concessions. Such reforms would provide a degree of relief to detainees and people with immigration cases. S. 744 may provide temporary relief for a selected group; however, it will not provide justice for migrants and their families over the long run. In fact all of these benefits come at a heavy cost for those who attempt to navigate the so-called pathway toward citizenship, for those who do not qualify, for the future flows of migrants, and for the prospects of having a meaningful democracy in the United States.

To qualify for the RPI status and start the legalization process, undocumented people will be required to pay a fine, pay back taxes, register with the government, and go through a series of background checks. From the commencement, a large number of migrants will not qualify for RPI status because of prior convictions and because many migrants arrived after December 31, 2011, both of which would disqualify them from the status. Moreover, as with DACA, there will be a large number of migrants who will not qualify because they cannot produce proper documentation within the brief one-year application filing period provided to apply for the RPI status.

For those undocumented migrants who successfully qualify for RPI status, the path toward citizenship is a gauntlet riddled with legal trip wires and requirements that will result in only a fraction of the undocumented population ever being able to apply for legal permanent residency status and even fewer able to apply for citizenship, if ever. In addition, there is a secondary set of fines and hurdles that must be met after six years to renew RPI status. For instance, to qualify for a renewed RPI status after six years, undocumented migrants will have to prove that they have not been unemployed for more than sixty days consecutively and that they have a yearly income 25% above the federal poverty line. These same requirements will apply four years later, along with an additional set of application fees, as part of the application for legal permanent residency status or the green card. Given the nature of the global economic crisis and the flexible segment of the labor economy that many undocumented Latino migrants occupy, it is highly unlikely that they will be able to navigate the ten-year process successfully to qualify for a green card, let alone citizenship. In a candid moment, while commenting on the requirements to meet the path for citizenship, Republican Senator Lindsey Graham noted, "Hell, half my family wouldn't qualify."[18]

Some immigration reformers maintain that S. 744 is a sweeping and historic reform. However, upon inspection, the bill appears to be designed to prevent people from successfully navigating the system and to expand the power of the homeland security state. The reputable immigration attorney Peter Schey of the Center for Human Rights and Constitutional Law noted that S. 744 may create a fair and straightforward path toward citizenship for the about two million Dreamers and agricultural workers out of the eleven million undocumented people in the United States. However, Schey emphasized, "The proposed program for 9 million undocumented immigrants is so complex, costly, drawn out over time, and burdened with obstacles that its implementation will likely legalize no more than half of the remaining 9 million undocumented immigrants now living in the US."[19] In addition, those who meet these requirements will be in a legal purgatory similar to that of youth who qualify for DACA, and they will not be able to apply for a green card for at least ten years or until the border is 90% "secured." [20] Moreover, those who obtain RPI status will have to go to the proverbial "back of the line" until all those who have applied for a green card have been processed. With such ambiguous language, the bill could potentially result in certain national groups such as Mexicans being given a temporary work permit and indefinitely waiting for a green card and perhaps citizenship because of the extensive backlogs in the system.[21] In short, S. 744 sets up a gauntlet of requirements designed to keep undocumented workers in a perpetual temporary legal status.

The Gang of Eight's S. 744 also calls for unabated political and economic support for the homeland security state. As originally passed by the Senate Judiciary Committee, S. 744 requests 3,500 new US Customs and Border Protection officers to be hired between 2014 and 2017. The bill also preserves the use of National Guard troops to be used to operate drones, install motion sensors, build fencing, and provide support including checkpoints and other duties in border regions at the request of the governor of a border state or the secretary of defense.

The border-enforcement provisions in S. 744 were problematic to begin with. However, as Gerald Lenoir of the Black Alliance for Just Immigration (BAJI) noted, S.744 "went from bad to worse" when Republican Senators Bob Corker and John Hoeven added the so-called border surge amendments designed to win Republican support for S. 744, which were approved on June 27, 2013.[22] The amended version of the bill will provide a total of $46.3 billion for migration control. According to the National Network for Immigrant and Refugee Rights, the border surge will provide $30 billion to double the number of Border Patrol agents from roughly 20,000 to 40,000 over the next ten years; provide $8 billion to add 700 miles of fencing along the US–Mexico border; provide $140 million for Blackhawk helicopters; deploy 160 drones for border enforcement; and recruit former members of the armed forces to be hired by Department of Homeland Security and its agencies.[23] This funding is a monumental amount of money to be spent on border security. If the Merida Initiative, a military aid package that the United States provided to Mexico in 2008—with disastrous human rights consequences—was for $1.9 billion, the proposed border surge would be twenty times larger and will likely yield the same results.

This border surge comes in the aftermath of the Secure Fence Act of 2006 and the Secure Border Initiative, which have resulted in a twenty-first-century state-of-the-art border-control strategy with ground sensors, aerial drones, and rapid-response teams. Such teams come from US counter-insurgency models in which special units comprising up to 500 Customs and Border Patrol agents can be rapidly deployed into the border to neutralize enemies. As the term *surge*, which was originally used by the United States armed forces to refer to the inten-sification of the war in Iraq, suggests, S. 744 will result in the intensification of the war on migrants along the US–Mexico border, which has already resulted in the deaths of thousands of migrants in the desert since the 1990s. Like the Merida Initiative, the border surge is likely to result in the intensification of state violence along both sides of the US–Mexico border while creating the appear-ance of stability and democracy. The border surge amendment was enough to win support for S. 744 among Arizona governor Janet Brewer and Senator John McCain, who frankly noted, "We will have the most militarized border since the fall of the Berlin Wall."[24]

This border-enforcement strategy is part of a broader migration-control paradigm that will also include expanding the police powers of the homeland security state for interior enforcement along with a system of employer verifica-tion. Interior enforcement has already been greatly expanded under the Obama administration, which has expanded the Secure Communities program from about a dozen police jurisdictions to almost every jurisdiction in the country.

The amended version of S. 744 that passed in the Senate will also empower the DHS to share information with local law enforcement agencies on people who have overstayed their visas. Such intelligence sharing will inevitably lead to ICE detainers being issued and hence more deportations. This unconditional sup-port for interior enforcement comes at a time when the House Appropriations Committee approved a bill that would provide $147 million more than what was originally allocated to the DHS in 2014 to keep the 34,000-bed quota in immi-gration detention centers and to fund deportation programs.[25]

The expanded capabilities of the homeland security state to police its bor-ders and the interior of the nation will take place in the context of the greatly expanded system of employer verification. As mentioned in the previous chap-ter, the current employment-verification program of the federal government, E-Verify, has become mandatory for all federal institutions and private employ-ers with a contract with the federal government under the Obama administra-tion. Moreover, many states have implemented the same program in their public facilities. Employment verification will be expanded to include all employ-ers across the nation in five years under S. 744. Finally, the Gang of Eight bill contains provisions for the expansion of a guest-worker program and visas for high-skilled workers in technology and science, among other critical areas. As we will see, the guest-worker program and the expansion of programs such as E-Verify are the linchpin of current immigration reform proposals.

All of these reforms come at a great expense for those who will not qualify for the RPI status, for those who fail to navigate the legalization gauntlet, and for future flows of migration. Undocumented migrants who do not qualify for RPI will be further criminalized and face a more powerful homeland security state through programs such as E-Verify and Secure Communities, which will starve and police them out of the United States. In fact, amendment 31 to S. 744, known as the Grassley Amendment, will require the United States Immigration and Citizenship Services to create a weekly report on individuals whose information did not match the E-Verify system, which, in turn, will be handed over to ICE. This requirement is likely to result in a witch-hunt against migrants that do not qualify for, or have lost, RPI status, people who have overstayed their visas, and future undocumented migrants.

The Gang of Eight's S. 744 creates a pipeline to the immigration detention system that will benefit the private detention corporations and the homeland security state. It does so by imposing the harshest penalties ever seen for illegal entry and illegal reentry. Currently being undocumented is a civil offense. Under S. 744, being undocumented in the United States will be punishable by one year in prison and reentry, that is returning after being deported or accepting a voluntary departure, will be punishable with three years of prison time.[26] The bill will also create the conditions for the maintenance of an immigration detention system to be filled with brown and black bodies for years to come long after S. 744, or similar legislation, becomes law.

As of this writing in August 2013, it is too early to predict if some version of S. 744 will become law, given Republican efforts to sink the bill in the House of Representatives. Most Democrats are expected to support any bill that includes a pathway toward citizenship and that lends unequivocal support for border and interior enforcement. Moreover, Democrats need to persuade twenty Republicans to support their legislation to reach the 218 votes necessary to pass the bill in the House.[27] In fact there is a memo circulating among House Democrats with a list of 99 House Republicans with a high concentration of Latino and Asian constituents or agriculture and high-tech industries in their districts.[28] Those on the list are being targeted by Democrats as potential supporters of a House bill. Regardless of the scenario that plays out in the House, Congress is bound to consider only reforms without justice similar to S. 744 unless the so-called bipartisan consensus made possible by anti-migrant hegemony is effectively challenged.

Beyond narrow discussions about House rules, or overly simplistic celebrations about the ascendency of Latino political power, we must begin to see that the Gang of Eight's S. 744, and most CIR bills for that matter, are destined to fail at their ostensible goal even if they become law. They will fail because they will not address the driving force behind mass migration from Latin America over the last thirty years—that is, US-backed neoliberal globalization, which was implemented through asymmetrical relations of domination with Latin

American and Caribbean nations particularly in the 1980s and 1990s. Moreover, most proposals are based on the same good immigrant–bad immigrant binary that has been used by both the anti-migrant bloc and immigration reformers over the last decade. This binary does not allow for proposals that recognize the fundamental and inalienable human rights of migrants. One audacious journalist, Meagan Ortiz, pointed out, "Embedded in the [Gang of Eight] principles is an emphasis of the economic versus the human worth of people and ensures a continuation of immigration policy that will divide the undocumented into the 'good and deserving' and the 'bad, criminal, and undesirable.' We have already seen what so-called 'smart enforcement' has yielded, record number deportations, even of 'good' immigrants."[29]

The Gang of Eight's S. 744 has not led us to a historic civil rights bill, as many had hoped and many will be tempted to argue still. Rather, it has resulted in a historic compromise between nativists and capitalists, who, only under the pressure of the migrant movement, changing demographics, and the Latino vote, may concede to a deal that will include legalization for some undocumented people but result in the emergence of a twenty-first-century migration- and labor-control system.

This system of labor-migration control will be unrivaled by any other in US history, including the Bracero Program, or others perhaps in the world. When one looks at all of the enforcement measures that have been put in place at the border and in the interior alongside the employment verification system of the homeland security state, there will be little room for undocumented workers to come to the United States except as guest workers. This is because E-Verify and similar programs are a key component in the enforcement-through-attrition strategy cooked up by the nativist Right several years ago. It will push undocumented workers either out of the United States because they will not be able to find work, or it will push them even deeper into the underground economy. Undocumented workers under such conditions will have no choice but to tell employers that they are undocumented to work in the most precarious labor sectors or face a dreaded no-match letter. This is nothing new per se.

Guest-worker programs have been at the heart of most immigration legislation since the notorious immigration reform negotiations between presidents George W. Bush and Vicente Fox. Indeed, before 9/11, before the Bolivarian movement led by the late Hugo Chávez effectively challenged the so-called Washington Consensus in Latin America, and before the Great Recession, a guest-worker program was seen as a natural corollary to NAFTA and the Free Trade Area of the Americas. According to labor historian Gilbert G. Gonzalez, there was an "upsurge of publicity as this matter swelled in the media, including research institutes. The Carnegie Endowment for International Peace, together with the Autonomous Technological Institute of Mexico, published a policy statement arguing that any 'comprehensive new strategy should match Mexico's surplus of young workers with the US industry's shortage of unskilled labor.' "[30] During this period when the so-called Washington Consensus appeared invincible, the United States sought to turn Latin America into a giant free trade zone, seal the border, and create a guest-worker program.

We now know that the post-9/11 climate created conditions in which such proposals fell apart. Yet after the Great Recession and the crisis of global capital more broadly, securing a flexible temporary labor force, or what Richard Vogal called "transient servitude," is still a necessity to the dominant classes in the United States and in Latin America.[31] Such a labor force will allow business to break the back of organized labor in the United States and provide an escape valve for Latin American countries, especially Mexico, to release social pressures brought about by economic crisis, endemic violence, and social and political polarization, not to mention maintain remittance-based economies. In fact, S. 744, the Secure Border Initiative, and the desire to invest in "border security" through the border surge and other proposals that will inevitably emerge should be viewed in the context of the relations of domination between the United States and Mexico. Indeed, a major pillar of the 2008 Merida Initiative, or Plan Mexico as it is known to many, is to create a "21st century border." According to the Congressional Research Service, some of the main goals of the initiative are "securing the cross-border flow of goods and people" and "expediting legitimate commerce and travel through investments in personnel, technology, and infrastructure."[32] The politics of migration control in the United States and so-called security in Mexico are two sides of the same transnational project to safeguard global capitalism.

This scheme for a twenty-first-century system of labor-migration control goes beyond "immigration enforcement," which implies that states are solely concerned with controlling who comes into their borders. In fact, states are concerned with migration control that regulates the importation of temporary workers when it is beneficial to certain fractions of capital but that can also remove such workers when they are unruly (i.e., become politicized) and or are no longer needed. Sociologist Robyn M. Rodriguez describes the role of guest-worker programs under the conditions of global capitalism in her writings on the Philippine state's labor export program. In her view, guest workers offer "a kind of institutional 'fix' resolving global capital's demand for labor and neoliberalizing labor-importing states' demand for temporary migrants who will not make claims for membership and will return to their countries of origin once their jobs are done."[33] Almost fifty years after the end of the Bracero Program (1942–64) and sixty years since Operation Wetback in the mid-1950s, the United States is forging a new migration control regime that could simultaneously import temporary flexible workers and deport those it does not need but this time with technologies of a twenty-first-century police state built for a global service-based economy. Indeed, those in RPI status will become the new braceros of the twenty-first century who have been lured into this status with the promise of legality and a pathway to citizenship.

This need for a flexible labor force is a recurring contradiction in the history of the United States since slavery; Anglo-American capital has had an unquenchable thirst for a racialized army of rightless workers to provide cheap labor when needed, but it has been unwilling to provide them with the same legal and substantive rights as white Americans. Many people of color have filled this role in the labor economy, albeit under different conditions. But for Mexicans in particular, we are always seen as the worker and never the citizen. The last thing that the major political parties, the Gang of Eight, and their associated corporate-funded think tanks on the right or the left seek to do is abandon the neoliberal model and asymmetrical relations between the United States and Latin America. Rather, they seek to fix the system by making it more efficient—not altering the relations of domination between states in North America, much less changing the system of racial domination that has characterized politics in the United States since its founding as an Anglo-American settler colony.

The Homeland Security State and Authoritarian Statism

Most CIR bills, including the Gang of Eight bill, raise questions around democracy and the relationship between popular movements and the homeland security state. All popular movements, even those that claim to be autonomous, must deal with the state at one point or another. In the case study offered here, Latino migrant activists and the migrant rights movement writ large are making demands vis-à-vis the homeland security state. As we saw, the homeland security state is neither a monolithic, homogenous, nor self-propelling force, nor is it simply a vehicle to be used by those who run the best campaign and get their candidate elected. It is a dynamic integral state with deep roots in a society divided over race and class and other forms of difference.

The homeland security state is also akin to a particular configuration of the modern capitalist state that Nicos Poulantzas described as authoritarian statism. In his formulation, authoritarian statism is a system in which states maintain all the formal and symbolic institutions of a representative democracy, such as elections, civil liberties, and constitutional guarantees, while they adopt draconian forms of social control that resemble those of a totalitarian regime. Poulantzas discusses aspects of authoritarian statism that are obviously relevant to the politics of migration control, such as the "rise of the administration" and the "rise of the mass party." The former refers to the rise of a powerful bureaucracy that gains power and autonomy, often in secrecy, from the traditional institutions of representative democracy such as parliament or congress. The latter refers to the converging of policy proposals among the dominant parties to those that guarantee the reproduction of global capitalism.

Poulantzas also noted that authoritarian statism "involves the establishment of an entire institutional structure serving to prevent a rise in popular struggles and the dangers which that holds for class hegemony."[34] Certainly one only need see the power of state repression during the May Day march of 2007 in Los Angeles or the violent repression and infiltration of the Occupy Wall Street movement in New York City in 2011 to witness authoritarian statism in full effect. Indeed, it is now clear that the FBI, DHS, and private security firms for some of the world's most powerful banks worked together to disrupt and repress leaders of the Occupy movement.[35] It would be a mistake to limit the analysis on authoritarian statism to racialized groups or "street radicals" like those in the Latino migrant or Occupy Wall Street movements. Rather, we must see this as part of broader authoritarian trends developing in the United States including, but not limited to, recent revelations of the National Security Agency spying on the international community and its massive domestic electronic surveillance program of personal phone and Internet records. These trends are all symptoms of a democracy in decay.

If we are to understand these distinct lines of resistance and domination, we must understand the nature of the global economic crisis for which authoritarian statism is a response. Poulantzas wrote that authoritarian statism has come to "define a structural characteristic of the present phase, namely the hidden but permanent instability of the bourgeoisie's hegemony in the dominant countries."[36] If this statement was true during the dawn of neoliberalism in the mid-1970s, it is profoundly evident today under the advanced stages of global capitalism, class polarization, nativism, and colorblindness. Indeed, we must understand the homeland security state and other configurations of state-led social and labor control as a response to the organic crisis of global capitalism and race relations over the last thirty years.

If a characteristic of state authoritarianism is to maintain all the formal constitutional mechanisms of a representative democracy while having the social control of a totalitarian state, then we must see the Latin Americanization of Latino politics in the specific context of the United States as a pernicious symptom of this project in a multiracial society. Thus we have a multiracial authoritarian statism, a situation in which the appearance of racial inclusion and representative democracy are maintained through the formal institution of governance—from minorities in office to minority police officers—but with the draconian policies and practices of a segregated racial totalitarian state.

This uniquely US brand of colorblindness and authoritarian statism is the political underbelly of the much-celebrated rise of Latino political power and the emerging Latino political elites including Julian Castro, Marco Rubio, Ted Cruz, and Bob Menendez, among others. As Michelle Alexander noted in her seminal work on mass incarceration, the ideology of colorblindness depends on stories of racial exceptionalism like that of Barack Obama.[37] This same need is also the case with the homeland security state, mass deportation, and the myth of a post-racial society. The state does not work through top-down repression only. It is a perpetual conduit for organizing the unity of the distinct factions of a society based on racialized class relations for the reproduction of that society. Thus the dominant classes dialectically make room for newcomers whom they can absorb more effectively vis-à-vis the state as they use the state to disorganize popular movements. Those it cannot co-opt or placate, it represses and marginalizes. Thus the dominant classes vis-à-vis the state give material concessions in the forms of special positions within the bureaucracy, high salaries, prestige, and grants (both governmental and from the private foundations of capital) to those in certain sectors of the Latino political elite who it can accommodate. At the same time it gives indictments, court cases, intimidation, mass incarceration, beatings, and mass deportation to those whom it cannot accommodate. Thus we have the former head of the National Council of La Raza, Cecilia Muñoz, appointed to the president's cabinet and defending the DHS-ICE's Secure Communities program, while community leaders Alex Sanchez, former executive director of the Los Angeles–based organization Homies Unidos, and Nativo Lopez, the former head of Hermandad Mexicana and key leader during the 2006 mega-marches in California, were both imprisoned for a significant period. Meanwhile, migrants Bernardo, Elsa, Miguel, Josue, Roberto, and Marcos, whom I interviewed for this book, have been deported or have self-deported variously to Mexico and El Salvador, along with millions of migrants who have been removed since 2001.

The homeland security state is a particular configuration of authoritarian statism, which is a response to the class and racial polarization brought about by the organic crisis of global capitalism and race relations in the United States over the last thirty years. We are still dealing with the global capitalist system that leads to what Poulantzas described as "real 'outsiders'. . . namely immigrant workers, the unemployed, women and a large proportion of the young and the old. . . whose real economic, social and cultural conditions of life not only diverge more and more from the legal-political representations of equality, but make increasingly fragile their participation in the institutions of political democracy."[38] In the context of the United States, Latinos and other people of color are disproportionally represented among those excluded from society.

Immigration reform is not enough. Unless there is a popular and democratic challenge to authoritarian statism and neoliberalism, the homeland security state will be a permanent feature of politics in the United States. Tanya Maria Golash-Boza courageously underscored a similar point when she wrote, "Legalization for all is not enough. . . . Even if undocumented migrants in the United States were able to legalize today, ten years from now, we would find ourselves in the same situation with a new population of undocumented migrants. This is the unspoken truth that rarely makes its way into the debates over immigration."[39] Indeed, if there is going to be a solution to the "immigration crisis" besides the proposed system of state-managed labor-migration control that seeks to preserve the neoliberal order and maintain a racialized rightless labor force, there must be an effective challenge to that very order.

Beyond Reform and Elections: Latino Youth and Democracy from Below

The politics of migration control, as Kathleen Arnold reminds us, "cannot be divorced from the status of democracy."[40] Democracy is conceived here as a system in which, at minimum, most people have relatively equal chances to effect the decisions that affect their lives and when people—regardless of legal status—can enjoy the right to have rights and protection from arbitrary abuse and coercion. The United States cannot claim to be a democracy, nor credibly promote democracy abroad, when under the homeland security state and the conditions of authoritarian statism it has incarcerated millions of black Americans and deported four million migrants since 1990. The consequences of such a system are inherently undemocratic, no matter how many black and Latino elites are incorporated into the upper echelons of formal state power. In the face of this inherently undemocratic system more broadly, there must be a movement to build Latino political power from below and forge new cross-racial and class-based coalitions in civil society if there is going to be a chance to democratize the United States.

This statement may seem counterintuitive, for much of the political science literature operates under the normative assumption that greater political incorporation under the traditional indicators will translate into greater political power. However, this formula does not necessarily guarantee a more democratic and just future under the conditions of authoritarian statism, in which the conditions of neoliberalism limit the power of elected officials and policy makers to create change in areas of governance that affect the everyday conditions facing Latinos. As Raymond Rocco reminds us, voting is a necessary but insufficient activity for guaranteeing the human rights of Latino communities.[41]

The insufficiency of electoral politics does not mean that traditional forms of political participation should be discarded; however, it means that those forms of political participation will not be enough and that a dual strategy should be pursued. Indeed, political parties and elected officials respond best to organized bases in Latino communities, which, regardless of their legal status, can hold elected officials accountable. However, Poulantzas warns, "unless the State is radically transformed by the Left in power," the opposition runs the risk of reproducing authoritarian statism.[42] Therefore there must be an effort to build political power that contests the power of the homeland security state and that pushes for democratic victories from below.

During the conjuncture between 2001 and 2012, several battles have been won and lost, but the greatest victories have not come from the corporate board rooms in Washington, D.C., but from Latino youth and politically autonomous movements that acted from below. In fact, we have seen that those closest to the upper echelons of state power have been most willing to compromise and those based in the barrios and that are often physically and political distant from the halls of Congress have taken a more oppositional stance. These divisions are most evident in the reactions to S. 744. On the one hand, Washington, D.C.-based leaders such as Frank Sherry of America's Voice issued a statement in which he heralded S. 744 as a landmark victory and thanked the Gang of Eight senators for their courage in passing a Senate immigration bill that, although imperfect, is "consistent with our movement's principles."[43] On the other hand, oppositional Latino migrant organizations such as Hermandad Mexicana, one of the oldest Latino migrant organizations founded by the legendary Mexican labor leader Bert Corona, issued the following statement:

> There is no Faustian bargain for us. S. 744 smells rotten to the core and the most recent border militarization amendment and the corollary House Judiciary Committee bills moved us to publicly oppose this legislation.. . . We admonish those "advocates" and union leaders who do not recognize the national security character of the proposed legislation and related amendments under the guise of "comprehensive immigration reform that moves the country closer to a police state with all the insidious totalitarian trappings."[44]

Such divisions over how to proceed should not be reduced to being a reflection of one group's pragmatism and another's idealism.

Such idealism, or principled demand for a democratic society, has often come from young people who have driven the migrant movement forward. Against horrible odds, there is reason to be optimistic for a new generation of seasoned and battle-tested Latino youth leaders who have emerged from California to

New York City and from Kansas City to Fort Meyers, Florida, and beyond. It was this generation of leaders that produced the firestorm of Latino migrant activism unleashed by Dreamer youth, especially in the months before the 2012 election, that helped create relatively more favorable relations for the migrant movement at the end of 2012 and the beginning of 2013. Even more so than the youth who took to the streets during the 2006 mega-marches, youth activism around the Dream Act was more structured and capable of moving the immigration debate. This youth activism was chaotic and contradictory, but it could not be completely detained by Washington, D.C., insiders and the Democratic Party, despite their efforts to do so. Although a certain faction bought into the same good immigrant–bad immigrant binary that many of their counterparts in the migrant rights movement helped to perpetuate, Dreamers became a liability for the Obama administration.

These youth were able to expose how the president and the Democratic Party failed to pass immigration reform and to pass the Dream Act in Congress. The Spanish-language media and even immigration reformers began to question the president in public about his lack of action on immigration reform. In the face of this pressure, the president instituted DACA in an effort to win over strategic sectors of the Latino vote. This action came at a moment when oppositional sectors of the migrant rights movement sought to denounce the president's deportation policies in the months before the election. Dreamer youth took over the president's headquarters in the heat of the election, and other Dreamers infiltrated Broward Detention Center in Florida to denounce the president's policies of going after only "high-priority" immigrants as a farce.

On July 22, 2013, nine undocumented Mexican youth who became known as the Dream Nine—Claudia Amaro, Adriana Gil Diaz, Luis Leon, Maria Peniche, Ceferino Santiago, Mario Felix, Lulu Martinez, Marco Saavedra and Lizbeth Mateo—attempted to enter to the United States without authorization from Nogales, Mexico, in an act of civil disobedience. Frustrated with the national debate on immigration reform and dressed in graduation robes, these valiant youth sought to denounce the Obama administration's deportation policies and position themselves in the debate on reform in a way that defies the good immigrant–bad immigrant binary and brings attention to the plight of detainees and deportees. They were immediately detained and some held in solitary confinement, a practice which has been denounced by human rights groups across the United States and the world, for their act of civil disobedience. While immigration reformers have been critical of their civil disobedience, and most silent on the detention of the Dream Nine, the actions of these youth have reenergized oppositional sectors of the movement, especially among the youth to continue to fight for reforms with justice while calling attention to the plight of all migrants and detainees.[45]

There is an entire generation of young leaders emerging like those that took over President Obama's headquarters and the Dream Nine. A significant portion of these oppositional leaders understand not only the urgency of winning immediate victories but they also know that if there is ever going to be a substantive multiracial and multilingual democracy in the United States, there must also be a concerted effort to fight for the rights of migrants and people of color beyond the Gang of Eight bill and any proposal for CIR. This sector of Latino migrant activists understands that even if S. 744 or any similar bill passes that it may bring temporary relief to some but that there will still be people dying at the border, there will still be a massive buildup of prisons (both private and state owned) to be filled with brown and black bodies, and that there will still be human suffering at the hands of the homeland security state. Beyond efforts to create a kinder and gentler "civil" homeland security state, these young leaders are pushing for the demilitarization and democratization of our society.

If we are to learn anything from the 2006 mega-marches that defeated HR 4437 and the movement of undocumented youth, which pressured the Obama administration to implement DACA, it is that for a popular sector to gain ideological leadership within the migrant rights movement and in society at large, the people directly affected must be in the lead. Moreover, for this leadership to be effective, it must have a great deal of political and financial autonomy from the dominant political parties and corporate forces that fund many of the leading advocacy organizations. This autonomy does not mean, in this case, that groups try to live "off the grid" by engaging in dumpster diving and wearing homemade clothes, or that they do not make demands to the state and its officials, or that allies cannot not play a support role. It means that the leading forces in the movement must be primarily accountable to organized social bases, not foundations or political cronies. Only a politically autonomous force can effectively lead a counterhegemonic movement that challenges the power of the homeland security state and fights for a more democratic society.

This new approach would require a subtle but important shift from a movement based primarily on professional leadership and dependent on a campaign strategy financed by the major foundations, union brass, and Democratic Party political operatives at the state–civil society nexus to a movement led by the people most affected, financed through alternative funding and predicated on a mass-based social movement strategy. The differences between these two approaches and forms of leadership may seem subtle, but they are important. In campaign mode, organizers attempt to win justice for migrants in the same way that a union wins a contract, or a community group shuts down a polluter, or a party gets a candidate elected. This tactic has essentially been the strategy used by groups such as Reform Immigration for America to try to win CIR in Congress. A mass-based social movement strategy requires that movement leaders distinguish between a nonviolent civic version of what Gramsci called a war of maneuver and a war of position. In the former, one struggles for a direct and immediate victory, via elections or through a campaign; in the latter, groups struggle to build forces in civil society to change the relations of force before transforming the state and society at large.

Gramsci argued that the fight against the Fascists needed to be a war of position. Along similar lines, I suggest that the struggle for the rights of Latino migrants but also racial justice and democracy more broadly goes beyond any immigration reform bill. Like the African American freedom struggle, which did not end with passage of the civil rights acts, state violence against Latino communities and migrants from the global south will not go away with immigration reform. While the challenges facing the migrant movement require it to be capable of winning short-term meaningful victories that improve people's lives, to be sure, it also requires that Latino migrant activists and their allies develop a long-term vision and strategy. This strategy requires challenging white supremacy and transforming the social and economic structures rooted in geopolitical asymmetries between the United States and Latin America that cause people to migrate and that allow society to consent to the production of state violence against brown bodies and racial others.

Winning a civic war of position, however, is a complicated and difficult task. It requires that a new social bloc, perhaps not even a Latino one, emerge to transform US politics. If such a movement congeals, it must be able to counter individual laws and state acts of violence against migrants, and it must also be able to dismantle and hence demilitarize specific police programs such as 287(g) or programs like Secure Communities. Moreover, it must also be able to win moral and intellectual authority on the issue of who belongs in the United States and what are the acceptable conventions of belonging. For such a movement to be successful, a new generation of leaders and intellectuals must grapple with people's common sense and try to create a new moral, intellectual, and ethical reformation in civil society. A new common sense must emerge among Latino migrant activists and their allies, those sectors of working-class communities of color—especially among those who do not consider themselves activists or who may not have ethnic and class consciousness. Otherwise, at best, the migrant movement will be led by the Latino political elite and their allied immigration reformers to fight for a CIR bill that will not get to the root of why people migrate in the first place (i.e., US-led global capitalism) and that will preserve the homeland security state and, more severely, authoritarian statism.

Such groups are emerging across the nation. One example of such a formation is the Migrant Power Alliance (MPA), or Alianza Poder Migrante, a promising group that has emerged in New York City. This multiethnic and multisector coalition comprised of and led by Caribbean, African, Mexican, and Filipino migrant, student, and worker organizations and their unique genealogies of struggle emerged with the goal of building migrant power, the social and political capacity of migrants to make rights claims in global civil society. Part of its organizational philosophy is that the people directly affected by the homeland security state should lead their own movement. Also by consciously using the word *migrant* versus *immigrant*, the group is asserting its right to have rights from a different epistemic location as part of a global diaspora of migrants displaced by the forces of global capitalism and asymmetric geopolitical relations of domination between North and South over the last thirty years.

In addition, the group's broad coalition that brings together black migrants with Latino and Asian migrants is fusing important genealogies of struggle to create a new migrant politics. Black migrants, who may be from any country in the Americas, the Caribbean, Africa, and sometimes Europe, are an especially potent force in the migrant rights movement because they serve as an important bridge between African Americans and Latinos (including Afro-Latinos). Moreover, black migrant organizations, such as BAJI, an organization founded by African Americans and black migrants that joined MPA, often emphasizes the need for rejecting the good immigrant–bad immigrant binary and stresses the relationship between the criminal justice system and the migration-control system. Perhaps most critically, black migrant organizations such as BAJI have a deep understanding of the history racial domination faced by African Americans that can enrich Latino and Asian migrant organizations by exposing the limits of formal citizenship in a society that practices racial policing and other forms of domination.

In the first months of the debate around what would become S. 744, immigration reformers provided a mariachi serenade in front of Senator Schumer's office thanking him for advancing what is now a flawed and problematic reform bill. In contrast, a young undocumented Jamaican working with MPA called S. 744 "fool's gold" as the coalition staged protests outside of the office of Senator Schumer demanding an end to all deportations and the criminalization of noncitizens, including the thirteen million legal permanent residents living in the United States who are still potentially subject to deportation due to the 1996 immigration laws. Such demands broke the code of silence that kept many immigration reformers applauding the bill and thanking the Republican senators for their support. MPA's call for an end to all deportations and its effort to build a multiethnic and multisector alliance are examples of fighting for the rights of migrants beyond immigration reform.

For the MPA to be effective, many more groups are needed like them throughout the country. Most critically, it will require what Gramsci called both pessimism of the mind and optimism of the spirit. When it comes to winning sustainable and transformative social justice victories for migrants, the struggle cannot be judged by its ability to arrive at the 279 votes in Congress needed to pass the Gang of Eight bill or any CIR bill. It must also move beyond immigration reform or getting more Latinos elected to office. Indeed, if anything, the first four years of the Obama administration exposed the structural limits of multi-culturalism in a world system dominated by hegemonic states and global capitalism. Latino politics, and all politics for that matter, is about the struggle for power, and power is much more than the ability to shape the outcome of an election, get a candidate elected, or have a place at the table in a meeting with White House staff. [45] Elections, voting, lobbying, and high-power meetings are simply a means to an end. Power is much more fluid and complex; it is the ability for groups with competing interests and values to have their needs and demands met in a polity shaped by racialized class relations. Power, in the end, determines a group's access to social justice. The ultimate measure of Latino political power in the twenty-first century will be to win a sustainable and transformative social justice for working-class Latinos, regardless of their legal status.

No one can precisely predict the future of the fifty-five million Latinos in the United States in light of the global economic crisis and authoritarian statism. History, while shaped by macrostructural forces, is always contested by rival forces and thus can unfold in any direction. Indeed, Gramsci noted, "the decisive element in every situation is the permanently organized and long prepared force which can be put into the field when it is judged that a situation is favorable (and it can be favorable only insofar as such a force exists, and is full of fighting spirit)."[46] Judging by the 2006 mega-marches and the struggle in defense of the undocumented through countless mobilizations, meetings, and actions that have taken place over the last two decades, it is clear that there is a fighting spirit in Latino communities. But just like the spirit needs the body to make concrete interventions in the material world, the fighting spirit of Latino migrant activists must find greater levels of organization and political clarity if they plan on being a democratizing force for turning the tide against not just the homeland security state but also, more profoundly, authoritarian statism. Regardless of what happens with immigration reform, there are no easy answers, just struggles to be fought.

Appendix

TOWARD A NEO-GRAMSCIAN APPROACH TO LATINO POLITICS RESEARCH: THEORY AND METHODS

The questions pursued in this book require an alternative to conventional theories and methodologies used in traditional American political science and its subfield of Latino politics. I say "methods" because the research questions pursued here cannot be reduced to a single methodology such as a large-n study where the researcher relies on a data set based on a survey such as the Latino National Survey.[1]

As even MIT professor Stephen Van Evera, a leading methodologist in traditional political science, noted, "Methodology classes cover large-n methods (or large n and rational choice) as if these were all there is...but political science should embrace the task of historical explanation among its missions."[2] He also wrote, "Political science field culture has avoided the application of theory to solve policy problems and answer historical questions."[3] Although I occasionally draw on such data to illustrate certain points, I rely on a unique theoretical framework, methods, and research design that is problem-oriented on the relations of force between the homeland security state, the anti-migrant bloc, and pro-migrant forces.

This historical problem requires theory and methods of political inquiry that can capture how power is exercised from above and resisted from below. To capture these multiple levels of analysis, I adopt a neo-Gramscian theoretical framework and variety of methods such as critical discourse analysis and critical ethnography. First I will discuss my reasons for drawing on neo-Gramscian theory, describe my methods that stem from this framework, and finally discuss how this approach could enrich our understanding of the politics of migration control and Latino politics.

Neo-Gramscian Theory

The argument advanced in this book rests on a particular Gramscian and neo-Gramscian understanding of the state, intellectuals, and relations of force in concrete historical conjunctures that was discussed in the introduction, and upon which my research design and methods are predicated.

The ideas of the twentieth-century political thinker Antonio Gramsci and the interpretation of his life works by neo-Gramscian scholars such as Stuart Hall, Nicos Poulantzas, and others can be used to illuminate Latino migrant politics in particular and Latino politics in general. Moreover, at a time when some scholars have proclaimed that Gramsci's ideas are no longer useful for understanding contemporary social movements, it is important to raise why I draw upon Gramsci and interpretations of his work for understanding the relations of force between Latino migrant activism and what I have referred to as the homeland security state.[4]

Neo-Gramscian scholars have used Gramsci's theoretical insights to understand the struggles between social movements and states in distinct conjunctures across the globe.[5] Although they are admittedly complex, Gramsci's conceptual insights have much to offer those who seek to gain greater clarity on the barriers facing Latino migrant activists and the migrant rights movement as they struggle for sustainable and transformative justice in the context of the homeland security state and global capitalism.

Although it is common for North American scholars to refer to Gramsci's use of the concept of hegemony, his writings offer far more complex tools and concepts for the study of conjunctures, including a methodology and philosophy of social science in which social, historical, and political research is conducted to inform practical social change.[6] In fact, Gramsci wrote, "The most important observation to be made about any concrete analysis of the relations of force is the following: that such analyses cannot and must not be ends in themselves, but acquire significance only if they serve to justify a particular practical activity, an initiative of will."[7]

Gramsci was a committed revolutionary who wanted to understand what went wrong with the Italian Left in a moment similar to the one facing Latino migrant activists and the broader migrant rights movement in 2006, when immediately after the mega-marches the movement seemingly was at the height of its power, only to see the expansion of the homeland security state and the deportation of millions of people thereafter. Gramsci wanted to understand how the Fascists in Italy were able to win consent for their reactionary project under the conditions of liberal democracy, *even among some socialists,* in the aftermath of the Italian factory workers' movement in the early 1920s, when over 500,000 workers took over factories and the Left seemed to be in its ascendancy. I recognize that there are important differences between Italian Fascism of the 1920s and 1930s and the fascistic elements of twenty-first-century state practices in the United States today, such as the degree of violence employed by both regimes, the nature of global capitalism, and the character of contemporary race relations. Nonetheless, I use a series of interrelated Gramscian concepts to understand why, despite intensified Latino migrant activism between 2001 and 2012, we have an ever more powerful and efficient homeland security state while receiving only relatively modest concessions and symbolic gestures toward Latino migrant activists and other people of color.

Methods

Neo-Gramscian theory, with its focus on power and resistance, requires methods that capture both these dynamics. To capture how power is exerted from above, from state actors and civil society organizations that comprise what I have termed the anti-migrant bloc, I employ discourse analysis. There are many forms of discourse analysis. In this case, I adopt a broad method known as critical discourse analysis for studying the relationship between language and power. Indeed, the leading social scientist who popularized critical discourse analysis, Teun A. Van Dijik, stated, "Critical discourse analysis (CDA) is a type of discourse analytical research that primarily studies the way social power abuse, dominance, and inequality are enacted, reproduced, and resisted by text and talk in the social and political context."[8] My approach to critical discourse analysis should be distinguished from formal approaches to the study of language coming out of contemporary linguistics that often focus on the structure of language such as the syntax or more quantifiable forms of content analysis. Rather, my approach highlights how language is deployed and consumed in the state–civil society nexus between micro actors and macro social and political structures. I use this method to illustrate how elite actors' discourse, whether written or spoken, is circulated in the context of the homeland security state and Latino migrant activism.

The discourse analysis is primarily of state documents related to migration control but also includes the speeches and documents of nativist think tanks and intellectuals who lobby to influence immigration policy at multiple levels of governance. Such methods are necessary when attempting to access elite actors, especially those located within the anti-migrant bloc, because elite actors most often make their political decisions behind closed doors and because they have the power to determine to whom they grant interviews. One advantage of studying elite actors in the deliberative institutions of the state is that they leave readily available public documents in the form of government press releases, transcripts of governmental proceedings, printed speeches, and other documents that can be found on governmental websites and that are often quoted in public media outlets. Thus, throughout this study I apply discourse analysis methods to the language of political elites in various sites of state power such as Congress, municipal government, foreign policy institutions, and so on. I also study the discourse of political elites in think tanks, media, and academic institutions, among other sites of knowledge production.

In a situation in which dominant groups are using the state and other institutions of power to police, detain, and deport subordinate groups, one must use alternative methods to reach those who resist this power from below. To get to these sources I draw upon critical ethnography rather than drawing upon a traditional data set. Critical ethnography is a method of study that draws its inspiration from critical theory and seeks to contribute to human liberation. Critical ethnographers recognize that the act of doing research is in itself a political act and attempt to identify their own positionality in the research. Soyini D. Madison noted, "The critical ethnographer also takes us beneath surface appearances, disrupts the status quo, and unsettles both neutrality and taken-for-granted assumptions by bringing to light underlying and obscure operations of power and control."[9]

This critical ethnography is based on over sixty interviews and participant observation with a range of Latino migrant activists, policy makers, and deportees in the US, El Salvador and Mexico. The interviews were done with activists, established community organizers, and labor leaders in Greater Los Angeles and New York City and with leading policy makers and advocates who are firmly rooted in Washington, D.C., immigration policy circles. To supplement these interviews, I also draw upon own participant observations drawn from hundreds of hours of meetings, protests, marches, and events organized by Latino migrant activists in Southern California, New York City, and Washington, D.C., from 2001 to 2012.

Researchers are never outside of the politics of the topics that they study. I gained access to the migrant leaders interviewed for this study based on long-established relationships that I built with Latino migrant activists in Southern California starting in the early 1990s, when I first became a participant in the Latino migrant movement as a high school student. Moreover, because many of these leaders were connected to national and transnational migrant activist networks, I was able to gain further access to these organizations and political operatives in Washington, D.C., New York City, Mexico, and El Salvador.

During the initial stages of my research program I used my positionality as a Chicano doctoral student at the University of California at Los Angeles to study the discourse and actions of the anti-migrant bloc in the United States and the Latino migrant movement in Southern California. Starting in the summer of 2008, as an assistant professor living and teaching in New York City, I began to build relationships and gain access to migrant activist networks in my new home.

I also drew on my own migration experience from Tijuana, Mexico, as a child and my relationships working with leading Latino migrant activists over the years to gain access to the various sectors of the migrant rights movement across the country and with deportees and policy makers in El Salvador. As a reflection of the racial, class, and geopolitical asymmetries that penetrate social and political research in any social formation, I was not able to gain access to many of the dominant sectors of the anti-migrant bloc in the United States, but I was able to gain access to many Latino political elites in the United States and in El Salvador.

It is also important to clarify that while the majority of people whom I interviewed are Latinos, Latino migrant activism does not occur in a vacuum but rather in the context of a multiethnic and multisector global migrant rights movement. Thus I also interview Asian, South Asian, African, and West Indian migrant activists and their Euro-American allies to understand the conjuncture in its complexity. Acknowledging this diversity, however, I focus on Latinos in the migrant rights movement because they are the largest and most visible group within the movement and because they are disproportionately the targets of vitriol and state violence in the United States and in the transnational spaces that they traverse in the conjuncture under study.

Implications for the Literature

The major challenge of writing this book is that the literature on migration control and Latino politics does not provide us with the theoretical and conceptual resources to develop the type of analysis needed to answer the questions pursued herein. While there are several books that cover parts and aspects of the themes and issues discussed here, there is no one book that tackles the admittedly large questions that I engage.

Most of the available literature is too narrowly focused on either aspects of migration control or Latino political behavior. The body of social science research on migration control, while certainly revealing much about the dynamics and evolution of state efforts to regulate migrants, most often assumes that Latino communities are passive victims or are otherwise powerless in shaping the policies that directly impact their lives.[10] Moreover, this literature is often focused on just one aspect of migration enforcement. For instance, the works of Wayne Cornelius and Joseph Nevins, among others, tend to focus on border enforcement.[11] Others such as Monica Varsanyi focus on local and state immigration policy, and Lina Newton focuses on congressional immigration policy.[12] A recent notable study, by sociologist Tanya Maria Golash-Boza, discusses DHS as the twenty-first-century enforcement regime but does not provide a theoretical foundation for conceptualizing DHS as part of a more complex and differentiated state apparatus. In other words, she limits her analysis to DHS, its agencies, and actions and provides scant discussion on the nature of the state or on Latino migrant activists' labor to counter such actions.[13] Scholars of migration control have produced insightful but atomized studies that focus on aspects of the matter, but few have developed theoretical or empirical work concerned with the dialectic between migration control and migrant resistance per se.[14] Yet for the millions of people like Bernardo, whose experience was discussed in the introduction and conclusion, migration control is infused with state power at multiple levels and is resisted almost every step of the way.

The difficulty with using the established research on Latino politics to answer the questions pursued in this study is almost the reverse of the literature on migration control. Latino politics research primarily focuses on political behavior, such as voting, naturalization, public opinion, and political incorporation, without taking into account the structural context for such behavior.[15] This research helps us understand with great precision certain aspects of Latino political life in the United States on a micro and individual level to be sure. Yet with few exceptions, the field of Latino politics has yet to develop a theory of the state, when almost everything that we study, from voter participation, transnationalism, identity formation, migrant activism, and so on takes place within the orbit of the state. One important exception to this work is that of Rodney Hero, who developed a theory of two-tiered pluralism to illustrate how despite the formal existence and recognition of democracy and equality in the American political system, there is only marginal inclusion of Latinos and other racial minorities within the polity.[16] Although Hero uses empirical data to effectively challenge the axiom of liberalism that all people have a relatively equal chance to affect the political system, he still works within a modified version of pluralism. The difficulty with the pluralist approach more generally is that it assumes that there is a functional separation of powers, a separation of the state and economy, and it assumes that the state has a transhistorical character. Yet as political theorist Raymond Rocco reminds us, Latino politics is taking place in the context of profound processes of neoliberal restructuring that limit the possibility of choice and justice afforded to Latino communities.[17]

As noted by Lisa García Bedolla, there is a tension between the study of structure and agency in Latino politics research.[18] Indeed, this brief review of the literature on migration control and Latino politics raises the question: how do we make sense of contemporary Latino political struggles, which include voting, running for office, the processes of voter preferences, forging congressional coalitions, and social movements, in the context of the marco-structural transformations taking place such as neoliberal globalization, the rise of a transnational civil society, and supranational institutions and regional trading blocs such as the NAFTA, the Dominican Republic–Central American Free Trade

Agreement (DR-CAFTA), and the United States–Colombia Trade Promotion Agreement? These realities require that we develop a theoretical approach to the study of migration control and Latino politics more broadly that could account for both the micro and macro levels of analysis.

Scholars working outside of what is traditionally considered Latino politics have recently begun to call for a different approach to understanding the politics of migration control and migrant activism as part of holistic problem facing democracy. One notable and recent example of this comes from political theorist Kathleen R. Arnold, in *American Immigration after 1996: The Shifting Ground for Inclusion*.[19] In this important book Arnold draws upon the theories of Michel Foucault and Giorgio Agamben to examine the militarization of US immigration policies after 1996. She argues that contrary to the idea that states are becoming weaker under neoliberal globalization, the United States is reasserting its sovereignty over borders and migrant flows. Unlike most researchers on the topic, she is concerned with the interactions between the efforts of groups in civil society and migration control. She argues that civil society groups on the Right such as Minutemen, the Federation for American Immigration Reform, and Save our State, although positioning themselves as critical "patriots" who are "doing what the government has failed to do," are supporting what she calls prerogative power, the legal suspension of constitutional and human rights norms in times of emergency in the name of anti-immigration and antiterrorism. Moreover, Arnold argues that demands from the "pro-immigrant" camp often reduce the undocumented to guest workers. In the final analysis, according to Arnold, demands from anti-migrant and pro-migrant groups are "mutually reinforcing" notions that migrants are either a threat to national security or a source of cheap labor.

Two other important books that speak to the issues addressed here are not coming from political scientists but from anthropologists, such as Nicholas De Genova and Leo Chavez. In the introduction to the edited volume *The Deportation Regime* (co-authored with Natalie Peutz) and in other writings, De Genova correctly argues that any effort to understand the politics of migration control and migrant rights activism must start with the state. In fact, I expand upon his notion of the homeland security state throughout this book. In *The Latino Threat*, Leo Chavez argues that there is a dominant narrative that portrays Latinos as a threat to the United States that can be found in the media and in the medical field, among other sites.[20] Moreover, Chavez writes about the spectacle of border enforcement and discusses how the 2006 marches were a form of performance politics in which Latinos were demanding full citizenship.

In this study, I attempt to build on the strengths of Chavez, De Genova and Peutz, and Arnold, while avoiding some of their conceptual pitfalls. *The Latino Threat* focuses almost entirely on civil society. Chavez does not provide an analysis of the state in the production of violence against migrants. Thus, he gives his concept of "the Latino threat" an agency of its own without providing a coherent explanation of the forces involved in producing the narrative and their relationship to the state. In *The Deportation Regime* and in other writings, De Genova's work correctly calls for studies of migration control to account for the state.[21] Moreover, he elucidates what he calls the securitization of citizenship and the emergence of the homeland security state.[22] However, De Genova attributes agency to the state and to immigration law themselves and does not reveal the structures and actors behind state migration control. Arnold, while giving one of the most penetrating analyses on this issue to date, homogenizes what she calls "pro-immigrant" groups and fails to account for oppositional migrant organizations that consciously resist the urge to reduce migrants to bare life in order to win short-term policy demands.

Reform Without Justice takes a different approach and endeavors to theorize state migration control in multiple spaces of governance through a neo-Gramscian framework. From this perspective, the state can be seen as an integral racial state rooted in civil society and shaped by concrete civil-society actors, similar to the way that Arnold accounts for nonstate actors. This approach complements De Genova's in that it accounts for the centrality of the state in migration control. However, unlike De Genova's approach, it also accounts for the ways that groups in civil society win consent for building the homeland security state not just among the general public, but also among immigration reformers. Approaching the state from the perspective of Gramsci's integral state, in which intellectual power is central to winning consent for state coercion, will allow us not only to decipher the interstices of the homeland security state—its juridical, legislative, intellectual, and ideological aspects—but also to name some of the concrete actors sustaining and resisting the homeland security state.

This book is part of a growing body of research that combines the insights from political theory and Latino studies to shed light on contemporary political issues for a transdisciplinary audience.[23] Indeed, I join the scholarship of my colleague Cristina Beltrán, who uses political theory to question the celebration of Latino political power and the insightful work of Kathleen R. Arnold.[24] However, my work should be distinguished from these authors', for it fuses neo-Gramscian theory with critical ethnography and discourse analysis from transdisciplinary approaches to anthropology and Latino studies. This allows me to ground my theoretical approach to Latino migrant politics and the homeland security state right down to meetings, protests, and on the streets where the rights of migrants, and democracy are violated and contested in the context of neoliberal globalization and post–civil rights racism.

NOTES

Introduction

1. Bernardo (pseudonym), interview, Mexico City, November 8, 2010.
2. Ibid.
3. See Nicholas De Genova, "The Production of Culprits: From Deportability to Detainability in the Aftermath of 'Homeland Security,'" *Citizenship Studies* 11, no. 5 (2007): 421. Also see Roberto Lovato. "One Raid at a Time: How Immigrant Crackdowns Build the National Security State," *Public Eye Magazine* 23, no. 1 (Spring 2008).
4. I use the term *migration control* instead of *immigration enforcement* in most cases, because the latter term assumes that the United States is only concerned with who enters the country, but as we shall see, recent efforts to build the homeland security state are just as concerned with controlling the flow of migrant labor coming into the United States and establishing the terms of their stay. However, I do use the term *immigration enforcement* when citing other works that use this term. For more on migration control as a form of labor control see, Gilbert Gonzalez, *Guest Workers or Colonized Labor: Mexican Labor Migration to the United States* (Boulder, CO: Paradigm Publishers, 2004).
5. For an analysis of post-1996 immigration politics, see Kathleen R. Arnold *Immigration Politics after 1996: The Shifing Ground of Political Inclusion* (College Park, PA: Pennsylvania University Press, 2011).
6. Migration Policy Institute, "US Spends More on Immigration Enforcement than on FBI, DEA, Secret Service & All Other Federal Criminal Law Enforcement Agencies Combined," press release, January 7, 2013, http://www.migrationpolicy.org/news/2013_1_07.php.
7. Ben Winograd, "Removals Remain the Starkest Measure of Immigration Enforcement," January 11, 2013, Immigration Impact, Project of the American Immigration Council, http://immigrationimpact.com/2013/01/11/removals-remain-the-starkest-measure-of-immigration-enforcement/.
8. Doris Meissner et al., *Immigration Enforcement in the United States: The Rise of a Formidable Machinery* (Washington, D.C.: Migration Policy Institute, January 2013), p.2, http://www.migrationpolicy.org/pubs/enforcementpillars.pdf.
9. Ibid.
10. Associated Press, "More Hispanics Go to Federal Prison," *USA Today*, June 4, 2011, http://usatoday30.usatoday.com/news/nation/2011-06-04-immigration-hispanic-offenders-federal-prison_n.htm.
11. I often use the word *migrant* versus *immigrant* when referring to Latino migrants, the migrant movement, and anti-migrant groups and policies. I regularly do this because the word *immigrant* as used in contemporary migration studies was developed on the Western European immigrant experience and assumes a unidirectional relationship in which people voluntarily come to the host country and permanently settle. I prefer to use the word *migrant*

in reference to Latino migrants and migrants from the global south because it indicates a more circular relationship in which people, like several that I interviewed for this book, plan on returning to their host country, or come from families in which people have migrated between two distinct nation states for generations. In some cases, as in the case of indigenous migrants it could be argued that their history of circular migration within the Americas actually predates the modern nation state. I do however, use the word *immigrant* when citing others who use this term, or as a generic reference to all people who have (im)migrated to the United States.

12. Irene Bloemraad, Kim Voss, and Taeku Lee, "The Protests of 2006: What Were They, How Do We Understand Them, Where Do We Go?" in *Rallying for Immigrant Rights: The Fight for Inclusion in 21st Century America*, ed. Irene Bloemraad (Berkeley, CA: University of California Press), 3–43.

13. Adrián Félix, Carmen Gonzalez, and Ricardo Ramírez, "Political Protest, Ethnic Media, and Latino Naturalization," *American Behavioral Scientist* 52, no. 4 (2008): 618–34.

14. Under the DACA program, DHS issued a memo in June 2012 stating that it would review the cases of undocumented youth who came to the United States before they were 16 years old, are under the age of 30, have lived in the United States for five consecutive years, and have not committed a felony or who have not committed a serious misdemeanor.

15. Iris Marion Young, *Justice and the Politics of Difference* (Princeton, NJ: Princeton University Press, 1990).

16. *The Antonio Gramsci Reader: Selected Writings, 1916–1935*, ed. David Forgacs (New York: New York University Press, 2000), 423.

17. Meissner et al., *Immigration Enforcement in the United States: The Rise of a Formidable Machinery*, 1.

18. Leisy Abrego and Cecilia Menjívar, "Immigrant Latina Mothers as Targets of Legal Violence," *International Journal of Sociology of the Family* 37, no. 1 (2012): 9–26.

19. Certainly we could find other anti-migrant discourses besides criminalization, such as the following: immigrants are responsible for the declining economy; immigrant women are having too many children; immigrants are responsible for the declining quality of public education and for the value of American citizenship; etc. In the public records I consulted in this study, however, I found criminalization of Latinos to be the dominant discourse.

20. Stuart Hall, "The Spectacle of the Other," chap. 4 in *Representation: Cultural Representations and Signifying Practices*, ed. Stuart Hall (London: Sage Publications, 1997), 223–90.

21. Factions refer to political ideological divisions such as libertarians versus traditional conservatives. When I refer to fractions, or fractions of capital, I am referring to groups located in a particular segment of the economy, such as private prison corporations, the meatpacking corporations, agricultural business, etc.

22. See Samuel P. Huntington, "The Hispanic Challenge," *Foreign Policy*, May 1, 2004, http://www.foreignpolicy.com/articles/2004/03/01/the_hispanic_challenge.

23. Here I am using organic intellectual in a slightly different way than Gramsci. He theorized several modes of being an intellectual. For instance, he distinguished between traditional intellectuals (professors, lawyers, priests, etc.) and non-traditional intellectuals such as workers, or a peasant who learns to produce knowledge with the aide of traditional intellectuals. In this book I refer to two types of organic intellectuals those of the homeland security state that produce knowledge to advance more authoritarian solutions to regulate migration, and to a particular strata of Latino migrant activists and their allies who draw upon their political traditions to produce knowledge for the migrant movement.

24. To understand this about Huntington's thesis on Latinos we must revisit his early writing in the study, titled "The Crisis of Democracy," written in the early 1970s in the aftermath of the watershed year of 1968. The study funded by the Trilateral Commission, a consortium convened by David Rockefeller brought together some of the most powerful corporate and governmental leaders to confront common problems. In this report Huntington argues that problem with democracy was that "marginal social groups, as in the case of the

blacks, are now becoming full participants in society." Huntington in Michel J. Crozier, Samuel P. Huntington, Joji Watanuki, *The Crisis of Democracy, Report Submitted to the Trilateral Commission Report on Governability* (New York, NY: New York University Press, 1973), 94.

25. Robert G Kaiser and Ira Chinoy, "Scaife: Funding Father of the Right," *Washington Post*, May 2, 1999, http://www.washingtonpost.com/wp-srv/politics/special/clinton/stories/ scaifemain050299.htm.

26. Luis Fernandez and Joel Olson, "To Live and Work, Anywhere You Please: Arizona and the Struggle for Locomotion," *Contemporary Political Theory* 10, no. 3 (2011): 412–19.

27. *The Antonio Gramsci Reader*, 211–12.

28. National Council of La Raza (NCLR), Corporate Board of Advisors, Commemorative Publication, http://www.nclr.org/images/uploads/pages/CBA_Pub_2011.pdf.

29. Aristride R. Zolberg, *A Nation by Design: Immigration Policy in the Fashioning of America* (Cambridge, MA: Harvard University Press, 2008).

30. *The Antonio Gramsci Reader*, 429.

31. Roberto Lovato, "One Raid at a Time: How Immigrant Crackdowns Build the National Security State."

32. Bob Jessop, *The Capitalist State: Marxist Theories and Methods* (New York, NY: New York University Press, 1982), 211–13.

33. Aníbal Quijano, "Coloniality of Power, Eurocentrisim, and Latin America," *Nepantla: Views from the South* 1, no. 3 (2000): 533–80.

34. Ibid., 533.

35. David Theo Goldberg, *The Racial State* (Malden, MA: Blackwell Publishing, 2002).

36. Bonilla-Silva, *White Supremacy and Racism*, 11.

37. Cristina Beltrán, *The Trouble with Unity: Latino Politics and the Creation of Identity* (New York: Oxford University Press, 2010).

38. Luis Fernandez and Joel Olson, "To Live and Work, Anywhere You Please: Arizona and the Struggle for Locomotion."

39. Gramsci distinguished between the conjunctural and the organic. The former represents the actors, personalities, and players of a "day-to-day character" that define a political moment. "Organic phenomena...give rise to social-historic criticism, whose subject is wider social groupings—beyond those people with immediate responsibilities and beyond the ruling personnel." Indeed Gramsci is talking about "something lasting decades," such as the changing mode of capitalist development or racial politics. As Gramsci noted, "when a historic period comes to be studied a great distinction becomes clear," but he also notes that "conjunctural phenomena too depend on organic movements to be sure"; thus his focus is on the nexus between these two levels of analysis, for it is the dialectic between the conjunctural and the organic from which the distinct political actors organize. *The Antonio Gramsci Reader*, 201.

40. William I. Robinson, *A Theory of Global Capitalism: Production, Class, and State in a Transnational World* (Baltimore: Johns Hopkins University Press, 2004).

41. United Nations Department of Economic and Social Affairs, Population Division, "Population Facts," no. 2010/6, November 2010, http://www.un.org/esa/population/ publications/popfacts/popfacts_2010-6.pdf.

42. Raúl Delgado-Wise, "Forced Migration and US Imperialism," *Critical Sociology* 35, no. 6 (2009): 793–810.

43. Ibid.

44. Pew Hispanic Center, "Statistical Portrait of the Hispanic Population in the United States," Table 6, Detailed Hispanic Origin 2009, http://pewhispanic.org/files/factsheets/ hispanics2009/2009%20Hispanic%20Profile%20Final.pdf.

45. Marilyn Espitia, "The Other 'Other Hispanics': South American Latinos in the United States," chap. 6 in *The Columbia History of Latinos in the United States since 1960*, ed. David Gutiérrez (New York: Columbia University Press, 2004).

46. For a discussion on post–civil rights racism, see Howard Winant, *The New Politics of Race: Globalism, Difference, Justice* (Minneapolis: University of Minnesota Press,

2004); Eduardo Bonilla-Silva, *White Supremacy and Racism in the Post–Civil Rights Era* (Boulder, CO: Lynne Rienner Publishers, 2001); and Michael Omi and Howard Winant, *Racial Formation in the United States: From the 1960s to the 1990s* (London: Routledge, 1994).

47. For more on this history, see Arnoldo De León, *They Called Them Greasers: Anglo Attitudes toward Mexicans in Texas* (Austin: University of Texas Press, 1983); Rodolfo Acuña, *Occupied America: A History of Chicanos.* 6th ed. (New York: Pearson Longman, 2000).

48. Manny Fernandez, "Prosecutors Describe Hunt for Hispanic Victim," *New York Times*, March 18, 2010.

Chapter 1

1. US. Library of Congress, Congressional Research Service, "Immigration Legislation and Issues in the 109th Congress," Andorra Bruno, CRS Report RL33125 (Washington, D.C.: Office of Congressional Information and Publishing, updated November 7, 2006), http://fpc.state.gov/documents/organization/76318.pdf.

2. Jean Stefancic and Richard Delgado, *No Mercy: How Conservative Think Tanks and Foundations Changed America's Social Agenda* (Philadelphia: Temple University Press, 1996).

3. Lisa McGirr, *Suburban Warriors: Origins of the New American Right* (Princeton, NJ: Princeton University Press, 2002).

4. *Selections from the Prison Notebooks of Antonio Gramsci,* ed. Quintin Hoare and Geoffrey Smith (New York: International Publishers, 1971), 157.

5. Ibid., 6.

6. "Center for Immigration Studies Staff List," accessed January 27, 2013, http://cis.org/Staff-List.

7. Mark Krikorian and Steven A. Camarota, *Immigration and Terrorism: What Is to Be Done?* (Washington, D.C.: Center for Immigration Studies, November 2001), http://www.cis.org/sites/cis.org/files/articles/2001/back1601.pdf.

8. Ibid.

9. Kathleen R. Arnold, *American Immigration after 1996: The Shifting Ground of Political Inclusion* (College Park, PA: Pennselvania State University, 2011), 10.

10. Gramsci used the concept of "war of position" to explain how groups from either the Right or Left could become hegemonic over a prolonged political struggle. In our case, I am talking about a reactionary racial war of position in which the radical right was able to become mainstream. "War of position" should be distinguished from Gramsci's concept of "war of maneuver," in which groups seek to overthrow the state to implement a revolution from above. For more on these concepts, see *The Antonio Gramsci Reader*, 225–30.

11. See John Tanton, interview by Otis L. Graham Jr. in Graham's *A Skirmish in a Wider War: An Oral History of John H. Tanton, Founder of FAIR* (Ann Arbor, MI: Bentley Historical Library, University of Michigan, 1992).

12. Eduardo Bonilla-Silva, *Racism Without Racists: Color-Blind Racism and the Persistence of Racial Inequality* (New York: Rowman & Littlefield, 2003); Howard Winant, *The World Is a Ghetto* (New York: Basic Books, 2001).

13. Deepa Fernandes, *Targeted: Homeland Security and the Business of Immigration* (New York: Seven Stories Press, 2007).

14. Graham, *A Skirmish in a Wider War*, 32.

15. SPLC, "John Tanton Is the Mastermind Behind the Organized Anti-Immigration Movement," *Intelligence Report*, no. 106 (Summer 2002), http://www.splcenter.org/get-informed/intelligence-report/browse-all-issues/2002/summer/the-puppeteer.

16. Graham, *Skirmish in a Wider War*, 15.

17. Ibid., 12.

18. These studies blamed so-called "inferior races" but conveniently overlooked the role of US- and Western European–backed military dictatorships and colonialism in creating poverty and so-called underdevelopment.

19. "Mexican Americans Sterilized Disproportionately In California Institutions, Study Says", *Huffington Post*, June 5, 2013, http://www.huffingtonpost.com/2013/06/05/mexican-americans-sterilized_n_3390305.html?view=print&comm_ref=false.
20. Graham, *Skirmish in a Wider War*, 37.
21. Tucker Carlson, "The Intellectual Roots of Nativism," *Wall Street Journal*, October 2, 1997.
22. Ibid.
23. Ibid.
24. Peter Brimelow, *Alien Nation* (New York: Random House, 1995), 59, quoted in Devin Burghart and Steven Gardiner, "Lady Liberty No More: The Rise of the New Nativism" (unpublished manuscript, 2011).
25. Ali Behdad, *Forgetful Nation: On Immigration and Cultural Identity in the United States* (Durham, NC: Duke University Press, 2005).
26. SPLC, "John Tanton Is the Mastermind."
27. Ibid.
28. Ibid.
29. Center for Immigration Studies, Board of Directors, http://cis.org/Staff-List.
30. Center for Immigration Studies, "Immigration and the SPLC" [video], National Press Club, Washington D.C., March 10, 2010 https://www.youtube.com/watch?v=R-DZK3J1Qao.
31. Jerry Kammer, *Immigration and SPLC: How the Southern Poverty Law Center Invented a Smear, Served La Raza, Manipulate the Press, and Duped its Donors* (Washington, D.C: Center for Immigration Studies, March 2010), http://www.cis.org/articles/2010/immigration-splc.pdf.
32. SPLC, "John Tanton Is the Mastermind." Emphasis in the original.
33. Burghart and Gardiner, "Lady Liberty No More." Emphasis in the original.
34. Bonilla-Silva, *Racism Without Racists*.
35. SPLC, "John Tanton Is the Mastermind."
36. Graham, *A Skirmish in a Wider War*.
37. For the mission statement of the Immigration Reform Law Institute, visit http://irli.org/about.
38. Southern Poverty Law Center, "When Mr. Kobach Comes to Town: Nativist Laws and the Communities they Damage" (Montgomery, AL, Southern Poverty Law Center, January 2011), http://cdna.splcenter.org/sites/default/files/downloads/publication/Kobach_Comes_to_Town.pdf.
39. Amanda Peterson Beadle, "Meet Mitt Romney's Immigration Advisors," http://thinkprogress.org/justice/2012/08/01/605121/meet-mitt-romneys-immigration-advisers/.
40. Burghart and Gardiner, "Lady Liberty No More."
41. Jessica M. Vaughan, "Attrition Through Enforcement: A Cost-Effective Strategy to Shrink the Illegal Population" (Washington, D.C.: Center for Immigration Studies, April 2006), http://www.cis.org/Enforcement-IllegalPopulation.
42. Ibid.
43. Angela Maria Kelley (vice president for immigration policy, Center for American Progress), personal interview, Washington, D.C., June 30, 2011.
44. Burghart and Gardiner, "Lady Liberty No More."
45. Robyn Rodriguez, *Migrant Workers for Export*, xxii.
46. For more on parochial nationalism, see Genova, "The Production of Culprits."
47. Devin Burghart (director of the Building Democracy Initiative), telephone interview, June 15, 2011.
48. Burghart and Gardiner, "Lady Liberty No More."
49. Ibid.
50. Stefancic and Delgado, *No Mercy*, 46.
51. Ibid.
52. The Sara Scaife Foundation broke off from the other foundations and was moved to West Palm Beach, Florida.
53. "Richard Mellon Scaife," IPS Right Web, updated February 26, 2009, http://www.rightweb.irc-online.org/profile/Scaife_Richard_Mellon.
54. Jessica M.Vaughan, "Attrition through Enforcement."

55. SPLC, "John Tanton Is the Mastermind."
56. Building Democracy Initiative, "Nativism in the House: A Report on the House Immigration Reform Caucus" (Chicago: Center for a New Community, 2007), http://www.buildingdemocracy.org/reports/HIRC.pdf.
57. Fernandes, *Targeted*, 225.
58. Building Democracy Initiative, "Nativism in the House," 6.
59. Ibid., 6
60. Ibid., 6
61. Examining the Need for Comprehensive Immigration Reform, Part II: Hearing Before the Committee on the Judiciary, US Senate, 109th Cong. (July 12, 2006) (statement of Michael W. Cutler, fellow, Center for Immigration Studies, Washington, D.C.), http://judiciary.senate.gov/hearings/testimony.cfm?id=e655f9e2809e5476862f735da118277a&wit_id=e655f9e2809e5476862f735da118277a-2-1.
62. Comprehensive Immigration Reform II: Hearing before the Committee on the Judiciary, US Senate, 109th Cong. (October 18, 2005) (statement of Frank Sharry, executive director of the National Immigration Forum), http://judiciary.senate.gov/hearings/testimony.cfm?id=e655f9e2809e5476862f735da10b35e4&wit_id=e655f9e2809e5476862f735da10b35e4-2-1.
63. Ibid.
64. I do not contend that there were no competing or overlapping discourses used by groups in the House. Some Republicans argued that immigrants are a drain on national resources, and others made the claim that Mexican migrants were anti-American. Nonetheless, it goes beyond the scope of this chapter to categorize and quantify all of the competing discourses.
65. James Sensenbrenner (Republican, Wisconsin), "Border Protection, Antiterrorism, and Illegal Immigration Control Act of 2005" (House of Representatives, December 15, 2005).
66. Steve King (Republican, Iowa), "Comparing the Statistics" (House of Representatives, May 3, 2006).
67. Ginny Brown-Waite (Republican, Florida), "The Senate Needs to Act on Immigration Reform" (House of Representatives, March 29, 2006).
68. John Carter (Republican, Texas), "The Senate Needs to Act on Immigration Reform" (House of Representatives, July 12, 2006).
69. John Carter (Republican, Texas), "Illegal Immigration" (House of Representatives, July 11, 2006).
70. James Sensenbrenner (Republican, Wisconsin), "Border Protection, Antiterrorism, and Illegal Immigration Control Act of 2005" (House of Representatives, December 15, 2005).
71. Of course, to the dominant society, most Latinos can appear to be Mexican.
72. Steve King (Republican, Iowa), "Border Protection, Antiterrorism, and Illegal Immigration Control Act of 2005" (House of Representatives, July 11, 2006).
73. For more on metaphors that compare immigrants to animals, see Otto Santa Ana, *Brown Tide Rising: Metaphors of Latinos in Contemporary American Discourse* (Austin: University of Texas Press, 2002).
74. Ginny Brown-Waite (Republican, Florida), "Border Protection, Antiterrorism, and Illegal Immigration Control Act of 2005" (House of Representatives, July 12, 2006).
75. "Border Protection, Anti-Terrorism, and Illegal Immigration Control Act of 2005" (House of Representatives, December 16, 2005).
76. Ibid.
77. Nancy Pelosi (Democrat, California), "Border Protection, Antiterrorism, and Illegal Immigration Control Act of 2005" (House of Representatives, December 16, 2005).
78. Sheila Jackson Lee (Texas, Democrat), "Border Protection, Antiterrorism, and Illegal Immigration Control Act of 2005" (House of Representatives, December 16, 2005).
79. Ibid.
80. Raúl Grijalva (Democrat, Arizona), "Border Protection, Antiterrorism, and Illegal Immigration Control Act of 2005" (House of Representatives, December 16, 2005).

81. Charles Gonzales (Democrat, Texas), "Border Protection, Antiterrorism, and Illegal Immigration Control Act of 2005" (House of Representatives, December 16, 2005).
82. For more on the lack of leadership among California Latinos in the House of Representatives, see Mindy Farabee, "Where Are Latino Elected Leaders in Immigration Reform Fight?" *Eastern Group Publications*, March 25, 2006, http://network.nshp.org/profiles/blogs/latino-leaders-need-to-be.
83. These politicians are located in an area stretching from downtown Los Angeles to the San Gabriel Valley that has one of the largest Latino voter blocs in the United States.
84. Paloma Esquivel, "From the Streets to the Polls," *The Nation*, August 15, 2006.
85. Chris Zepeda-Millán, "Dignity's Revolt: Threat, Identity, and Immigrant Mass Mobilization" (PhD diss., Cornell University, 2011).

Chapter 2

1. Field notes, San Bernardino, California, December 3, 2005.
2. At this protest and others in the Inland Empire, Joseph Turner appeared at protests alongside neo-Nazi skinheads and purposely taunted counter-protesters and sought to incite violence. Turner, a local anti-migrant activist who harassed day laborers and migrant rights protesters throughout Southern California, worked for FAIR but was reportedly let go thirteen months after being hired in November 2006. See Heidi Beirich, "Controversial Official Leaves FAIR," *SPLC Hatewatch*, January 8, 2008, http://www.splcenter.org/blog/2008/01/08/controversial-official-no-longer-at-fair.
3. For more on the role of the media in the 2006 mobilization, see Félix, "Political Protest."
4. Zepeda-Millán, "Today We March, Tomorrow We Vote."
5. One could certainly describe particular aspects of the 2006 mega-marches by taking one of the more traditional approaches to social movements, such as resource mobilization theory, political opportunities theory, or some of the theories to come out of the new social movement literature. Unlike scholars working from these perspectives, I am not interested in understanding the mobilization structures used in 2006, how organizers seized the opportunity created by HR 4437, or how they used identity for mobilization per se. However, I seek to analyze the marches within the analysis of conjunctures between 2001 and 2010 and to theorize the implication of the marches from a Gramscian framework.
6. While I focus on Latinos, it should be made clear that many other ethnic groups participated in organizing the marches. Perhaps most profoundly Filipino organizations drew on their knowledge and style of organizing for the mega-marches in Greater Los Angeles and nationally.
7. Indigenous Mexicans and other indigenous groups often found themselves siding with the "Latino" migrant bloc, but as they often point out they are not Latinos or Hispanics who have ancestral connections to the Iberian Peninsula. Rather, as these indigenous migrants correctly point out, their ancestors have been on this continent since time immemorial.
8. *Caciquismo* refers to a style of leadership in which one autocratic individual dominates, as opposed to a collective and democratically run leadership structure.
9. Zepeda-Millán, "Today We March."
10. Zepeda-Millán, "Today We March"; Monica Varsanyi, *Taking Local Control: Immigration Policy Activism in U.S. Cities and States* (Stanford, CA : Stanford University Press, 2010).
11. Jessie Diaz and Javier Rodriguez, "Undocumented in America," *New Left Review* 47 (September–October 2007): 93–107, http://newleftreview.org/II/47/jesse-diaz-javier-rodriguez-undocumented-in-america. Interview conducted by William Robinson.
12. Ponce, "Racialization, Resistance, and the Migrant Rights Movement."
13. The struggle for the rights of Mexican migrants goes back to the 1920s and to the civil rights activism of Mexican and Latino organizations in the 1950s. I provide analysis of these three genealogies because the people who were at the center of the organizing leading to the spring 2006 mobilizations had undisputable roots in these genealogies of struggle. For more on these earlier forms of migrant activism, see Ponce, "Racialization, Resistance, and the Migrant Rights Movement."
14. I realize that Gramsci spoke about the need for a party structure to form organic intellectuals during the specific moment that he was writing in Italy in the 1920s and 1930s. In our

twenty-first-century case study, however, there was not a formal or significant party structure yet capable of forming organic intellectuals. Thus I am taking the liberty to write about the formation of organic intellectuals as something that could happen inside a party structure to be sure but also in a more horizontal constellation of social movements spanning a period, as in the case of the Latino genealogies of struggle that led to the formation of the Latino social bloc.

15. Javier Rodríguez and Nativo Lopez had their roots in CASA; Armando Navarro and Carlos Montes came from the Brown Berets.

16. For more on Corona, see Mario T. García, *Memories of Chicano History: The Life and Narrative of Bert Corona* (Berkeley: University of California Press, 1994). For more on the evolution and eventual decline of CASA, see Ernesto Chávez, *Mi Raza Primero! (My People First!): Nationalism, Identity and Insurgency in the Chicano Movement in Los Angeles, 1966–1978* (Berkeley: University of California Press, 2002).

17. Laura Pulido, *Black, Brown, Yellow, and Left: Radical Activism in Los Angeles* (Berkeley: University of California Press, 2006).

18. Ibid.

19. Nora Hamilton and Norma S. Chinchilla, *Seeking Community in a Global City: Guatemalans and Salvadorans in Los Angeles* (Philadelphia: Temple University Press, 2001).

20. Susan Bibler Coutin, "Cultural Logics of Belonging and Movement: Transnationalism, Naturalization, and US Immigration Politics," in *The Anthropology of the State: A Reader*, ed. Sharma Aradhana and Akhil Gupta (Malden, MA: Blackwell Publishing, 2006), 310–36.

21. Lisa García Bedolla, *Fluid Borders: Latino Power, Identity, and Politics in Los Angeles* (Berkeley: University of California Press, 2005).

22. Carlos Mora, *Latinos in the West: The Student Movement and Academic Labor in Los Angeles* (New York: Rowman & Littlefield, 2007).

23. William I. Robinson, "'Aquí Estamos y No Nos Vamos!' Global Capital and Immigrant Rights," *Race and Class* 48, no. 2 (2006): 77–91.

24. See Armando Navarro, *La Raza Unida Party: A Chicano Challenge to the US Two-Party Dictatorship* (Philadelphia: Temple University Press, 2000); Michael C. Dawson, *Behind the Mule: Race and Class in African-American Politics* (Princeton, NJ: Princeton University Press, 1994); and Robert C. Smith, *We Have No Leaders: African Americans in the Post-Civil Rights Era* (Albany: State University of New York Press, 1996).

25. Gloria Saucedo (executive director, Hermandad Mexicana Nacional), interview, North Hollywood, California, February 5, 2008.

26. Armando Navarro, *The Immigration Crisis: Nativism, Armed Vigilantism, and the Rise of a Countervailing Movement*. (Boulder: Alta Mira Press, 2009), 321.

27. Esther Portillo (board member, Salvadoran American National Association), interview, Fontana, California, February 1, 2008.

28. Rosalio Muñoz (*People's Weekly World*), interview, Highland Park, California, February 13, 2008; Victor Narro (director of the UCLA Labor Center), interview, Westlake, California, February 11, 2008.

29. Juan Gómez-Quiñones, "Toward a Perspective on Chicano History," *Aztlán* 2, no. 2 (1971): 1–49.

30. Claudia Núñez, "La Clave Está en la Radio," *La Presna* (Riverside, California), March 31, 2006.

31. Ibid.

32. "Obispos y Empresarios Apoyan El Gran Paro Nacional," *El Sol: Voz Latina del Inland Empire*, April 19, 2006.

33. Amalia Pallares and Nilda Flores-Gonzalez, *Marcha! Latino Chicago and the Immigrant Rights Movement* (Chicago: University of Illinois Press, 2010).

34. Field notes, Los Angeles, March 25, 2006.

35. Narro, interview, Westlake, California, February 11, 2008.

36. Carlos Muñoz, *Youth, Identity, Power: The Chicano Movement* (New York: Verso Books, 2007); Juan Gómez-Quiñones, *Mexican Students por La Raza: The Chicano Student Movement in Southern California, 1967–1977* (Santa Barbara, CA: Editorial La Causa, 1978).

37. Narro, interview, Westlake, California, February 11, 2008.

38. Cynthia H. Cho and Joel Rubin, "High School Students Extend Immigration Protests into Fourth Day," *Los Angeles Times*, March 27, 2006.

39. Robert Jablon, "School Walkouts Continue in California to Protest Immigration Bill," Associated Press, March 27, 2006.

40. Field notes, Santa Ana, California, March 27, 2006.

41. Mario Martínez (field organizer, Hermandad Mexicana-Latinoamericana), interview, Riverside, California, February 9, 2008.

42. Jose Ortega, "Mega-Marcha," *La Opinión* (Los Angeles), March 26, 2006.

43. Ron Gochez (coordinator, Union Del Barrio), interview, Los Angeles, California, June 8, 2008.

44. Field notes, Santa Ana, California, March 27, 2006.

45. Angelica Salas (executive director, Coalition for Humane Immigrant Rights of Los Angeles), interview, Los Angeles, California, February 21, 2008.

46. Narro, interview, Westlake, California, February 11, 2008.

47. Gochez, interview; Juan Jose Gutiérrez, interview, East Los Angeles, California, February 21, 2006.

48. Gochez, interview, Los Angeles, California, June 8, 2008.

49. Rachel L. Swarns, "Cardinal Mahoney: Immigrant Groups Plan Campaign to Bring Legal Changes," *New York Times*, April 20, 2006.

50. Teresa Gaouette and Nicole Watanabe, "Marchers Fill LA's Streets," *Los Angeles Times*, May 2, 2006.

51. Gaouette and Watanabe, "Marchers Fill LA's Streets."

52. David Streitfeld, "Throngs Show Their Potent Role in Economy," *Los Angeles Times*, May 2, 2006.

53. Nancy Cleeland, "Boycott Turns Panorama City Mall into Ghost Town," *Los Angeles Times*, May 2, 2006.

54. Streitfeld, "Throngs Show Potent Role."

55. Pallares and Flores-González, eds., *¡Marcha!*

56. P. J. Huffstutter, "Cities' Immigrants Spoke One Language This Time," *Los Angeles Times*, May 2, 2006.

57. Gillian Flaccus, "From LA to NY, Immigrants Raise Peaceful, But Boisterous Voices," *Press-Enterprise* (Riverside, California), May 2, 2006.

58. "Obispos y Empresarios," *El Sol.*

59. Ibid.

60. Arturo Carmona (executive director of COFEM), interview, Los Angeles, California, January 29, 2008.

61. Santa Ana, *Brown Tide Rising.*

62. Gaouette and Watanabe, "Marchers Fill LA's Streets"; Scott Gold, "When I See This I See Strength," *Los Angeles Times*, May 2, 2006; Ana Gorman and Marjorie Miller, "Immigrants Demonstrate Peaceful Power," *Los Angeles Times*, May 2, 2006.

63. Streitfeld, "Throngs Show Potent Role."

64. "Millions of Immigrants to Take Part in Mass Protest," *China Daily*, April 29, 2006, http://english.peopledaily.com.cn/200604/29/eng20060429_262132.html.

65. Securing America's Borders Act, S. 2454, 109th Cong. (2006). *Congressional Record* 152, no. 37 (March 29, 2006): S2511–S2526. http://www.gpo.gov/fdsys/pkg/CREC-2006-03-29/html/CREC-2006-03-29-pt1-PgS2511.htm.

66. Kelley, interview, Washington, D.C., July 1, 2010.

67. Salas, interview, Los Angeles, California, February 21, 2008.

68. Ali Noorani (RIFA chair and executive director of the National Immigration Forum), interview, Washington, D.C., June 29, 2011.

69. Nativo Lopez (executive director, Hermandad Mexicana-Latinoamericana), interview, Ontario, California, February 25, 2008

70. Ibid.

71. Manuel Roman (lead organizer, UNITE-HERE Local 11), interview, Chino, California, February 11, 2006.

72. Ibid.

73. Lopez, interview, Ontario, California, February 25, 2008.

74. *Selections from the Prison Notebooks of Antonio Gramsci*, 12.

75. Martínez, interview, Riverside, California, February 9, 2008.
76. Angelica Rivera, "Chicago Grassroots Resistance to Racial Profiling, Deportations, and Empire Building: The Case of Elvira Arellano y un Pueblo Sin Fronteras (One People Without Borders)" (paper presented at the Nuestra América Conference, Kansas University, Lawrence, Kansas, February 9, 2008).
77. Adalijiza Sosa Riddell, "Chicanas and El Movimiento," *Aztlán* 1, no. 2 (1974): 359–70.
78. *The Antonio Gramsci Reader*, 97.
79. Portillo, interview, Fontana, California, February 1, 2008.

Chapter 3

1. Emilio Amaya (executive director, San Bernardino Community Service Center), interview, San Bernardino, California, March 25, 2011.
2. Zepeda-Millán, "Today We March."
3. Alexandra Delano and Adrián Félix, "From Migrants to New Americans: Latinos and Civic Integration in the US" (paper presented at the International Studies Association Annual Meeting, New Orleans, February 2010), 24.
4. Varsanyi, *Taking Local Control* (see chap. 2, no. 10).
5. Board of Supervisors, Riverside County of California, http://www.countyofriverside.us/government/boardofsupervisors.html.
6. Hans Johnson, Deborah Reed, and Jose Hayes, *The Inland Empire in 2015* (San Francisco: Public Policy Institute of California, 2008).
7. Ibid.
8. For a discussion on Mexican Americans and the citrus industry in Riverside County, see José Alamillo, *Making Lemonade Out of Lemons: Mexican American Labor and Leisure in a California Town, 1880–1960* (Urbana: University of Illinois Press, 2006).
9. Despite this growth of Mexican and Central American communities in the Inland Empire, there is virtually no available research on this demographic phenomenon in Riverside County. Inland Southern California is not exactly a new destination for Latino migrant labor, given that the region has largely consisted of Mexican communities since it was part of Mexico. Nonetheless, the region has much in common with new destinations for migrants, where the emerging Mexican and Latino communities are upsetting the demographic balance in conservative areas, whose local state institutions often respond with coercive policies.
10. Sherry McNary, "Deporting Inmates: Program Aims to Save Money, Relieve Crowding Doing More Time," *Press-Enterprise*, January 27, 2007.
11. Agenda no. 3.23, Minutes of the Riverside County Board of Supervisors, April 11, 2006, Riverside, California.
12. Aarti Kohli and Deepa Varma, *Borders, Jails, and Jobsites: An Overview of Federal Immigration Enforcement Programs in the United States* (Berkeley: Chief Justice Earl Warren Institute on Race, Ethnicity, and Diversity, the University of California Berkeley School of Law, 2001), 13.
13. Ibid.
14. Tom Barry, "The Deterrence Strategy of Homeland Security," *CounterPunch*, June 7–9, 2008, http://www.counterpunch.org/2008/06/07/the-deterrence-strategy-of-homeland-security/.
15. McNary, "Deporting Inmates."
16. Kohli and Varma, *Borders, Jails, and Jobsites*, 13.
17. Ibid., 14.
18. Daniel Mears, "Immigration and Crime: What Is the Correlation?" *Federal Sentencing Reporter* 14, no. 2 (2002): 284–88.
19. Johnson et al., *The Inland Empire in 2015*.
20. Ibid.
21. For an excellent analysis of culture and the production of luxurious suburban spaces in the Inland Empire, see Juan D. De Lara, "Remapping Inland Southern California: Global Commodity Distribution, Land Speculation, and Politics in the Inland Empire" (PhD diss., University of California Berkeley, 2009).
22. Mario Barrera, *Race and Class in the Southwest: A Theory of Racial Inequality* (Notre Dame, IN: University of Notre Dame Press, 1979).

23. For a history of Southern California Indians, see Eduardo D. Castillo, "Short Overview of California Indian History" (California Native American Heritage Foundation, 1998), http://www.nahc.ca.gov/califindian.html.

24. Alamillo, *Making Lemonade*.

25. Mike Davis, *City of Quartz: Excavating the Future of Los Angeles* (New York: Verso Books, 1990).

26. Raymond Rocco, "Latino Los Angeles: Reframing Boundaries/Borders in Los Angeles" (unpublished manuscript, 2006).

27. Jeff Horsemen, "Southwest Part of County Still Mostly White," *Press-Enterprise*, March 14, 2011.

28. For a discussion on gentrification and Latino families leaving Los Angeles for the Inland Empire, see Steve Bender, *Tierra y Libertad: Land, Liberty, and Latino Housing* (New York: New York University Press, 2010).

29. Horsemen, "Southwest Part of County Still Mostly White."

30. Tiffany Ray and Vanessa Franco, "Change in Inland Landscape," *Press-Enterprise*, March 16, 2011.

31. David Gutiérrez, "Globalization, Labor Migration, and the Demographic Revolution: Ethnic Mexicans in the Late Twentieth Century," chap. 1 in *The Columbia History of Latinos in the United States since 1960*, ed. David Gutiérrez (New York: Columbia University Press, 2004), 43–86.

32. Robin M. Law and Jennifer R. Wolch, "Social Reproduction and the City: Restructuring in Time and Space," in *The Restless Urban Landscape*, ed. Paul Knox (Princeton, NJ: Princeton Hall, 1993), 165–206.

33. Delgado-Wise, "Forced Migration" (see introduction, n. 43).

34. Edna Bonacich and Jake B. Wilson, *Getting the Goods: Ports, Labor, and the Logistics Revolution* (Ithaca, NY: Cornell University Press, 2008), 136.

35. Formally unicorporated Mira Loma became part of the City of Jurupa Valley in 2011.

36. California Public Interest Research Group, *Citizen's Agenda* 13, no. 3 (1997): 4.

37. Martin Valdez Torres, "Indispensible Migrants: Mexican Workers and the Making of Twentieth-Century Los Angeles," in *Latino Los Angeles: Transformations, Communities, and Activism*, ed. Enrique C. Ochoa and Gilda L. Ochoa (Tucson: Arizona University Press, 2005), 23–37.

38. As geographer Juan de Lara noted in a conversation with the author, the number of Latino workers is actually much higher when one takes into account temporary workers in the region.

39. Agenda no. 3.23, Minutes of the Riverside County Board of Supervisors.

40. Ibid.

41. Ibid., emphasis added.

42. Ibid.

43. Ibid.

44. Ibid.

45. Ibid.

46. Amaya, interview, San Bernardino, California, March 25, 2011.

47. Ibid.

48. Ibid.

49. Daniel Guzmán (coordinator of the Diocese of San Bernardino Justice for Immigrants Campaign), interview, Fontana, California, March 26, 2011.

50. This statement is not to suggest that African Americans are exempt from racial profiling and police violence in Riverside County. On the contrary, the African American community was subject to profiling and racial violence in Riverside long before the Tyishia Miller case in 1995. However, Latinos are profiled in a different way, one in which their phenotypic features and cultural characteristics make them subject to the homeland security state and potential targets for deportation.

51. Guzmán, interview, Fontana, California, March 26, 2011.

52. Ibid.

53. Estela (pseudonym; community organizer from Temecula), interview, March 26, 2011. Pseudonym used by mutual agreement.

54. Sonja Bjelland, "In Deputy-Involved Fatal Shootings, Riverside County Tops LA County," *Press-Enterprise*, June 25, 2007.
55. Kenneth B. Noble, "Videotape of Beating by Authorities Jolts Los Angeles," *New York Times*, April 3, 1996.
56. Don Terry, "California Officers Cleared in Killing of Young Woman, Prompting Protests," *New York Times*, May 7, 1999.
57. "Border Patrol Remains Silent about Immigration Raids This Summer" (American Civil Liberties Union, December 15, 2004), http://www.aclu-sc.org/releases/view/100794.
58. Guzmán, interview, Fontana, California, March 26, 2011.
59. Jacquie Welsh and John Paul, "Officers, Family Differ over Death," *Press-Enterprise*, December 22, 2004.
60. Richard K. Atley, "Attorney General Says Deputies' Names Should Be Disclosed," Press-Enterprise, April 22, 2008.
61. Agenda no. 3.23, Minutes of the Riverside County Board of Supervisors.
62. Esther Portillo, interview, Brooklyn, New York, March 27, 2011.
63. Guzmán, interview, Fontana, California, March 26, 2011.
64. Ibid.
65. Amaya, interview, San Bernardino, California, March 25, 2011.
66. Ibid.
67. Estela interview, March 26, 2011.
68. Amaya, interview, San Bernardino, California, March 25, 2011.
69. Víctor Zúñiga and Rubén Hernández-León, *New Destinations: Mexican Immigration in the United States* (New York: Russell Sage Foundation, 2006).

Chapter 4

1. Mirna Perla (Supreme Court Justice, Supreme Court of El Salvador), interview, San Salvador, El Salvador, January 14, 2007. *"La gente que viene deportada, la tratan como el peor criminal que pueda haber en el mundo."*
2. Meissner et al., *Immigration Enforcement,* 118.
3. Elana Zilberg, *Spaces of Detention: The Making of a Transnational Gang Crisis Between Los Angeles and San Salvador* (Durham, NC: Duke University Press, 2011).
4. I do not engage the entire debate around the state and globalization in this chapter; scholars generally view the relationship between them along two ends of the same pole. At one end there is a tendency to view the state as "withering away." On the other end, the state is viewed as retaining its primacy in the international system. For a synopsis of the literature on the state in the era of globalization, see Aradhana Sharma and Akhil Gupta, "Introduction: Rethinking Theories of the State in the Era of Globalization," in *The Anthropology of the State,* ed. Sharma and Gupta, 1–41.
5. For a discussion on the nature of the state under capitalist globalization see Bob Jessop, "Narrating the Future of the National Economy and National State: Remarks on Remapping Regulation and Reinventing Governance," in *State/Culture: State Formation after the Cultural Turn,* ed. George Steinmetz (Ithaca, NY: Cornell University Press, 1999), 378–406; and Leslie Sklair, *Sociology of the Global System* (Baltimore: Johns Hopkins University Press, 2001).
6. Robinson, *A Theory of Global Capitalism,* 88 (see introduction, n. 40).
7. For more on Salvadoran transnationalism, see Leisy Abrego, "Rethinking El Salvador's Transnational Families," *NACLA Report on the Americas* 42, no. 6 (2010): 28–32; Cecilia Menjívar, *Fragmented Ties: Salvadoran Immigrant Networks in America* (Berkeley: University of California Press, 2000); Susan Coutin, "Cultural Logics of Belonging and Movement"; William I. Robinson, *Transnational Conflicts: Central America, Social Change, and Globalization* (New York: Verso Books, 2003).
8. Robinson, *Transnational Conflicts.*
9. Menjívar, *Fragmented Ties.*
10. De Genova, "The Production of Culprits" (see introduction, n. 3).
11. "Statement of Principles" (Project for a New American Century, June 3, 1997), http://www.newamericancentury.org/statementofprinciples.htm.

12. For more on Bush-era neoconservatives, see Greg Grandin, *Empire's Workshop: Latin America, the United States, and the Rise of the New Imperialism* (New York: Macmillan, 2007).

13. "El Salvador Withdraws Last Soldiers from Iraq," *USA Today*, February 7, 2009.

14. "Military and Police Aid and All Program Entire Region, 1996–2012," Just the Facts, accessed on February 5, 2013, http://justf.org/Print_All_Grants_Country?country=&year1=1996&year2=2012&subregion=Entire+Region&funding=All+Programs&x=212&y=14.

15. see Leslie Gil, *School of the Americas: Military Training and Political Violence in the Americas* (Durham, NC: Duke University Press, 2004); and Jennifer Schirmer, *The Guatemalan Military Project: A Violence Called Democracy* (Philadelphia: University of Pennsylvania Press, 1998).

16. For more on US military involvement in El Salvador, see Mario Lungo Ucles, *El Salvador in the Eighties: Counterinsurgency and Revolution* (Philadelphia: Temple University Press, 1990); William Stanley, *The Protection Racket State: Elite Politics, Military Extortion, and Civil War in El Salvador* (Philadelphia: Temple University Press, 1996); and Tommie Sue Montgomery, *Revolution in El Salvador: From Civil War to Civil Peace*, 2d ed. (Boulder, CO: Westview Press, 1996).

17. For more on national security regimes in Latin America, see Charles Call, "War Transitions and the New Civilian Security in Latin America," *Comparative Politics* 35, no. 1 (2002): 1–20; Paul Zagorski, *Democracy vs. National Security: Civil-Military Relations in Latin America* (Boulder, CO: Lynne Rienner, 1992); and Brian Loveman and Thomas M. Davies Jr., *The Politics of Anti-Politics: The Military in Latin America* (Wilmington, DE: Scholarly Resources, 1997).

18. Tom Barry, "Mission Creep" in Latin America–US Southern Command's New Security Strategy (International Research Center, America's Program, July 2005), http://nlgmltf.org/pdfs/Mission_Creep.pdf.

19. *Posture Statement of General Bantz J. Craddock, United States Army Commander US Southern Command, before the 109th Congress Senate Armed Services Committee*, US Southern Command, March 14, 2006, http://www.armed-services.senate.gov/statemnt/2005/March/Craddock%2003-15-05.pdf.

20. Ibid.

21. M. V. Bhatia, "Fighting Words: Naming Terrorists, Bandits, Rebels, and Other Violent Actors," *Third World Quarterly* 26, no. 1 (2005): 5–22.

22. Alberto Gonzales, "Prepared Remarks of Attorney General at the Press Conference Following Bilateral Meetings in El Salvador," *San Salvador*, February 5, 2007, http://www.justice.gov/archive/ag/speeches/2007/ag_speech_070205.html.

23. Manuel Bermúdez, "Central America: Gang Violence and Anti-Gang Death Squads," Inter Press Service, September 6, 2005, http://www.ipsnews.net/2005/09/central-america-gang-violence-and-anti-gang-death-squads/.

24. Kathryn Tarker, "Too Close for Comfort: El Salvador Ratches Up US Ties," *Council on Hemispheric Affairs*, July 19, 2005, http://www.coha.org/too-close-for-comfort-el-salvador-ratchets-up-its-us-ties/.

25. For more on conservative think tanks, see Stefancic and Delgado, *No Mercy* (see chap. 1, n. 2).

26. Exxon Mobil Corporation, 2010 Contributions and Community Investments, accessed on February 5, 2013, http://exxonmobil.com/Corporate/Files/gcr_contributions_pubpolicy-2010.pdf.

27. Stephen Johnson and David B. Muhlhausen, *North American Transnational Youth Gangs: Breaking the Chain of Violence* (Washington, D.C.: Heritage Foundation, 2005), http://www.heritage.org/research/reports/2005/03/north-american-transnational-youth-gangs-breaking-the-chain-of-violence.

28. Ibid.

29. Ibid.

30. For more on neoliberalism and migration among Salvadorans, see Edur Velasco Arregui and Richard Roman, "Perilous Passage: Central American Migration through Mexico," in *Latino*

Los Angeles: Transformations, Communities, and Activism, ed. Enrique C. Ochoa and Gilda L. Ochoa (Tucson: University of Arizona Press, 2005), 38–62.

31. Robinson, *Transnational Conflicts,* 309–10.
32. Ibid.
33. Ibid.
34. Fundación de Estudios para la Aplicación del Derecho and Centro de Estudios Penales de El Salvador, *Informe Anual Sobre Justicia Penal Juvenil en El Salvador 2004* (San Salvador, El Salvador: Fundación de Estudios para la Aplicación del Derecho, 2005).
35. Alfonso Gonzales, *Rethinking US Involvement in the War on Gangs in Central America: The Case of El Salvador* (Washington, D.C.: Institute for Policy Studies, 2006).
36. "Informe de PDDH confirma existencia de Escuadrones de la Muerte," *Diario CoLatino* (San Salvador), June, 28, 2005.
37. Manuel Bermúdez, "Gang Violence and Anti-Gang Death Squads," Inter Press Service, September 6, 2005, http://www.ipsnews.net/news.asp?idnews=30163.
38. Mirna Perla, interview, San Salvador, January 15, 2007. *"Aquí a cualquier persona que mandan de ayá, seguro que lo van a matar. Eso, lo van a matar, o destruir moralmente."*
39. Javier (pseudonym), interview, San Salvador, El Salvador, January 14, 2007.
40. Zilberg, *Spaces of Detention,* 11.
41. Javier, interview, San Salvador, El Salvador, January 14, 2007.
42. Ibid.
43. Ibid.
44. Zilberg, *Spaces of Detention,* 46.
45. Javier, interview, San Salvador, El Salvador, January 14, 2007.
46. For more on El Salvador's post-peace accord security system, see Call, "War Transitions"; and Mary Popkin, *Peace Without Justice: Obstacles to Building the Rule of Law in El Salvador* (Philadelphia: Pennsylvania State University Press, 2000).
47. Marcos (pseudonym), interview, San Salvador, El Salvador, January 14, 2007.
48. Ibid.
49. Bureau of Democracy, Human Rights, and Labor, US Department of State, Country Report on Human Rights Practices 2005—El Salvador, March 8, 2006, http://www.state.gov/j/drl/rls/hrrpt/2005/61727.htm.
50. Javier, interview, San Salvador, El Salvador, January 14, 2007.
51. David C. Brotherton and Luis Barrios, *Banished to the Homeland: Dominican Deportees and Their Stories of Exile* (New York: Columbia University Press, 2011).
52. Marcos, interview, San Salvador, El Salvador, January 14, 2007.
53. Carlos (pseudonym), interview, San Salvador, El Salvador, January 13, 2007.
54. An important exception to this was Dr. Esencio, who was a subcommissioner of the PNC and a Farabundo Marti Front for National Liberation combatant during the civil war. He often spoke about neoliberalism and social exclusion as the main reason why gangs and crime had gotten out of control.
55. Roberto (pseudonym), interview, San Salvador, El Salvador, January 3, 2007. (*Bueno aquí de deportados ay realmente... que el gobierno le ha dado mucha propaganda negativa. Porque ahora si los problemas sociales que el país tiene se lo quieren hacerlo ver a otra gente ósea,... cuando el gobierno no puede con lo que tiene entonces tratando de hacerla la manera de que alguien page por lo que hiso. Cuando yo llegue en el 2003 esto aquí no estaba. Entonces ahora la criminalidad ha aumentado, y el gobierno no puede estar en el lugar equivocado y la hora equivocado. Entonces alguien tiene que pagar los platos rotos y que mejor que el deportado.*)
56. Perla, interview. (*Por supuesto, ósea ellos nunca les dan protección la policía. Si ellos dicen miren yo quiero que me ayuden, me están amenazando, me están persiguiendo, me está extorsionando, me están... ni siquiera dentro de la prisión se hace. Por qué ayá extorsionan a la gente, les dicen si no me das 500 dólares el día. Cuando venga tu familia, te vamos a matar o te vamos a violar, o te vamos hacer esto. A la gente la agreden ahí. Y la policía no es capaz de hacer nada menos hacer algo. Ah esta gente normalmente, no les da ningún tipo de protección. Al contrario los tienen estigmatizados y cada vez han resuelto algún crimen a ellos los van a traer. Aunque no hayan cometido nada y estén tratando de portarse bien. Algunos de ellos incluso cuando salen de la cárcel, se quedan solo en la casa con miedo que no salgan. Pero, ahí los capturan o los persiguen. Y si van a pedir una ayuda obviamente no se la pueden dar.*)

57. International Human Rights Clinic, *Nowhere to Hide: Gang, State, and Clandestine Violence in El Salvador* (Cambridge, MA: Harvard Law School, 2007), http://www.law.harvard.edu/programs/hrp/documents/FinalElSalvadorReport%283-6-07%29.pdf.

58. Brotherton and Barrios, *Banished to the Homeland*.

Chapter 5

1. Julia Preston, "In Big Shift, Latino Vote Was Heavily for Obama," *New York Times*, November 6, 2008.

2. Erin Kelly, "Obama's 1st Year Sets Record for Hispanic Nominations," *Arizona Republic*, August 31, 2009, http://www.azcentral.com/arizonarepublic/news/articles/2009/08/31/20090831hispanics0831.html.

3. Forgacs, ed., *The Antonio Gramsci Reader*, 423.

4. Ibid.

5. Stuart Hall, *Hard Road to Renewal: Thatcherism and the Crisis of the Left* (New York: Verso, 1988), 132.

6. I use pseudonyms for all of the activists whom I interviewed at actions or marches in Washington, D.C., and in New York City, unless given permission to use the actual name of the interviewee. Interviews were conducted in English and in Spanish. I asked people their name, country of origin, and why there were participating. I conducted all of these interviews on the street during an action or march, with noise and a heavy police presence in most cases. In contrast, the interviews that I conducted with organizers and political operatives associated with the migrant rights movement were almost always conducted in English and in an office or calm spaces, where they retrospectively reflected on the broader movement and the specific actions such as marches, rallies, or lobby efforts.

7. Forgacs, ed., *The Antonio Gramsci Reader*, 250.

8. Ibid., 218.

9. Ibid.

10. Félix et al., "Political Protest, Ethnic Media, and Latino Naturalization"; Zepeda-Millán, "Today We March."

11. Eliseo Medina (secretary-treasurer, SEIU), interview, Washington, D.C., June 28, 2011.

12. Ricardo Ramírez and Olga Medina, *Catalysts and Barriers to Attaining Citizenship: An Analysis of Ya Es Hora ¡Ciudadania!* (Washington, D.C.: National Council of La Raza, 2011).

13. "Barack Obama at the LULAC Convention," YouTube video, posted by BarackObama.com, July 8, 2008, http://www.youtube.com/watch?v=fx8-h1WdEbg. From a speech at the League of United Latin American Citizens convention on July 8, 2008.

14. Matt Barreto. "Record Latino Voter Turnout in 2008 Helps Obama Win Key Battleground States," *Latino Decisions*, November 19, 2008, http://www.latinodecisions.com/blog/2008/11/19/record-latino-voter-turnout-in-2008-helps-obama-win-key-battleground-states/.

15. Noorani, interview, Washington, D.C., January 29, 2011.

16. Ibid.

17. Ibid.

18. Ibid.

19. Michael Scherer, "Inside Obama's Factory of Ideas," *Time*, November 21, 2008, http://www.time.com/time/politics/article/0,8599,1861305,00.html#ixzz1V2V2hNIh.

20. Kelley, interview, Washington, D.C., July 1, 2011.

21. Scherer, "Inside Obama's Factory of Ideas."

22. Carrie Budoff Brown, "Dems' Tough New Immigration Pitch," *Politico*, June 10, 2010, http://www.politico.com/news/stories/0610/38342.html.

23. Kelley, interview, Washington, D.C., June 30, 2011.

24. Gustavo Andrade (organizing director, CASA de Maryland), interview, Washington, D.C., June 28, 2011.

25. Noorani, interview, Washington, D.C., June 29, 2011.

26. Elsa (pseudonym), interview, Washington, D.C., January 26, 2010.

27. Fernandez and Olson, "To Live and Work" (see introduction, n. 26).

28. Tony (pseudonym), interview, Washington, D.C., January 27, 2010.

29. Kelley, interview, Washington, D.C., June 30, 2011.
30. María (pseudonym), interview, Washington, D.C., January 27, 2010.
31. Gustavo Torres (executive director, CASA De Maryland), public speech, Washington D.C., January 27, 2010.
32. Javier Valdez (co-executive director, Make the Road New York), interview, Brooklyn, New York, June 23, 2010.
33. Andrade, interview, Washington, D.C., June 28, 2011.
34. Alonso (pseudonym), interview, Washington, D.C., March 21, 2010.
35. Alyssa (pseudonym), interview, Washington, D.C., March 21, 2010.
36. Ibid.
37. Sylvia Herrera (organizer, Puente Arizona), interview, Washington, D.C., March 21, 2010.
38. Jamie Contreras (capital-area district chair, SEIU Local 32BJ), interview, New York City, June 8, 2011.
39. Janis Rosheuvel (executive director, Families for Freedom), interview, Brooklyn, New York, May 17, 2011.
40. Contreras, interview, New York City, June 8, 2011.
41. Ibid.
42. Kelley, interview, Washington, D.C., June 30, 2011.
43. Charles Schumer and Lindsey Graham, "The Right Way to Mend Immigration," *Washington Post*, March 19, 2010.
44. Clarrisa Martinez de Castro (director of immigration and national campaigns, National Council of La Raza), interview, Washington, D.C., July 1, 2011.
45. Perry Bacon Jr., "Democrats Unveil Immigration-Reform Proposal," *Washington Post*, April 29, 2010.
46. Emphasis in the original. "Real Enforcement with Practical Answers for Immigration Reform (REPAIR) Proposal" (Immigration Policy Center, American Immigration Council, May 3, 2010), http://www.immigrationpolicy.org/just-facts/real-enforcement-practical-answers-immigration-reform-repair-proposal-summary.
47. Emphasis in the original, Ibid.
48. Reform Immigration for America, "Immigration Reform Gathers Steam as Democrats Release Comprehensive Outline" (press release), April 29, 2010.
49. Kelley, interview, Washington, D.C., June 30, 2011.
50. Melanie Dulfo (BAYAN USA), interview, Manhattan, June 10, 2011.
51. Teresa Gutiérrez (coordinator, May 1 Coalition for Immigrant and Workers Rights), interview, Queens, New York, June 3, 2011.
52. Rhamades Rivera (vice president, SEIU Local 1199), interview, New York City, June 24, 2011.
53. Guitiérrez, interview, Queens, New York, June 3, 2011.
54. The organizers from these unions supported the May 1 rally at Union Square in direct defiance of the union leadership.
55. Juan (pseudonym) interview, New York City, May 1, 2010.
56. Zoila (pseudonym) interview, New York City, May 1, 2010.
57. Sabia (pseudonym) interview, New York City, May 1, 2010.
58. Rivera, interview, New York City, June 24, 2011.
59. Valdez, interview, Brooklyn, New York, June 23, 2010.
60. Clarissa Martínez De Castro (director of Immigration and National Campaigns, National Council of La Raza), interview, Washington, D.C., July 1, 2011.
61. Juan Carlos Ruiz (New Sanctuary Movement), interview, Manhattan, New York, June 10, 2011.
62. Meissner et al., *Immigration Enforcement in the United States,* 129–30.
63. Department of Homeland Security, "Secretary Napolitano Announces Record-Breaking Immigration Enforcement Statistics Achieved Under the Obama Administration" (press release), October 6, 2010, http://www.dhs.gov/ynews/releases/pr_1286389936778.shtm.
64. Spencer S. Hsu, "Obama Revives Bush Idea to Catch Illegal Workers," *Washington Post*, July 9, 2009.
65. Meissner et al., *Immigration Enforcement in the United States,* 84.
66. Ibid.
67. Ibid., 113.

68. Ibid., 115.
69. Shankar Vedantam, "No Opt-Out for Immigration Enforcement," *Washington Post,* October 1, 2010.
70. Meissner et al., 116.
71. Meissner et al., 26.
72. Meissner et al., 31.
73. Fernandez and Olson, "To Live and Work."
74. RIFA would argue otherwise and point to its polling on support for CIR.
75. Kelley, interview, Washington, D.C., June 30, 2011.
76. This term has many meaning in Mexican Spanish, but in this context it has the English equivalent to the word *dude.* Manuel (pseudonym), interview, Brooklyn, New York, February 2013

Chapter 6

1. Mark Hugo Lopez and Ana Gonzalez-Barrera, Inside the 2012 Latino Electorate (Pew Hispanic Center, June 3, 2008). http://www.pewhispanic.org/files/2013/05/the-latino-electorate_2013-06.pdf.
2. Matt Barreto and Gary Segura, 2012 Election Eve Poll (ImpreMedia/Latino Decisions, November 7, 2012), http://www.latinodecisions.com/files/3513/5232/9137/LEE_PRESENTATION_2012.pdf.
3. Ibid.
4. Ibid.
5. Ibid.
6. Ibid.
7. Lopez and Gonzalez-Barrera, Inside the 2012 Latino Electorate.
8. Oakford and Vanessa Cardenas, Infographic: The Growth of the Latino Electorate in Key States (Center for American Progress, February 28, 2013), http://www.americanprogress.org/issues/race/news/2013/02/28/54251/infographic-the-growth-of-the-latino-electorate-in-key-states-2/.
9. Paul Taylor, Ana Barrera-Gonzalez, Jeffery Passel, and Mark Hugo Lopez, Awakened Giant, Hispanic Electorate Is Likely to Double by 2030, (Pew Hispanic Center, November 14, 2012). http://www.pewhispanic.org/2012/11/14/an-awakened-giant-the-hispanic-electorate-is-likely-to-double-by-2030/.
10. Matt Barreto and Gary Segura, 2012 Election Eve Poll.
11. "Raul Ruiz Defeats Mary Bono Mack in Riverside County Upset," *Los Angeles Times,* November 7, 2012.
12. Ibid.
13. Joe Feagin, *White Party, White Government: Race, Class, and US Politics* (London: Routledge, 2012), 206.
14. Pete Kasperowicz, "House Votes to Defund Obama's 'Administrative Amnesty' for Immigrants," *The Hill,* June, 6, 2013, http://thehill.com/blogs/floor-action/house/303869-house-votes-to-defund-obamas-administrative-amnesty-for-immigrants#ixzz2VbW2cNLd.
15. Although the racial dimensions to the Latin Americanization of Latino politics are strong, it should be noted that this does not mean that Latinos of Afro or indigenous descent cannot become honorary parts of this elite. Eduardo Bonilla-Silva and David R. Dietrich, "The Latin Americanization of US Race Relations: A New Pigmentocracy," in *Shades of Difference: Why Skin Color Matters,* ed. Evelyn Nakano Glenn (Stanford, CA: Stanford University Press, 2009) 40–60.
16. Arnold, *American Immigration Politics after 1996.*
17. Ibid.
18. Albert R. Hunt, "Republicans to Watch on Immigration," *New York Times,* June 16, 2013, http://www.nytimes.com/2013/06/17/us/17iht-letter17.html?_r=1&.
19. Peter Schey, Analysis of Senate Bill 744's Pathway to Legalization and Citizenship (Center for Human and Constitutional Rights, June 2013), http://www.centerforhumanrights.org/6-18-13%20CHRCL-Peter%20Schey%20Analysis%20Senate%20Bill%20Legalization%20Program.pdf.

20. Elise Foley, "Immigration Reform Framework Includes Citizenship, Drones, and Dreamers," *Huffington Post*, January 28, 2013, http://www.huffingtonpost.com/2013/01/28/immigration-reform-framework_n_2566494.html.

21. Foley, "Immigration Reform Framework."

22. Black Alliance for Just Immigration, "Senate Immigration Bill Goes from Bad to Worse," June 28, 2013, http://www.blackalliance.org/senate-immigration-bill-goes-from-bad-to-worse/.

23. National Network for Immigrant and Refugee Rights, "Senate Nears Vote on Flawed Immigration Bill" [press blog], June 26, 2013, http://www.nnirr.org/drupal/senate-nears-vote-on-flawed-immigration-bill.

24. "McCain: US Will Have 'The Most Militarized Border Since the Fall of the Berlin Wall,'" *RT*, June 25, 2013, http://rt.com/usa/mccain-border-berlin-wall-226/.

25. Detention Watch Network, "House Appropriations Committee Approves $147 Million More to Detain Immigrants" [press release], May 23, 2013, http://detentionwatchnetwork.wordpress.com/2013/05/23/house-appropriations-committee-approves-147-million-more-to-detain-immigrants/.

26. National Immigrant Justice Center, Heartland Alliance Program, "The Good & Bad in S. 744: Border Security, Economic Competitiveness, and Immigration Modernization Act of 2013," http://www.immigrantjustice.org/immigrationreform/s744analysis#.UdFYsvlgdrt.

27. Greg Sargent, "Can Immigration Reform Pass in the House? Maybe," *Washington Post*, July 8, 2013, http://www.washingtonpost.com/blogs/plum-line/wp/2013/07/08/can-immigration-reform-pass-the-house-maybe/?print=1.

28. Ibid.

29. Maegan Ortiz, "Hispanic Caucus Repeats Same Old Immigration Reform Policy," *Politics365*, November 28, 2012, http://politic365.com/2012/11/28/hispanic-caucus-reiterates-same-old-comprehensive-immigration-reform-principles/.

30. Gonzalez, *Guest Workers or Colonized Labor*, 154.

31. Richard Vogal, "Transient Servitude: The Guest Workers Program For Exploiting Mexican and Central American Workers," *Monthly Review* 25, no. 8 (2007), http://monthlyreview.org/2007/01/01/transient-servitude-the-u-s-guest-worker-program-for-exploiting-mexican-and-central-american-workers.

32. Clare Ribando Seelke and Kristen M. Finklea, "US–Mexican Security Cooperation: The Merida Initiative and Beyond," Congressional Research Service, June 12, 2013, 22. http://fpc.state.gov/documents/organization/210921.pdf.

33. Robyn Magalit Rodriguez, *Migrants for Export: How the Philippine State Brokers Labor to the World* (Minneapolis: University of Minnesota Press, 2010), xxii

34. Nicos Poulantzas, *State Power Socialism* (London: Verso Books) 1978, 211.

35. Jason Cherkis and Zach Carter, "FBI Surveillance of Occupy Wall Street Detailed," *Huffington Post*, January 5, 2013, http://www.huffingtonpost.com/2013/01/05/fbi-occupy-wall-street_n_2410783.html.

36. Poulantzas, *State Power Socialism*, 212.

37. Michelle Alexander, *The New Jim Crow: Mass Incarceration in the Age of Colorblindness* (New York: New Press, 2010).

38. Ibid., 215.

39. Tanya Maria Golash-Boza, *Immigration Nation: Raids, Detentions, and Deportations in Post-9/11 America* (Boulder, CO: Paradigm Publishers, 2012), 169.

40. Ibid, 141.

41. Raymond Rocco, "The Structuring of Latino Politics: Neoliberalism and Incorporation," *NACLA Report on the America* 43, no. 6 (2010): 40–43.

42. Poulantzas, *State Power Socialism*, 237.

43. Americas Voice, "Landmark Immigration Bill Passes" [blog], June 27, 2013, http://americasvoiceonline.org/blog/landmark-immigration-bill-passes-senate-68-32/.

44. Hermandad Mexicana, "Border Militarization Amendment Prevails with Majority Democratic Vote: No Faustian Barging for Us" [press release], June 27, 2013.

45. Michelle Chen, "No Papers, No Fear" In *These Times*, August 6, 2013, http://inthesetimes.com/article/15402/no_papers_no_fear_9_activists_push_the_boundaries_of_the_immigrant_rights_m/

46. Alfonso Gonzales, "Power, Justice, and Survival: Latino Politics in the 21st Century," *NACLA Report on the Americas* 43, no. 6 (2010): 13–14, https://nacla.org/news/power-justice-and-survival-latino-politics-21st-century.

47. Forgacs, ed., *The Antonio Gramsci Reader*, 209.

Appendix

1. I do not wish to suggest that data from the Latino National Survey cannot be used to highlight, sustain, and perhaps even challenge certain aspects of Latino political life. It provides an important set of data, but it is limited for understanding the politics of the homeland security state and of Latino migrant activism to a certain extent.

2. Stephen Van Evera, *Guide to Methods for Students of Political Science* (Ithaca, NY: Cornell University Press, 1997), 4–5.

3. Ibid.

4. Richard J.F. Day, *Gramsci Is Dead: Anarchist Currents in the Newest Social Movements* (London: Pluto Press, 2005).

5. For discussions of Gramsci and social movements, see Stuart Hall, Chas Critcher, Tony Jefferson, and Brian Roberts, *Policing the Crisis: Mugging, The State and Law and Order* (London: McMillan, 1978); David Morton, *Unravelling Gramsci: Hegemony and Passive Revolution in the Global Political Economy* (London: Pluto Press, 2007); and William I. Robinson, "Gramsci and Globalization: From Nation-State to Transnational Hegemony," *Critical Review of International Social and Political Philosophy* 8, no. 4 (2005): 1–16. For a Gramscian analysis of Afro-Brazilian social movements, see Michael G. Hanchard, *Orpheus and Power: The "Movimento Negro" of Rio de Janeiro and São Paulo, Brazil, 1945–1988* (Princeton, NJ: Princeton University Press, 1994). For more on the uses of Gramsci by movements in Latin America, see Raúl Burgos, "The Gramscian Intervention in the Theoretical and Political Production of the Latin American Left," trans. Carlos Pérez, *Latin American Perspectives* 29, no. 1 (2002): 9–37.

6. A wider set of conceptual tools such as "historic bloc," "integral state," "organic intellectuals," "common sense," and "passive revolution" are among his most important contributions.

7. Forgacs, ed., *The Gramsci Reader*, 209.

8. Teun A. Van Dijk, "Critical Discourse Analysis," in *The Handbook of Discourse Analysis*, ed. Deborah Schiffrin, Deborah Tannen, and Heidi E. Hamilton (Malden, MA: Blackwell Publishers, 2001), 352–71. Emphasis in the original.

9. Soyini D. Madison, *Critical Ethnography, Method, Ethics, and Performance* (Thousand Oaks, CA: SAGE Publications, 2005), 1–16.

10. Douglas S. Massey, Jorge Durand, and Nolan Malone, *Beyond Smoke and Mirrors: Mexican Immigration in an Era of Economic Integration* (New York: Russell Sage Foundation, 2002); Wayne Cornelius, "Death at the Border: Efficacy and Unintended Consequences of US Immigration Control Policy," *Population and Development Review* 27, no. 4 (2001): 661–85; Timothy Dunn, *Militarization of the US–Mexico Border: Low Intensity Conflict Doctrine Comes Home* (Austin: University of Texas Press, 1996); and Joseph Nevins, *Operation Gatekeeper: The Rise of the "Illegal" Alien and the Making of the US–Mexico Boundary* (London: Routledge, 2002).

11. Cornelius, "Death at the Border"; and Nevins, *Operation Gatekeeper*.

12. Varsanyi, *Taking Local Control* (see chap. 2, n. 10); also see Lina Newton, *Illegal, Alien, or Immigrant: The Politics of Immigration Reform* (New York: New York University Press, 2008).

13. Tanya Maria Golash-Boza, *Immigration Nation: Raids, Detentions, and Deportations in Post-9/11 America* (Boulder, CO: Paradigm Publishers, 2012).

14. For an important exception to this, see Arnold, *Immigration Politics after 1996*.

15. For an example, see Fraga et al., *Making It Home*, and Rodolfo Espino, David Leal, and Kenneth Meier, eds., *Latino Politics: Identity, Mobilization, and Representation* (Charlottesville: University of Virginia Press, 2008).

16. Rodney E. Hero, *Latinos and the US Political System: Two-Tiered Pluralism* (Philadelphia: Temple University Press, 1992), 190.
17. Rocco, "The Structuring of Latino Politics."
18. Lisa García Bedolla, *Introduction to Latino Politics in the US* (Cambridge, UK: Polity Press, 2009).
19. Arnold, *American Immigration after 1996.*
20. Leo Chavez, *The Latino Threat: Constructing Immigrants, Citizens, and the Nation* (Stanford, CA: Stanford University Press, 2008).
21. See Nicholas De Genova and Nathalie Peutz, eds., *The Deportation Regime: Sovereignty, Space, and the Freedom of Movement* (Durham, NC: Duke University Press, 2010); and Nicholas De Genova, "The Legal Production of Mexican/Migrant 'Illegality,'" *Latino Studies*, no. 2 (2004): 160–85.
22. Also see De Genova, "The Production of Culprits" (see introduction, n. 3).
23. For more on this approach, see Paul Apostolidis, *Breaks in the Chain: What Immigrant Workers Can Teach America about Democracy* (Minneapolis: University of Minnesota Press, 2010); Cristina Beltrán, *The Trouble with Unity: Latino Politics and the Creation of Identity* (New York: Oxford University Press, 2010); Edwina Barvosa, *Wealth of Selves: Multiple Identities, Mestiza Consciousness, and the Subject of Politics* (College Station: Texas A&M University Press, 2008); and Victor M. Valle and Rodolfo D. Torres, *Latino Metropolis* (Minneapolis: University of Minnesota Press, 2000).
24. Beltrán, *The Trouble with Unity.*

SELECTED BIBLIOGRAPHY

Abrego, Leisy. "Rethinking El Salvador's Transnational Families." *NACLA Report on the Americas* 42 no. 6 (2010): 28–32.

Abrego, Leisy, and Cecilia Menjívar. "Immigrant Latina Mothers as Targets of Legal Violence." *International Journal of Sociology of the Family* 37, no. 1 (2012): 9–26.

Acuña, Rodolfo. *Occupied America: A History of Chicanos.* 6th ed. (New York: Pearson Longman, 2000).

Alamillo, José. *Making Lemonade Out of Lemons: Mexican American Labor and Leisure in a California Town, 1880–1960* (Urbana: University of Illinois Press, 2006).

Apostolidis, Paul. *Breaks in the Chain: What Immigrant Workers Can Teach America about Democracy* (Minneapolis: University of Minnesota Press, 2010).

Arregui, Edur Velasco, and Richard Roman. "Perilous Passage: Central American Migration Through Mexico." In *Latino Los Angeles: Transformations, Communities, and Activism,* edited by Enrique Ochoa and Gilda L. Ochoa, 38–62 (Tucson: University of Arizona Press, 2005).

Barrera, Mario. *Race and Class in the Southwest: A Theory of Racial Inequality* (Notre Dame, IN: University of Notre Dame Press, 1979).

Barvosa, Edwina. *Wealth of Selves: Multiple Identities, Mestiza Consciousness, and the Subject of Politics* (College Station: Texas A&M University Press, 2008).

Behdad, Ali. *Forgetful Nation: On Immigration and Cultural Identity in the United States* (Durham, NC: Duke University Press, 2005).

Beltrán, Cristina. *The Trouble with Unity: Latino Politics and the Creation of Identity* (New York: Oxford University Press, 2010).

Bender, Steve. *Tierra y Libertad: Land, Liberty, and Latino Housing* (New York: New York University Press, 2010).

Bhatia, M. V. "Fighting Words: Naming Terrorists, Bandits, Rebels, and Other Violent Actors." *Third World Quarterly* 26, no. 1 (2005): 5–22.

Bloemraad, Irene, and Kim Voss. *Rallying for Immigrant Rights: The Fight for Inclusion in 21st Century America* (Berkeley: University of California Press, 2011).

Bonacich, Edna, and Jake B. Wilson. *Getting the Goods: Ports, Labor, and the Logistics Revolution* (Ithaca, NY: Cornell University Press, 2008).

Bonilla-Silva, Eduardo. "The Latin Americanization of U.S. Race Relations: A New Pigmentocracy." In *Shades of Difference: Why Skin Color Matters,* edited by Evelyn Nakano Glenn, 40–60 (Stanford, CA: Stanford University Press, 2009).

———. *Racism Without Racists: Color-Blind Racism and the Persistence of Racial Inequality* (New York: Rowman & Littlefield, 2003).

———. *White Supremacy and Racism in the Post–Civil Rights Era* (Boulder, CO: Lynne Rienner, 2001).

Brotherton, David C., and Luis Barrios. *Banished to the Homeland: Dominican Deportees and Their Stories of Exile* (New York: Columbia University Press, 2011).

Burghart, Devin, and Steven Gardiner, *"Lady Liberty No More: The Rise of the New Nativism."* Unpublished manuscript, 2011.

Burgos, Raúl. "The Gramscian Intervention in the Theoretical and Political Production of the Latin American Left." Translated by Carlos Pérez. *Latin American Perspectives* 29, no. 1 (2002): 9–37.

Call, Charles. "War Transitions and the New Civilian Security in Latin America." *Comparative Politics* 35, no. 1 (2002): 1–20.

Chávez, Ernesto. *Mi Raza Primero! (My People First!): Nationalism, Identity, and Insurgency in the Chicano Movement in Los Angeles, 1966–1978* (Berkeley: University of California Press, 2002).

Cornelius, Wayne. "Death at the Border: Efficacy and Unintended Consequences of US Immigration Control Policy." *Population and Development Review* 27, no. 4 (2001): 661–85.

Coutin, Susan Bibler. "Cultural Logics of Belonging and Movement: Transnationalism, Naturalization, and US Immigration Politics." In *The Anthropology of the State: A Reader*, edited by Sharma Aradhana and Akhil Gupta, 310–36. (Malden, MA: Blackwell Publishing, 2006).

———. *Nation of Emigrants: Shifting Boundaries of Citizenship in El Salvador and the United States* (Ithaca, NY: Cornell University Press, 2007).

Davis, Angela. *Are Prisons Obsolete?* (New York: Seven Stories Press, 2003).

Davis, Mike. *City of Quartz: Excavating the Future of Los Angeles* (New York: Verso Books, 1990).

Dawson, Michael C. *Behind the Mule: Race and Class in African-American Politics* (Princeton, NJ: Princeton University Press, 1994).

De Genova, Nicholas. "The Legal Production of Mexican/Migrant 'Illegality.' " *Latino Studies* 2, no. 2 (2004): 160–85.

———. "The Production of Culprits: From Deportability to Detainability in the Aftermath of Homeland Security." *Citizenship Studies* 11, no. 5 (2007): 421–48.

De Genova, Nicholas, and Nathalie Peutz, eds. *The Deportation Regime: Sovereignty, Space, and the Freedom of Movement* (Durham, NC: Duke University Press, 2010).

Delano, Alexandra, and Adrián Félix. "From Migrants to 'New Americans': Latinos and Civic Integration in the US." Paper presented at the International Studies Association Annual Meeting, New Orleans, February 2010.

De Lara, Juan D. "Remapping Inland Southern California: Global Commodity Distribution, Land Speculation, and Politics in the Inland Empire." PhD diss., University of California Berkeley, 2009.

Delgado-Wise, Raúl. "Forced Migration and US Imperialism: The Dialectic of Migration and Development." *Critical Sociology* 35, no. 6 (2009): 793–810.

Delgado-Wise, Raúl, and Humberto Marquez Covarrubias. "The Reshaping of Mexican Labor Exports Under NAFTA: Paradoxes and Challenges." *International Migration Review* 41, no. 3 (2007): 656–79.

Dunn, Timothy. *Militarization of the U.S.–Mexico Border, 1978–1992: Low-Intensity Conflict Doctrine Comes Home* (Austin: University of Texas Press, 1996).

Earl Warren Institute on Race, Ethnicity, and Diversity at the University of California, Berkeley School of Law, 2001.

Espino, Rodolfo, David L. Leal, and Kenneth J. Meier, eds. *Latino Politics: Identity, Mobilization, and Representation* (Charlottesville: University of Virginia Press, 2008).

Espitia, Marilyn. "The Other 'Other Hispanics': South American Latinos in the United States." In *The Columbia History of Latinos in the United States since 1960*, edited by David Gutiérrez, 257–80 (New York: Columbia University Press, 2004).

Feagin, Joe. *White Party, White Government: Race, Class, and U.S. Politics* (London: Routledge, 2012).

Félix, Adrián, Carmen Gonzales, and Ricardo Ramírez. "Political Protest, Ethnic Media, and Latino Naturalization." *American Behavioral Scientist* 52, no. 4 (2008): 618–34.

Fernandes, Deepa. *Targeted: Homeland Security and the Business of Immigration* (New York: Seven Stories Press, 2007).

Fernandez, Luis, and Joel Olson. "To Live and Work, Anywhere You Please: Arizona and the Struggle for Locomotion." *Contemporary Political Theory* 10, no. 3 (2011): 412–19.

Fraga, Luis R., John A. García, Gary M. Segura, Michael Jones-Correa, Rodney E. Hero, and Valerie Martínez-Ebers. *Making It Home: Latino Lives in America* (Philadelphia: Temple University Press, 2010).

Frymer, Paul. *Uneasy Alliances: Race and Party Competition in America* (Princeton, NJ: Princeton University Press, 1999).

García Bedolla, Lisa. *Fluid Borders: Latino Power, Identity, and Politics in Los Angeles* (Berkeley: University of California Press, 2005).

———. *Introduction to Latino Politics in the U.S.* (Cambridge, UK: Polity Press, 2009).

García, Mario. T. *Memories of Chicano History: The Life and Narrative of Bert Corona* (Berkeley: University of California Press, 1994).

Gill, Leslie. *School of the Americas: Military Training and Political Violence in the Americas.* (Durham, NC: Duke University Press, 2004).

Gilmore, Ruthie Wilson. *Golden Gulag: Prisons, Surplus, Crisis, and Opposition in Globalizing California* (Berkeley: University of California Press, 2007).

Golash-Boza, Tanya Maria. *Immigration Nation: Raids, Detentions, and Deportations in Post-9/11 America* (Boulder, CO: Paradigm Publishers, 2012).

Goldberg, David Theo. *The Racial State* (Malden, MA: Blackwell Publishing, 2002).

Gómez-Quiñones, Juan. *Mexican Students por La Raza: The Chicano Student Movement in Southern California 1967–1977* (Santa Barbara, CA: Editorial La Causa, 1978).

Gonzales, Alfonso. "The 2006 Mega Marchas in Greater Los Angeles: Counter-Hegemonic Moment and the Future of El Migrante Struggle." *Latino Studies* 7, no. 1 (2009): 30–59.

———. "Power, Justice, and Survival: Latino Politics in the 21st Century," *NACLA Report on the Americas* 43, no. 6 (2010): 13–14.

———. *Rethinking U.S. Involvement in the War on Gangs in Central America: The Case of El Salvador* (Washington, D.C.: Institute for Policy Studies, 2006).

Gonzalez, Gilbert G. *Guest Workers or Colonized Labor: Mexican Labor Migration to the United States* (Boulder, CO: Paradigm Publishers, 2004).

Graham Jr., Otis L. *A Skirmish in a Wider War: An Oral History of John H. Tanton, Founder of FAIR* (Arbor, MI: Bentley Historical Library, University of Michigan, 1992).

Gramsci, Antonio. *The Antonio Gramsci Reader: Selected Writings 1916–1935.* Edited by David Forgacs (New York: New York University Press, 2000).

———. *Selections from the Prison Notebooks of Antonio Gramsci.* Edited by Quintin Hoare and Geoffrey Smith (New York: International Publishers, 1971).

Grandin, Greg. *Empire's Workshop: Latin America, the United States, and the Rise of the New Imperialism* (New York: Macmillan, 2007).

Gutiérrez, David. "Globalization, Labor Migration, and the Demographic Revolution: Ethnic Mexicans in the Late Twentieth Century." In *The Columbia History of Latinos in the United States since 1960*, edited by David Gutiérrez, 1–42 (New York: Columbia University Press, 2004).

Hall, Stuart. "The Spectacle of the Other." In *Representation: Cultural Representations and Signifying Practices*, edited by Stuart Hall, 223–90 (London: SAGE Publications, 1997).

———. *Hard Road to Renewal: Thatcherism and the Crisis of the Left* (New York: Verso, 1988), 132.

Hall, Stuart, Chas Critcher, Tony Jefferson, and Brian Roberts. *Policing the Crisis: Mugging, the State, and Law and Order* (London: McMillan, 1978).

Hamilton, Nora, and Norma S. Chinchilla. *Seeking Community in a Global City: Guatemalans and Salvadorans in Los Angeles* (Philadelphia: Temple University Press, 2001).

Hanchard, Michael G. *Orpheus and Power: The "Movimento Negro" of Rio de Janeiro and São Paulo, Brazil, 1945–1988* (Princeton, NJ: Princeton University Press, 1994).

Hero, Rodney E. *Latinos and the U.S. Political System: Two-Tiered Pluralism* (Philadelphia: Temple University Press, 1992).

Huntington, Samuel. *Who Are We: Challenges to Americas National Identity* (New York: Simon and Shuster, 2004).

Jessop, Bob. "Narrating the Future of the National Economy and National State: Remarks on Remapping Regulation and Reinventing Governance." In *State/Culture: State Formation After the Cultural Turn*, edited by George Steinmetz, 378–406 (Ithaca, NY: Cornell University Press, 1999).

———. *The Capitalist State: Marxist Theories and Methods* (New York: New York University Press, 1982).

Johnson, Hans, Deborah Reed, and Jose Hayes. *The Inland Empire in 2015* (San Francisco: Public Policy Institute of California, 2008).

Kohli, Aarti, and Deepa Varma. *Borders, Jails, and Jobsites: An Overview of Federal Immigration Enforcement Programs in the United States*. Berkeley, CA: Berkeley Law Center for Research and Administration. http://www.law.berkeley.edu/files/WI_Enforcement_Paper_final_web.pdf.

Law, Robin M., and Jennifer R. Wolch. "Social Reproduction and the City: Restructuring in Time and Space." In *The Restless Urban Landscape*, edited by Paul Knox, 165–206 (Princeton, NJ: Princeton Hall, 1993).

Loveman, Brian, and Thomas M. Davies, Jr. *The Politics of Anti-Politics: The Military in Latin America* (Wilmington, DE: Scholarly Resources, 1997).

Lusane, Clarence. *Pipeline Dreams: Racism and the War on Drugs* (Boston: South End Press, 1991).

Madison, Soyini D. *Critical Ethnography, Method, Ethics, and Performance* (Thousand Oaks, CA: SAGE Publications, 2005).

Massey, Douglas S., Jorge Durand, and Nolan Malone. *Beyond Smoke and Mirrors: Mexican Immigration in an Era of Economic Integration* (New York: Russell Sage Foundation, 2002).

McGirr, Lisa. *Suburban Warriors: Origins of the New American Right* (Princeton, NJ: Princeton University Press, 2002).

Mears, Daniel. "Immigration and Crime: What Is the Correlation?" *Federal Sentencing Reporter* 14, no. 2 (2002): 284–88.

Meissner, Doris, Donald M. Kerwin, Muzaffar Chishti, and Claire Bergeron. *Immigration Enforcement in the United States: The Rise of a Formidable Machinery*. Washington, D.C.: Migration Policy Institute, January 2013. http://www.migrationpolicy.org/pubs/enforcementpillars.pdf.

Menjívar, Cecilia. *Fragmented Ties: Salvadoran Immigrant Networks in America* (Berkeley: University of California Press, 2000).

Montgomery, Tommie Sue. *Revolution in El Salvador: From Civil War to Civil Peace*. 2d ed. (Boulder, CO: Westview Press, 1996).

Mora, Carlos. *Latinos in the West: The Student Movement and Academic Labor in Los Angeles* (New York: Rowman & Littlefield, 2007).

Morton, David. *Unravelling Gramsci: Hegemony and Passive Revolution in the Global Political Economy* (London: Pluto Press, 2007).

Muñoz, Carlos. *Youth, Identity, Power: The Chicano Movement* (New York: Verso Books, 2007).

Navarro, Armando. *La Raza Unida Party: A Chicano Challenge to the U.S. Two-Party Dictatorship* (Philadelphia: Temple University Press, 2000).

Nevins, Joseph. *Operation Gatekeeper: The Rise of the "Illegal" Alien and the Making of the U.S.–Mexico Boundary* (London: Routledge, 2002).

Newton, Lina. *Illegal, Alien, or Immigrant: The Politics of Immigration Reform* (New York: New York University Press, 2008).

Omi, Michael, and Howard Winant. *Racial Formation in the United States: From the 1960s to the 1990s* (London: Routledge, 1994).

Pallares, Amalia, and Nilda Flores-González, eds. ¡*Marcha! Latino Chicago and the Immigrant Rights Movement* (Urbana: University of Illinois Press, 2010).

Ponce, Albert. "Racialization, Resistance, and the Migrant Rights Movement: A Historical Analysis." *Critical Sociology*, in press (prepublished online). doi:10.1177/0896920512465210.

Popkin, Mary. *Peace without Justice: Obstacles to Building the Rule of Law in El Salvador* (Philadelphia: Pennsylvania State University Press, 2000).

Poulantzas, Nicos. *Political Power and Social Classes* (London: Verso Books, 1968).

————. *State Power Socialism* (London: Verso Books, 1978).

Pulido, Laura. *Black, Brown, Yellow, and Left: Radical Activism in Los Angeles* (Berkeley: University of California Press, 2006).

Quijano, Aníbal. "Coloniality of Power, Eurocentrisim, and Latin America." *Nepantla: Views from the South* 1, no. 3 (2000): 533–80.

Ramírez, Ricardo, and Olga Medina. *Catalyst and Barriers to Attaining Citizenship: An Analysis of the Ya Es Hora ¡Ciudadania!* (Washington, D.C.: National Council of La Raza, 2011).

Rivera, Angelica. "Chicago Grassroots Resistance to Racial Profiling, Deportations, and Empire Building: The Case of Elvira Arellano y un Pueblo Sin Fronteras (One People Without Borders)." Paper presented at Nuestra América Conference, Kansas University, Lawrence, 2006.

Robinson, William I. "'Aquí Estamos y No Nos Vamos!': Global Capital and Immigrant Rights." *Race and Class* 48, no. 2 (2006): 77–91.

————. *A Theory of Global Capitalism: Production, Class, and State in a Transnational World* (Baltimore: Johns Hopkins University Press, 2004).

————. "Gramsci and Globalization: From Nation-State to Transnational Hegemony." *Critical Review of International Social and Political Philosophy* 8, no. 4 (2005): 1–16.

————. *Transnational Conflicts: Central America, Social Change, and Globalization* (New York: Verso Books, 2003).

Rocco, Raymond. "Latino Los Angeles: Reframing Boundaries/Borders in Los Angeles." Unpublished manuscript, 2006.

————. "The Structuring of Latino Politics: Neoliberalism and Incorporation." *NACLA Report on the Americas* 43, no. 6 (2010): 41–43.

Santa Ana, Otto. *Brown Tide Rising: Metaphors of Latinos in Contemporary American Discourse* (Austin: University of Texas Press, 2002).

Scherer, Michael. "Inside Obama's Factory of Ideas." *Time*, November 21, 2008. http://www.time.com/time/politics/article/0,8599,1861305,00.html#ixzz1V2V2hNIh.

Schirmer, Jennifer. *The Guatemalan Military Project: A Violence Called Democracy* (Philadelphia: University of Pennsylvania Press, 1998).

Sharma, Aradhana, and Akhil Gupta. "Introduction: Rethinking Theories of the State in the Era of Globalization." In *The Anthropology of the State: A Reader*, edited by Aradhana Sharma and Akhil Gupta, 1–41 (Malden, MA: Blackwell Publishing, 2006).

Singh, Nikhil. *Black Is a Country: Race and the Unfinished Struggle for Democracy* (Cambridge, MA: Harvard University Press, 2004).

Sklair, Leslie. *Sociology of the Global System* (Baltimore: Johns Hopkins University Press, 2001).

Smith, Robert Charles. *We Have No Leaders: African Americans in the Post–Civil Rights Era* (Albany: State University of New York Press, 1996).

Sosa Riddell, Aldajiza. "Chicanas and El Movimiento." *Aztlán* 5, no. 1 (1974): 27–56.

Stanley, William. *The Protection Racket State: Elite Politics, Military Extortion, and Civil War in El Salvador* (Philadelphia: Temple University Press, 1996).

Stefancic, Jean, and Richard Delgado. *No Mercy: How Conservative Think Tanks and Foundations Changed America's Social Agenda* (Philadelphia: Temple University Press, 1996).

Tarker, Kathryn. *Too Close for Comfort: U.S. Ratches Up Central American Ties.* Washington, D.C.: Council on Hemispheric Affairs, 2005. http://www.coha.org/too-close-for-comfort-el-salvador-ratchets-up-its-us-ties/.

Ucles, Mario Lungo. *El Salvador in the Eighties: Counterinsurgency and Revolution* (Philadelphia: Temple University Press, 1990).

U.S. Bureau of the Census. "Census Shows America's Diversity." Press release. March 24, 2011. http://www.census.gov/newsroom/releases/archives/2010_census/cb11-cn125.html.

Valdez Torres, Martin. "Indispensible Migrants: Mexican Workers and the Making of Twentieth Century Los Angeles." In *Latino Los Angeles: Transformations, Communities, and Activism*, edited by Enrique C. Ochoa and Gilda L. Ochoa, 23–37 (Tucson: University of Arizona Press, 2005).

Valle, Victor M., and Rodolfo D. Torres. *Latino Metropolis* (Minneapolis: University of Minnesota Press, 2000).

Van Evera, Stephen. *Guide to Methods for Students of Political Science* (Ithaca, NY: Cornell University Press, 1997).

Van Dijk, Teun A. "Critical Discourse Analysis." In *The Handbook of Discourse Analysis*, edited by Deborah Schiffrin, Deborah Tannen, and Heidi E. Hamilton, 352–71 (Malden, MA: Blackwell Publishers, 2001).

Varsanyi, Monica. *Taking Local Control: Immigration Policy Activism in U.S. Cities and States* (Stanford, CA: Stanford University Press, 2010).

Winant, Howard. *The World Is a Ghetto* (New York: Basic Books, 2001).

_____. *The New Politics of Race: Globalism, Difference, Justice* (Minneapolis: University of Minnesota Press, 2004).

Young, Iris Marion. *Justice and the Politics of Difference* (Princeton, NJ: Princeton University Press, 1990).

Zagorski, Paul. *Democracy vs. National Security: Civil–Military Relations in Latin America* (Boulder, CO: Lynne Rienner, 1992).

Voss, Kim and Irene Bloemraad. *Rallying for Immigrant Rights: The Fight for Inclusion in 21st Century America* (Berkeley: University of California, 2011).

Zepeda-Millán, Chris. "Dignity's Revolt: Threat, Identity, and Immigrant Mass Mobilization." PhD diss., Cornell University, 2011.

_____. "Today We March, Tomorrow We Vote: The Effects of the 2006 Immigrant Rights Protest-Wave." Paper presented at the American Political Science Association Annual Meeting and Exhibition, Washington, D.C., September 2010.

Zilberg, Elana. *Spaces of Detention: The Making of a Transnational Gang Crisis between Los Angeles and San Salvador* (Durham, NC: Duke University Press, 2011).

Zolberg, Aristride R. *A Nation by Design: Immigration Policy in the Fashioning of America* (Cambridge, MA: Harvard University Press, 2008).

Zúñiga, Víctor, and Rubén Hernández-León. *New Destinations: Mexican Immigration in the United States* (New York: Russell Sage Foundation, 2006).

INDEX

Page numbers followed by *f* or *t* indicate figures or tables, respectively. Numbers followed by "n" indicate endnotes.